Syriza in Power

To Joanna
and
Phaedra

Syriza in Power

Reflections of an Accidental Politician

Costas Douzinas

polity

First published in 2017 by Polity Press

Polity Press
65 Bridge Street
Cambridge CB2 1UR, UK

Polity Press
101 Station Landing
Suite 300,
Medford, MA 02155
USA

ISBN-13: 978-1-5095-1157-0 (hardback)
ISBN-13: 978-1-5095-1158-7 (paperback)

A catalogue record for this book is available from the British Library.

Typeset in 10.5 on 12 pt Sabon by Toppan Best-set Premedia Limited
Printed and bound in the UK by CPI Group (UK) Ltd, Croydon

The publisher has used its best endeavours to ensure that the URLs for
external websites referred to in this book are correct and active at the time of
going to press. However, the publisher has no responsibility for the websites
and can make no guarantee that a site will remain live or that the content is
or will remain appropriate.

Every effort has been made to trace all copyright holders, but if any have
been inadvertently overlooked the publisher will be pleased to include any
necessary credits in any subsequent reprint or edition.

For further information on Polity, visit our website: politybooks.com

Contents

Prologue:
The Accidental Politician

I was elected a Syriza Member of Parliament on 20 September 2015. I had not planned it, I did not want it, the idea had not even crossed my mind. I had lived in London since 1974. All my adult life and career had been spent in the protected and until recently gentle environment of British universities. In 1992, I had the great fortune to be appointed with Peter Goodrich to set up a Law School at Birkbeck College, the radical part of the University of London. Over twenty years, the School moved from three to thirty members of staff and acquired a reputation as the headquarters of Critical Legal Studies (CLS), a movement of radical academics and lawyers. The movement had started in the United States but has flourished in Britain. Its annual conference has been taking place every first weekend of September for some thirty years. On 5 September 2015, at the annual Critical Legal Conference at the University of Wroclaw, Poland my life changed. It was the first time the conference was taking place in Eastern Europe. I opened the conference offering a review of the history of CLS, its theoretical pluralism and the long campaign to export critical teaching, research and lawyering to other parts of the world.

It was a relaxing and pleasant occasion until Saturday morning. I was in my hotel room when a flurry of telephone calls from the Athens headquarters of Syriza turned my life upside down. Alexis Tsipras, the Prime Minister who had resigned a few weeks earlier after losing his parliamentary majority, had announced new elections for the end of September. I was asked to stand. I refused. The calls kept coming. I offered to come to Athens and campaign for the party in its hour of need, even to have my name on the ballot paper in a non-electable position. Eventually, I was told that if I were placed on the list of my hometown Piraeus, I would considerably help the campaign but with a minimal chance of getting elected. After consulting Joanna and Phaedra, my partner in Australia and my daughter in Manchester, I nervously accepted.

The election campaign was short – just a couple of weeks. I toured central Piraeus with fellow candidates and party members. We visited public service and utilities offices, shops and markets. I was embarrassed and kept apologizing to fellow candidates and potential voters for my relative ignorance of local problems. The greatest fear, however, was appearing on TV. I was worried that my rusty Greek and lack of experience would work against the party. I was wrong. Everyone treated me with unexpected respect except for a notorious right-wing candidate, who attacked me on live TV for leaving London to stand for a loser party and a totalitarian ideology. I replied by telling her that she had paraphrased the inimitable Groucho Marx who defending an outrageous lie quipped 'Are you going to believe your eyes or what I am telling you?' I shared another TV debate with a former right-wing Secretary of Education. I spoke about the way European universities have turned into moneymaking degree-issuing assembly lines, about their extensive bureaucratization, about the abandonment of the humanities. I praised the Greek constitution, which, in a world first, makes higher education state-provided and free. The social democratic and right-wing parties (Pasok and New Democracy) have repeatedly tried to amend article 16 of the constitution which keeps universities public. The resistance of academics and students, however, condemned every attempt to failure. The private universities affair and education more generally are key battlegrounds for the government. After this rather didactic TV performance, I became 'the professor' and lost my TV fright. I was placed in the position of someone who is supposed to know things that are crucial but generally unknown. For Jacques Lacan this is the position of the analyst. The patient must assume that the analyst can interpret dreams and symptoms and can divine the deepest secrets of the psyche. The analyst's significance does not lie, however, in his ability to uncover the secrets of the analysant but in his position. He personifies knowledge, a guarantee that an answer to the psychic disturbance exists even if it is not forthcoming. Later, some people added the moniker 'philosopher' to that of 'the professor'. I knew immediately that the honeymoon period was coming to an end. Being called a philosopher is usually a term of mild ridicule. Professors are experts, philosophers are figures of unscrupulous obfuscation and unnecessary incomprehension. This ambiguous attitude, half admiring half dismissive, characterizes every part of life. Syriza cadres want me to speak in their constituencies but they will not vote for me in party elections. The academic caché brings people who would not otherwise come to a Syriza event. But as I was told early on, if I want to be elected to a party office or appointed to a ministry I should join a party faction or tendency. I have not done so, staying away from Syriza tribes. I remain an insider politically but an outsider organizationally, an apt metaphor for Syriza's wider position vis-à-vis the Greek state.

A couple of weeks after the opening of Parliament, I was elected Chair of the House Standing Committee on Defence and Foreign Relations. It is perhaps the most senior, although not the busiest committee. It scrutinizes bills from the two ministries and carries out, like the other five standing committees, a basic oversight of the executive. Part of my duty is to represent Parliament in various international and European conferences and meet a steady flow of ambassadors and visiting dignitaries. Speaking fluent English, the lingua franca of international politics, and letting it be known that I am a London Law professor does give an advantage. This is one of the few instances where my previous life and skills are of help. Otherwise my academic, research and publishing experience is largely irrelevant. I believed that I could help government and Parliament through a better use of my expertise. It was the wrong assumption. People who say that political and academic life cannot combine are right. What they mean is that politics and academic skills are mostly incompatible. The two could cohabit only if they are kept strictly separate. The ministers I have to work with and hold to account are the two most difficult members of the government. Panos Kammenos, the Minister of Defence, is the leader of the small right-wing Independent Greeks (AnEll) party, Syriza's coalition partner. He is a nationalist and cultural conservative with occasional bursts of emotional rhetoric. Nikos Kotzias, the Foreign Secretary, is a former Foreign Office official and an international relations expert. Kotzias has a good understanding of the arcane machinations of diplomacy and links with the post-Soviet world. He is the leader of a small 'left patriotic' group, which veers towards nationalism. Kotzias is authoritative and friendly outwards but secretive and controlling in his dealings. Having to work with these two highly experienced but unpredictable politicians is a challenging task. As many people tell me, my ticket drew the hardest lot among government ministers.

My involvement with foreign relations and defence taught me two things. First, the various European and international conferences to which MPs are invited regularly are less about business and more about self-esteem. Very little happens in the many inter-parliamentary conferences. This is in part the result of the global reduction in the significance of parliaments and the almost complete control of foreign relations by the executive and cliquish Foreign Office. An inverse relationship exists between the small significance of these conferences and the pomp and circumstance that accompanies them. People who have travelled overseas only for short holidays find themselves in exotic places in Latin America, Asia and Africa and are treated like minor royalty. Parliamentary tourism gives MPs a sense of importance, which is shared by the population at large. When my sophisticated brother met a number of MPs whom I had invited for drinks, he told me how surprised he was when he realized that they are 'normal' people. Appearing as someone of higher knowledge or greater power than the normal person is part of the deputy's mystique. In reality, both are in short supply.

The second lesson is related to academic work. Lawyers live by the text. They learn to speak, write and interpret in particular ways. As a legal philosopher, I wrote and practised hermeneutics, rhetoric and semiotics. Deconstruction teaches that the meaning of texts continuously slides; hermeneutics, the importance of authorized communities of interpreters. I now moved to the other side as an occasional draughtsman of legal texts. The most important was a parliamentary resolution recognizing Palestine. It was drafted with the assistance of advisers and senior diplomats. We had to negotiate with the Palestinian and Israeli Embassies and all parties in Parliament to ensure the widest possible consensus. After three weeks of negotiations, in which every word and punctuation mark was pored over, we arrived at a final text acceptable to the opposition. The Speaker would read it in the Chamber on Friday 22 December 2015. I would then give the oration welcoming President Abbas, who was attending the session. While preparing the talk on the previous Sunday, I received a strange phone call from a senior opposition politician. I was asked whether the resolution referred to '*the* Palestinian state' or '*a* Palestinian state'. The text was embargoed until its reading later that week so I prevaricated. I soon realized that the concern was generalized. I spent the following three hours on the phone with assorted diplomats and politicians being lectured about the benefits or defects of the 'the'. Its inclusion in the text would make little difference to the resolution and would certainly have no effect whatsoever on the intractable Palestinian problem. People were prepared to argue, however, as if their lives depended on it. It was a mild instance of what we can call 'text fetishism': the belief that the text of the law determines the future and should aim to police strictly all possible interpretations and applications.

'You should forget about academic life and about writing books', a Syriza MP told me soon after I joined Parliament. Others repeated the warning and an academic friend and former MP confirmed it. 'Work in Parliament is all consuming', she said. 'You would not have time to do anything else. Forget about continuing your academic life.' I did not have a yardstick against which to judge the accuracy of the warnings, so I believed them and negotiated unpaid leave with the University of London. Luck intervened. By the time I had decided to stand in the elections, the teaching programme for the new academic year had already been set by the law school. I was starting my Masters' degree class on the philosophy and history of human rights a week after the 20 September elections. It would have been impossible for the Law school to arrange an alternative lecturer. I was asked to help out and decided to continue with my teaching duties. For twelve weeks I commuted, spending a couple of days in central London and the rest of the week in Athens. I started the weekly commute with trepidation. By the end of the teaching term, I decided that continuing my academic activities was the only way to cope with the unplanned reversal of life. Going back to London, teaching, supervising doctoral students, reading and writing articles and books (including this one), meeting academic friends and sharing my experience kept me sane. Commuting weekly to teach for twelve weeks, rather than tiring me physically, relaxed and comforted me spiritually. Parliamentary life has minimal overlap with the life of the mind.

In the Chamber and the committee rooms, debates are often parallel monologues repeating the briefing 'non-papers' sent to MPs by the parties' spin-doctors. Deputies read their prepared speeches and rarely engage in the arguments of the previous speakers. Parliamentary rules, unlike those of the House or Commons, do not allow MPs to 'give way' to opponents while speaking. As a result, a genuine exchange of views seldom takes place. When senior ministers or opposition leaders speak, the Chamber is full; when ordinary members or Chryssi Avgi MPs take the floor, the Chamber empties. There is a strong impression that deputies make speeches in order to upload them later on YouTube and social media for the benefit of voters. I decided to speak only when I have something different and hopefully enlightening to say and only on topics about which I have some knowledge. Since I have many opportunities to speak publicly and publish in newspapers, websites and magazines, I decided not to create a Facebook page or a Twitter account. I told TV Channels that I was not prepared to participate in their political 'panels' which unfailingly end up in verbal and occasionally physical brawls. Sticking to the old, perhaps ancient, rituals of debate and communication means that I am not recognised in the street and will ensure that my life as a politician will probably be short.

Learning the rules, customs and etiquette of parliamentary life, following the set-piece debates and chairing committee meetings is often boring. Little intellectual effort is demanded, many hours are spent in the cafés waiting around for a leaders debate or for a vote on a government bill. Parliamentary café life is interesting. The smaller and unadorned cafeteria is frequented by Syriza MPs. It is a smoking den with a thick cloud of smoke engulfing the conversations. There is laughter, bonhomie and anxiety. Syriza members found themselves unexpectedly in Parliament, have little experience as politicians and treat the whole thing with a sense of historic responsibility and a dose of self-irony and deprecation. The larger and 'posher' lounge is a New Democracy lair. It is dominated by some sixty moustaches of all styles. Portraits of serious looking men ranging from revolutionary heroes to major politicians and former Speakers emphasize the gender division of politics. Respect for gender equality, minority identities and political correctness are not the strongest suits of my new environment. When I chide colleague for sexist language or the endless stories about 'stupid blondes' I am told that it is all a joke; don't I understand, am I a politically correct killjoy?

This book is a sequel to *Philosophy and Resistance in the Crisis: Greece and the Future of Europe* published by Polity in 2013. In that book, written in 2012 at the height of the economic and political crises, I adopted 'strategic optimism': 'Europe used Greece as a guinea pig to test the conditions for restructuring late capitalism in crisis', I wrote. 'What the European and Greek elites did not expect was for the guinea pig to occupy the lab, kick out the blind scientists and start a new experiment: its own transformation from an object to a political subject.' My optimism was met with disbelief. I was repeatedly accused in Britain and Greece of taking leave of reality and turning wishes into facts. My predictions came true three years later, however. Syriza, the radical left party, won handsomely two elections and a referendum in 2015 and has undertaken the salvation of the country after six years of economic, political and moral devastation.

Personal vindication was followed by a major life transformation. As Syriza MP for my home city of Piraeus, I was now a part of the Left, the unlikely arrival of which I had predicted. My wager had come through but I was caught in its after effects. On arriving in Parliament, I started taking notes about life as a politician. It was an alien environment; the early pages are full of incomprehension and excitement. I did not know the rules of the political game, how to speak on TV and debate in Parliament, how to chair Committee meetings. It was all terribly new, intriguing, even thrilling. This early note-taking was a mnemotechnic device: an aid to memory, somewhere to register the names of the tens and hundreds of new people I was meeting every day. Soon, however, the tone of the notes started changing. A great deal of what I was experiencing was no longer agreeable. Opposition deputies, initially polite, turned out to be narcissistic, impolite, almost brutish in their behaviour. The excitement of debate began to wear off when it became clear that very little exchange of views was taking place. The taking down of names, dates and events in order to remember gradually turned into a more organized journal. Sitting in the Chamber and following an uninteresting debate, I retreated to writing the journal in an attempt first to understand the scene around me and then to uncover the deeper meanings behind the often offensive words exchanged. It soon became clear that my professional deformation was turning me into an ethnographer of a strange and powerful tribe. I decided to turn my sketchy notes into a book. Writing a book about the politics of the Left, I became both the observer of strange situations and people and the object of observation as a member of the target group. The position of participant observer who is at the same time observed does not always lead to accurate self-reflection. The observer aims at an ethnographically accurate presentation of events, rituals, ways of life. The observer as observed aims at a phenomenologically accurate presentation of states of mind, intentionality and psychology. The two tasks overlap but also resist each other. I claim no objectivity or neutrality in the analysis of the events. These hugely overrated attributes are necessarily absent from the political arena. I hope, however, to give an accurate representation of events and a self-reflective impression of states of mind.

The events narrated in this book are based on personal experience, publicly available sources and only exceptionally on private information. The book reveals no great secrets and discloses no confidences. It aims, however, to confront the many lies against Syriza the Greek establishment circulates in the West with little correction. My position as a deputy at the time of writing adds certain constraints. Party members and deputies (ought to) remain separate from the government; they have an important role in passing popular complaints to ministers, reminding them of left principles and holding them to account. However, the difficulty of running the state while under continuous attack makes us temper our critique and offer greater support to government than some actions deserve. I do not parade my ideological disagreements and conscience pangs as an excuse for my flawless voting record; nor do I apologize for sticking with government and party in its hour of need. I left the comforts of a pure conscience and the Pontius Pilate-like consolations of clean hands when I joined Parliament. I have no regrets or apologies. Angels and furies are my own private business at the midnight hour.

Over the last few years, I have been contributing articles and commentary in Britain, Greece and other parts of the world. In London, I have been writing for the *Guardian*, *Open Democracy* as well as various newspapers and websites. In Athens, I have been contributing since 2014 a fortnightly column entitled *Πολιτικά και Φιλοσοφικά Επίκαιρα* (Current Political and Philosophical) to the leading centre-left newspaper, the cooperative *Efimerida Syntakton* (Newspaper of Journalists). The *Efimerida Syntakton* is perhaps the one entrepreneurial success story of the crisis. Most electronic and print media lose money and operate to serve business interests and political campaigns. The *Efimerida Syntakton* is an exception. Writing regularly a 1,500-word article that puts forward some abstract idea in a comprehensive way is a difficult task. It is not a skill that can be mastered; one has to wrestle with it every time. Columns often start with a vignette or event in the news (the 'political' part) and then proceed to a theoretical generalization (the 'philosophical' part) that helps understand our predicament and hopes. Many ideas and chapters were rehearsed first in *Efimerida Syntakton* and other newspapers and websites. They have all been re-written with the generous and forgiving privilege of hindsight, to which a chapter of the book is devoted.

The book is divided into seven parts and twenty-one chapters. The first part (Resistance Rising) is a direct continuation and conclusion of the earlier book on the theory and practice of resistance. It charts debates in radical political philosophy and encounters with some of its leading thinkers. The final chapter ('A Philosophy of Resistance') offers an analytics of resistance that emerges out of recent experience and forms the basis of a separate book that will appear soon. The second part ('Syriza Agonistes') has the two longest chapters ('A Very European Coup' and 'Contradiction is the Name of the Governing Left'), which offer a critical description of the dense two years since Syriza's victory in January 2015. They do not offer a chronicle of events; they have the minimal presentation of facts necessary for the accompanying theoretical reflection. The protagonists of the dramatic events have spoken little so far in interviews and articles. I am sure that we will hear more in years to come. This most political part of the book describes briefly what happened in 2015 and 2016, offering a correction to the widespread inaccuracies about Greece and Syriza. It presents my reflections about the unprecedented victories of 2015, the July defeat and the prospects of the Left in the twenty-first century. The third part ('Reflections on Life as a Politician') is the most personal. Based on my journal, it mobilizes theoretical resources in order to make sense of the strange world I found myself in. It is a work of reflection and self-reflection even though the latter part will have to wait a quieter moment for its completion.

But what is the Left of the twenty-first century? There is no widely acceptable left theory and certainly no account of what left governmentality might be. This absence places added responsibility on Syriza as party and government. The inventors of the 'left interval' idea believe that Syriza's failure will put the left project back for a generation. This adds extra pressure and demands, I believe, to start the theoretical reconstruction before all relevant information is in or reflection and self-reflection have been concluded. The book starts this difficult task. Its writing in the midst of a state of emergency makes it refer elliptically only to existing theories without extensive exegesis. The theoretical forays assume some familiarity with its basic premises and often refer obliquely to my earlier work. The hope is that the theory on offer contributes novel ways of understanding political events and cultural arguments. The rise of Syriza has reversed the well-known one-way street from theory to practice. Left theory has to learn from best (or worst) political practice, extract its live kernel and generalize into a coherent vision and a workable plan. Governmental practice has often been problematic, tortuous, failing, winning elections is far removed from gaining power. But when governance serves the values of equality, social justice and democracy, it offers the foundations for a revitalization of theory that could be of importance for the Left internationally.

The middle section of the book could be described as an intervention in the Greek culture wars. It starts with a look at the greatest advantage of the Left: morality and ethics as against the emphasis on economics, possessive individualism and consumer satisfaction ('The Ethos of the Left'; 'Greeks or Europeans', 'The Euro, the Sacred and the Holy'). The book then turns to the philosophy of history and the way Greek historiography is being rewritten by the Syriza victory ('The Left and the Philosophy of History'; 'The Cycles of History: 1949, 1969, 1989'). Most chapters in this section are short, polemical and punchy. Many started as articles in Efimerida Syntakton trying to help people make sense of a time out of joint.

The final section moves back to politics. Part 6 examines the similarities and differences between the Grexit and Brexit campaigns. It advocates a left Euroscepticism that could save Europe. Part 7 looks at the current existential crisis of Europe, placing it in the *longue durée* of its civilizing mission. Finally, Part 8 examines the refugee crisis, the Greek and European responses and the role of humanity and human rights in its evolution and solution. It calls for a revitalization of the classical tradition of the Cities of Refuge.

The final draft was written in the village of Dryos, Paros in August 2016. I have been spending August in Dryos for some twenty-five years. The year 2016 was strange. I came to Dryos as an MP. Unlike Piraeus and Athens where, after my forty-one years in London, few people know me, the Dryos locals recognize me. Their attitudes changed. Exaggerated greetings, unusually respectful words and gestures, occasional requests for minor favours made me realize that my status was now different, something of which I am not fully conscious in everyday life. When locals saw me driving a rather large car, they thought that it was given to me by Parliament and expressed their fulsome admiration. It was the only one left at the car rental shop, which had rented out all small and economical cars. When I told them that I was renting because I had not accepted the car given to all MPs by Parliament (accompanied by two policemen), I sensed that people were taken aback. I was either stupid or not important enough to be given a large car. For the first time, I realized fully the gap between reality and appearance, or between presumed status and power. Power does not exist if it does not come with a modicum of pomp and circumstance.

Joanna Bourke was the most careful, critical and supportive reader of the manuscript as always. She was the key person in my decision to stand in the elections. We have both adjusted our life so that we can be together as often as before the fateful election. Joanna is fully responsible for my ability to lead a double life, political and academic, in Athens and London. A number of people facilitated the transfer from Academic Hall to Parliamentary Chamber. Phaedra Douzina, Alexandra Bakalaki, Nikos Douzinas, Akis Papataxiarchis, Christos Lyrintzis, Yanna Kandilorou, Efi Avdela Nikos and Anna Tsigonia and Lois Lambrianidis corrected various errors and misunderstandings and offered solid advice against the innocence and naivete of the neophyte. Konstantinos Tsoukalas has been an imaginative inspiration, a wise friend and adviser and a soul comrade. He insisted that I should stand in the elections, after he decided to stand down himself. I blame him for both. Parliament is missing his sage prudence and I miss his elegant presence of mind. Dimitris Emmanouilidis, Sakis Papadopoulos, Foteini Vaki, Kostas Gavroglu, Nikos Xydakis, Yota Kozompoli, Maria Theleritou, Themis Moumoulidis, Kostas Morfidis, Spyros Lappas, Anneta Kavadia, Maria Triantafyllou, Dimitris Sevastakis and Michalis Sotiropoulos became parliamentary companions, social friends and spiritual comrades, giving me advice when ignorant, sympathy when low and drinks when desperate. Dimitris Tzanakopoulos moved effortlessly from star researcher to star politician and has been a theoretical companion. The members of the 'Ideas Lab', we hold every second Wednesday in Parliament, made me reconsider and nuance my thinking about the Left in the twenty-first century in theory and everyday practice. There is no indignation or desperation that cannot be soothed by a calm discussion, a good heart-to-heart and a visit to a taverna. Maria Spanou and Peggy Smyrnioti, two great parliamentary officials, helped me in the difficult early days and became friends. When I publicly thank some officials in the Chamber, thus entering their names into the parliamentary record, I am taken aback by their delighted surprise. It had not been done before, I was told. Greek politicians do not do much politeness. Finally, the bar *Resalto* and DJ Apostolis in Dryos, Paros, offered occasional respite during the obsessive writing, while the bakery *Takis* in Koukaki, one of the best in Athens, offers the necessary tasty sustenance that keeps us going.

This book was written in medias res. It was penned and edited in the Parliamentary Chamber and committee rooms, on trains, airplanes and terminals. Some repetitions and the odd unconscious contradiction must have crept in. Its peripatetic composition is evident: some chapters follow academic protocols, others are more journalistic, still others are existential explorations of philosophical conjecture and political impasse. It follows the difficult journey of return and the painful initiation to active politics. Its mood changes from avowed optimism to strategic optimism to the odd bouts of melancholy. I kept this vacillation, which follows the mood at the time of writing, as an 'authentic' representation of emotionally turbulent times, even though I may be seeing things differently now.

The next elections in the ordinary run of things will take place in late 2019. But Greek Parliaments rarely finish their term. Perhaps I should have waited. However, the lies told about the government and the Left are so many and outrageous that I believe that a mid-term setting the record straight – if that is even possible – is necessary. A more considered view will have to wait until after the end of my life as accidental politician.

Part I
Resistance Rising

1

From Utopia to Dystopia and Resistance, a Short Run

Michael Anderson's science fiction *Logan's Run* (1976) opens with these words: 'Sometime in the twenty-third century, the survivors of a war, overpopulation and pollution are living in a great domed city, sealed away from the forgotten world outside. Here, in an ecologically balanced world, mankind lives only for pleasure, freed by the servo-mechanisms which provide everything. There's just one catch: "Life must end at thirty unless reborn in the fiery ritual of carousel."' The film offers a standard description of utopia. A society cut off from a threatening environment lives secluded in a land of peace and plenty. There is no conflict, people are happy, needs and desires are fully catered for. People can call in sex partners or go to orgy rooms but they cannot have long-term relationships. All utopias, however, have a little flaw that eventually turns them into dystopias. The dome dwellers are programmed to accept that life will be 'renewed' at the age of thirty. Implanted 'life-clocks' with changing colours following the advancing age of their holders prepare them for 'lastday', their thirtieth birthday. Assembled at the 'carousel' to be 'reborn', they are exterminated.

The cosmopolitan utopia of perpetual peace, human rights and a life of plenty, promised in 1989, followed a similar pattern. Unlimited and continuous growth would be delivered by the close link between globalization, neoliberal capitalism and a light type of liberal democracy. The reality was different. After the flight of industry and agriculture to the developing world, debt for consumption became the growth strategy of the West. In our post-Fordist societies of services, possessive individualism and consumerism fuelled by credit and debt became sole criteria of success. Life-long savings were turned into financial 'products'; working people became shareholders directly or though the investments of insurance and pension funds. Proliferating individual and consumer rights deepened the fake socio-economic integration. Desire, rights and morality became intimately linked. Every desire could become entitlement, every 'I want X' 'I have a right to X' and 'it is moral to X'.[1] On the surface, the interests of working people and capitalists started converging. In reality, the income and inequality gap grew to unprecedented levels. The sub-prime mortgages disaster showed that financialized capitalism must 'invest in the bare life of people who cannot provide any guarantee, who offer nothing apart from themselves.'[2]

Michel Foucault, Gilles Deleuze and Giorgio Agamben have explained how, in a biopolitical world, power is exercised over life. It extends from the depths of consciousness to the bodies of individuals. Whole populations are targeted on the basis of characteristics such as gender, race, health, age or profession. Collective strategies of power are supplemented by 'technologies of self'. People are asked to adjust their behaviour through practices of self-improvement and discipline in the name of individual happiness, health, success and collective well-being. Two types of strategy target the self. The first inscribes needs, desires and expectations in the individual, making her feel free, autonomous, creative. Only as disciplined by the symbolism of power do people acquire the imaginary of freedom. The second targets populations with policies on birth rate and life expectancy, sexuality and health, education and training, work and leisure. This double-pronged register aims at disciplining and controlling behaviour. Biopolitical power pays little attention to ideas: you can be a Communist or an anarchist as long as your behaviour and comportment follow the prescribed life choices.

Greece is a textbook case of the complex entanglement of population control and the disciplining of individuals. After entry to the Euro, the government promoted extreme hedonism. Conspicuous consumption was the neoliberal dream. Easy and cheap loans, rewards for market speculation, rapid increase of real estate values became instruments of economic policy as well as criteria of social mobility and individual well-being. The moral imperative of the period was 'enjoy', 'buy' and 'live as if this is your last day'. Satisfying desire was mandatory, linking psychological drive with policy direction. This distorted economic model came to an end in 2009. Austerity reversed priorities and imposed a brutal administration of population and individuals. The 'rescue' of Greece became tantamount to a return to fiscal 'probity'. Public spending cuts, tax hikes and privatizations were the tools. People had been told for twenty years that the main concern of power was their economic success and happiness. Now the earlier policies were overturned. The politics of personal desire and enjoyment turned into a strategy of saving the nation by abandoning its individual members. Population was everything; the individual nothing. Mandatory individual pleasure turned into a prohibition of pleasure.

Austerity policies divide the population according to skills, age, economic, gender, race and work criteria and impose radical behavioural reform for the sake of fiscal discipline and competitiveness. The measures cover every aspect of life from basic food consumption to health, education, work and leisure. People are asked to align their behaviour with the 'needs' of the nation and to be subjected to extensive controls, which aim at recovering 'social health'. The behavioural change was initially demanded of the low paid and pensioners; it eventually spread to everyone. Every new austerity wave extended the measures to ever-increasing groups of population and pulling into the vortex the middle class with the imposition of large property taxes. Population strategies were supplemented with extensive interventions at the individual level. Twenty years of individual hedonism had to be brought to a rapid and violent end. An extreme version of the 'shock doctrine' recipe was imposed in the hope that the violent introduction of austerity would reduce resistance and re-arrange behaviour.[3] It privatized social provision making it scarce and helped individualize the disciplining process. Money, work, rights and aspirations were rationed. People were asked to find private replacement for hitherto public services and to accept that the reversal of fortunes was the just result of their sinful profligacy.

The 2006 film *The Children of Man*, directed by Alfonso Cuaron, is an extreme parable of the Greek predicament. Humanity is facing extinction after a long period of global infertility. Britain has been deluged by refugees and has become a police state with concentration camps. A brutal war rages between the government and bands of immigrants. Kee, the only pregnant woman alive, is escorted by a state bureaucrat and radical immigrants through the war zone and the camps towards the sea where a ship will take her to a 'human project' trying to reverse infertility. Kee gives birth in a room provided by a Roma woman and eventually makes it to the ship called 'Tomorrow' and the possibility of redemption.

Greek resistance was a long journey through the austerity desert. The Pasok and right-wing governments used migrants and women to display toughness and ideological purity. A disgraceful incident came close to Cuaron's nightmare. Before the May 2012 elections, ministers launched a campaign against 'foreign-looking' sex workers. They were rounded up, tested for HIV and detained pending trial for unspecified crimes. Their names and photos were publicized in newspapers and websites. The practice copied the infamous British Contagious Diseases Acts of the 1860s, which authorized the rounding up of prostitutes and women judged to be promiscuous for mandatory venereal diseases testing and subsequent imprisonment. As Joanna Bourke drily comments, 'the legislation treated women as a whole as nothing more than contagious animals, while at the same time they identified the real "mute creatures" in class terms'.[4] The contemporary operation added race to class and gender. The government was protecting the 'health' of family men from foreign sex 'predators'. When it became known that almost all detained women were Greek and many of them not sex workers, the publicity subsided. In May 2014, Katerina, one of these women, committed suicide. She had been kept in prison for a year, prosecuted for prostitution and intention to inflict grievous bodily harm. She was acquitted and later awarded €10 a day for the period of imprisonment. In May 2016, she was followed by Mary, another of the targeted

HIV women. Mary's mother wrote that their family was humiliated by health inspectors testing her grandson in his school. 'They disgraced us publicly', she added, 'now the [minister who launched the campaign] can sleep at ease.'[5] The persecution of the wretched of the crisis did not stop there. During the May 2012 election campaign, the Ministers of Health and Public Order launched a campaign to remove immigrants from city centres, calling them 'human trash' and accusing them of spreading infectious diseases. It was just for show; those arrested soon returned to the city centre. The right-wing government, elected in June 2012, promised to 're-conquer' central Athens from the 'invaders'. Once in power, it launched a campaign ironically called 'Xenios (hospitable) Zeus' to arrest and remove immigrants from cities. Detention camps spread everywhere. Calling the rounding of immigrants 'Xenios' indicated a certain postmodern irony if it was not ignorance of the meaning of the word.

Is there an escape from this catastrophic cycle of biopolitical neoliberalism? In John Carpenter's film *They Live* (1988), the protagonist John Nada – the Homeric *outis*, anyone and everyone – finds a pair of magic glasses. When he puts them on he sees the world in black and white. Commands appearing over the omnipresent media and subliminal advertising messages order people to obey, to consume, to conform. With the glasses on, however, the messages change. 'What you hear is lies.' 'The people of wealth and power are aliens with skulls for faces.' The sunglasses demystify dominant ideology and reveal the oppressive reality beneath the consumer heaven. The multiple resistances of the Greeks acted precisely as deconstructive spectacles.

The direct integration of workers into the debt economy can turn into the Achilles heel of late capitalism. If one of the links in the integration chain breaks the worker withdraws abruptly and violently. This can happen through the sudden loss of job, major deterioration in conditions of life or expectations, frustration of desires or promises. It is not enough. The protests, occupations and insurrections around the world from Tahrir to Syntagma, Puerta del Sol, OWS and Taksim demystified the dominant ideology and taught the power of collective resistance. Resistance disarticulates identities from the circuit of desire–consumption–frustration and helps to see through the secrets and lies of power. When life becomes unlivable and subjection intolerable, the refusal to obey the law and the invention of new types of resistance turns disobedience into a 'political baptism' that releases the subject from the consolations of normality and the numbing of normalization.[6]

In *Logan's Run*, those who realize that the carousel 'renewal' is a ruse leading to mass extinction, escape the city. They become 'runners' seeking a 'sanctuary' beyond the city walls. They are pursued by 'sandmen', special policemen, authorized to exterminate. Logan, a sandman pursuing a runner, realizes that there is no sanctuary and returns to the domed city to lead the resistance. This causes its demise, with the captive citizens released onto the outside. The South Europe utopia turned into the dystopia of unemployment, poverty and death. Like Logan and Kee, the answer is to escape, to exit the false paradise of obedient consumer happiness and of the state of exception of camps and riot police fighting the population. Utopias turn into dystopias when their kernel of 'truth' is revealed to be their fatal flaw. Dystopias on the other hand are a fertile ground for disobedience and resistance. The Greeks saw through the myth of consumer 'happiness' when the preconditions of pleasure became the portents of disaster. They persevered by using all sorts of resistance and eventually elected a radical left government. Did they exit biopolitical control? No, this is a much longer struggle; it is not simply a matter of parties, elections and governments.

2

Hunger Strikers
and Hunger Artists

2.1   The hunger strikers

Athens, January 2011. While the Egyptian revolution was in full flow, three hundred *sans papiers* immigrants from the Maghreb took refuge in *Hepatia*, a neo-classical building in central Athens, and staged a hunger strike. They had lived and worked in Greece for up to ten years doing the jobs the Greeks didn't want to do for a fraction of the minimum wage without social security. When the crisis struck they were unceremoniously kicked out. They had no Greek documents, work or residence permits and were liable to immediate deportation. During the period of fake growth their underpaid and uninsured work did the necessary 'dirty' jobs the locals would not do. When the crisis struck, they became surplus to requirement. After forty days, with several strikers in hospital with irreversible organ failure that would lead to death, the government accepted the bulk of their demands.

Athens, December 2014. Nikos Romanos, a young anarchist went on hunger strike while in prison. Romanos was a close friend of Alexis Grigoropoulos, who was murdered in central Athens by the police on 6 December 2008. Alexis died in the arms of his friend Nikos, whose life was marked by the death. The murder led to a two-week insurrection by Greek youth, which began the long spring of Greek resistance. In 2012, Romanos was tried for robbing a bank with anarchist comrades and was sentenced to a fifteen-year imprisonment. While in prison, Romanos took university entry exams and was admitted to the Athens School of Business and Economics. Prisoners were entitled to follow university classes under guard. Following the escape of another prisoner while on leave, however, leave privileges were cancelled. Romanos' hunger strike was a protest against the deprivation of his right to education. Eventually, after thirty-one days of strike and with pressure from social movements and Syriza, the right-wing government relented and Romanos ended his strike.

2.2   The hunger artist

Kafka's short story 'A Hunger Artist'[1] is set at a time and place where fasting was an art performed in public. Kafka's artist carried out his popular starvation act in a cage. A large number of spectators came to see the artist, with the public's excitement increasing with every passing hour. Full-time watchers, usually butchers, kept a continuous guard to ensure the artist did not cheat. But the artist was not satisfied. People did not believe him when he said that it was easy not to eat. Even worse his manager limited his fast to forty days believing that the public would get bored after that. As a result, the artist was not able to display his virtuosity fully. Interest in the art of fasting was diminishing, the crowds thinned and eventually disappeared. The artist joined a circus with his cage in a quiet corner and started his most audacious fast. Spectators scarcely glanced at him, however, as they went past on the way to a cage with wild animals. The artist was forgotten but persevered. One day a passerby asked the guards why his cage was empty and unused. When they entered and poked at the dirty straw, they discovered the famished remnants of the artist. After his death the attendants placed a well-fed and lively panther into his cage. The excited crowds returned to view the new resident.

2.3   Autonomy

The sense of freedom as autonomy brings together the hunger striker and the hunger artist. Jean-Jacques Rousseau wrote in the *First Discourse*: 'A pigeon would die of hunger near a basin filled with the best meats. And a cat upon heaps of fruits or grain, although each could very well nourish itself on the food it disdains, if it made up its mind to try some.' Compare the pigeon and the cat with the suicide, the martyr, the hunger striker. '[The beast] chooses or rejects by instinct and [man] by an act of freedom, so that a beast cannot deviate from the rule that is prescribed to it even when it would be advantageous for it to do so, and a man deviates from it often to his detriment.'[2]

Animals follow the law; they cannot break it. Man on the contrary is free to die of freedom. Autonomy is to create your own law and go against nature's law telling the hunger striker to eat and survive. Anti-naturalism is the morality of modernity. For Immanuel Kant, action is moral if motivated exclusively by respect for a law which demands that needs, passions and interests are set aside. The law and reason demand the renunciation of the flesh. For Sigmund Freud, civilization is the attempt to renounce sexual desires and drives and leads inevitably to discontent. For Jacques Lacan, modernity is symbolized by Kant's sadistic renunciation of the flesh. Bartleby's mantra 'I would prefer not to' differentiates humanity from animality. Before his death, Bartleby changed it: 'I prefer not to dine today...it would disagree with me; I am unused to dinners.'

Throughout history 'Freedom or Death' has been inscribed on the banners of warriors for religion, nation or ideology. Life is worth living, they proclaim, for values it is worth dying for. Terence MacSwinney, the lord mayor of Cork, died in Brixton Prison after 74 days of hunger strike in 1920. Mac-Swinney's cry was 'It is not those who can inflict the most, but those who can suffer the most who will conquer.'[3] His *cris de coeur* has echoed through the ages. Nikos Romanos' hunger strike belongs to the same project. He was prepared to die, if he was not allowed an education. From Samson to Christian martyrs, from suffragettes to anti-colonial fighters and hunger strikers, martyrdom performs man's essence in the form of departure from nature's call to survive and from the second 'nature' of social codes. Autonomy as defiance of the law is the highest moral achievement of modernity. This is why Bartleby is the most sacred modern saint.

2.4 Desire

Suicide and martyrdom are as ancient as Socrates and Jesus and as modern as Emily Pankhurst and Bobby Sands. In the arsenal of sacrificial self-harm, hunger and self-starvation have pride of place. Why? Eating is indispensable to life. Stopping to eat is the simplest negation of life's demands. There is more. For Hegel, Marx and Freud, eating lies at the origin of subjectivity. Hunger discloses a constitutive lack in the subject who needs food to survive. Lack gives rise to desire. Desire makes the subject aware of its difference and dependence on the not-I, the object world and the other person. Initially desire negates the not-I; the subject devours and assimilates the foodstuff, the object. But this devouring negation is not enough. It abolishes the object and throws the subject back to his illusory self-sufficiency. Desire must be displaced from food, the object, towards another subject. The other's desire and recognition gives rise to the full self, who sees himself reflected in the other's desire. This way the other becomes a substitute for food and is partly introjected through the constitutive action of her desire. In the dialectics of desire, the other is inside me and I am inside the other through our reciprocal recognition necessary for reaching self-consciousness. In this sense, food gets sacralized, every encounter with the other becomes a Eucharistic meal.

Hegel's phenomenology of identity is an invitation to the other to come dine with me. The subject negates the reality of objects by digesting them. But as food is not enough eating must take place in a romantic dinner setting. I become who I am only when I realize that I cannot fully enjoy food without a companion to praise and criticize the cuisine and each other. The ego is a digestive economy and a weight-watchers' meeting. Consciousness incorporates the object transforming it into thought and then excreting it back into material existence in the company of men. Freud and Lacan adopted the Hegelian dialectic with little recognition of the Master. Sexual desire is a displacement of the desire for food, of the demand for and pleasure from mother's breast. The ego comes to existence by identifying with another. We assimilate the object we long for by both eating and preserving it. No one who has seen a baby sinking back satiated from the breast and falling asleep with flushed cheeks and a blissful smile, wrote Freud, can escape the reflection that this picture persists as the prototype of the expression of sexual satisfaction in later life. For Lacan, this will become the equation 'desire is demand minus need'. The infant asks the breast for nourishment; this is not enough. He additionally demands the mother's unreserved love, opening the vista of the desire for the other over and above the need for the object. There is hunger in desire and insatiability. It goes back to the desperate need for the breast and for the love of the other.

2.5   Political hunger

Exodus or martyrdom is a common form of resistance by the contemporary *homines sacri*. Suicide, self-mutilation and immolation, boarding the floating coffins that daily sink in the Mediterranean are desperate acts used by those treated as expendable, redundant beings. The Arab Spring started with the self-immolation of Muhammad Boazizzi in Tunisia. The Athens hunger strikers realized that in a biopolitical world, life exists as registered life; undocumented life without birth certificates and IDs, visas and work permits is not recognized. Minimum humanity is created through what the immigrants lacked: *papiers*, IDs, documents. To retrieve life from this administrative void, they had to come to the threshold of death.

The immigrant hunger strikers and Romanos were martyrs in the double meaning of the word: witnesses and sacrificial victims. As witnesses, they stated that there are higher truths than life; life is worth living for values worth dying for. The hunger striker disrupts sovereign power. It is the Sovereign's prerogative to demand martyrdom and to sacrifice subjects and enemies. He negotiates the link between secular and holy by making sacred (*sacer facere*): war, the death penalty, mercy, the rituals of sacrifice and consecration are ways through which the transcendent is both acknowledged and kept at a distance. The hunger strikers take a wager with mortality. They remind us that the theologico-political order, based on the ability to take life and let live, can be disrupted by removing from the Sovereign the power of life and death. In doing so collectively, they trace the promise of a new type of power not based on imposed or voluntary sacrifice. A type of power that goes to the edge of finitude and touches it but does not pierce or transcend it, as Jean-Luc Nancy puts it.[4] Their gift to the immigrants all over Europe was to tell them that they can take their lives in their hands against the iniquities and humiliations of governments, authorities and paper pushers.

2.6   Food and words

Food and words are eternally competing. 'Don't speak with your mouth full' my mother used to say. I wondered why. Eating and speaking are the greatest pleasures, why not enjoy them together? She had a point, though. Food and speech engage the same orifice. They compete for mouth, tongue, saliva; when one takes over, the other withdraws. Words replace food, as Deuteronomy puts it: 'Man doth not live by bread only, but by every word that procedeeth out of the mouth of the Lord doth man live' (8: 3). The Book of Revelation 10: 9 takes it further. The anger of the Lord tells man 'to eat the sacred book, it shall make thy belly bitter, but it shall be in thy mouth sweet as honey'.

Eating silences words. Starving on the other hand hungers for sense and craves for meaning. Starvation may be involuntary, during a famine, the failure of crops, a bout of anorexia. Or, it can be voluntary. Religious fasting differs from dieting or a hunger strike. Hunger has its histories and cadence, its symbolism and purpose. Medieval saints fasted to control sexual desire, to cleanse and mortify the body. Contemporary dieters fast to serve sexual desire, to cleanse and beautify the body. For the striker, hunger is a political speech act. Political fasting is temporally and spatially situated. René Girard argues that at times of great conflict, the community projects its tensions onto a victim whose sacrifice temporarily pacifies it.[5] Hunger strike is a personal sacrifice that aims to rebuild community. Eating supports subjectivity; starving reassembles the fissured community.

What about the hunger artist? Hunger as performance aims at whittling away and eventually depriving the striker of body. Hunger makes the body depart from itself. Starvation is not just a cleansing or purification, but a disembodiment, a body eating itself away, becoming pure soul or air. The striker is inebriated by air, as Emily Dickinson said. The hungering person negates food, the not-I, creating a figure of autarchy, self-sufficiency and auto-desire. I don't need the other, I do not lack, I am complete in myself. The hunger artist wants to go to the end. But he is not interested in sacrifice or death. The artist becomes himself by eating himself up, by showing that he can survive the absence of the other, the not-I. His purpose is not to die but to perfect his art, to become the best hunger artist, to bring the ejection and redundancy of the other to completion. He is the absolute figure of sovereignty, greater than his manager, more powerful than the panther. The artist expels himself, spits himself out in the same movement that establishes himself. The *telos* is not death but self-sufficiency, becoming an independent *causa sui*.

The earlier *fames interruptus* of the hunger artist was stopped at forty days, the time Moses spent on Mount Sinai before receiving the covenant or Christ in the wilderness. The hunger artist seeks not sacrifice but deification, a self created by excluding the not-self, sustained by ceaseless purification. He succeeds only in part. He rejects the other as object but cannot survive without the other as subject. When the spectators stop observing and admiring him, he wilts and withers away. Starving like all performance needs spectators, admiration, commentary. We come to life through the gaze of the other and we survive in her regard. We cannot live on unless seen by others. Starvation acquires meaning through its spectacularization. Similarly with the hunger striker. He does not want death but victory, he is not suicidal but militant. Romanos repeatedly stated that he did not want to die but to exercise his right to education. The striker's strategy is to overpower the oppressor with the spectacle of his disempowerment. In the case of the Egyptian hunger strikers, the lack of *papiers*, documents, letters – the institutional recognition by the other – is complemented by the rejection of food, the not-I as object. Lack of papers and lack of food offer a reversed but symmetrical refutation of the world. The same happens when refugees and immigrants sow their lips up. Romanos linked denial and lack of education with the absence of food; for him, education was food for life.

Acts of disempowerment must be communicated. Others must be implicated in the strikers' performance, they must witness the act. The starving body performs only when it communicates. Bobby Sands and the Irish hunger strikers spoke to each other and the outside world by means of minuscule written scrolls hidden in the body orifices, called 'comms' for communication.[6] The Egyptian strikers created the conditions that led to victory by using press conferences and releases to describe their predicament to the initially hostile public and media. Romanos kept issuing statements encouraging his supporters, explaining his motives, asserting his right to a life examined. This is the main reason why the hunger strike is the preferred mode of sacrificial self-annihilation. Unlike self-immolation or a bullet in the head, it uses time to increase interest and anxiety. Its news reporting always starts with the number of days the strike has been going on, each day another nail in the coffin but also a further call to the people to rally around and to the authorities to concede. Passing time turns the strike from *sacri-fice* to *commu-fice*, from making sacred to making community.

The hunger artist too lives for the other and by the other. This is why he found enough strength at the end to whisper his last words into the ear of the overseer, pursing his lips as in a kiss. 'You should not admire my fasting', the artist said, 'I can't help it. The only reason I starved was that I've never been able to find the food I like. If I had found it, believe me, I should have made no fuss and stuffed myself like you and everyone else.'[7] The artist had not found the food he needs. This is why it was easy to fast. It is not that he did not eat; he ate nothing. He ingested the hole in the midst of existence. Insatiability is the same whether you eat or starve. Only the other could give the nourishment he longed for, by gifting him the desire in her eyes, turning him into an artwork. In the absence of the other, the artist turned art into starvation unto death. He was no longer a hunger artist but a hunger striker. His sacrifice allowed the crowd to gather again, the community to reassemble.

Starvation reveals the alternating and mutually exclusive place from which eating and speaking proceed. As a collective performance, voluntary starvation gathers together and creates community in the spectacle of its autarchic self-annihilation. Such foundation could eventually constitute a community that jettisons sacrifice and retains autarchy. The three hundred *Hepatia* strikers are the only immigrants who, against the atomizing tactics of the immigration and refugee law, managed to retrieve their life from the administrative void that had engulfed them. Collective anti-naturalism and sacrificial autarchy – this is how victories are won. They are collective victories; only collectivities can win political battles. The new community is founded on the disappearing body of the hunger striker/artist. Life wins over death.

3

Radical Philosophy Encounters Syriza

A strange incident in June 2011 changed my research interests first and my life later. I had just finished my invited address to the Syntagma Square occupation in Athens and members of the multitude were lining up to speak. A man in the queue was showing strong symptoms of stage fright. But he proceeded to give a beautiful speech. When I inquired, he nonchalantly told me that when he started speaking he was just mouthing the words. A stranger inside him was dictating what to say.[1] I heard a similar story in December 2015. A taxi-driver who recognized me confessed that he had voted Left for the first time in the September elections. He came from a right-wing family, his father had fought the Communists, he had never voted for anything but conservative parties. When he entered the polling station and was given the Syriza ballot paper a 'powerful force' inside him made him 'cross the line'. Before putting the envelope in the ballot box he crossed himself – the act was too transgressive. Voting Left had been dangerous for many years. After the vote, he added, he felt a new man. Attacking the government in front of 10,000 people is not the same as crossing a ballot paper in the privacy of the polling booth. Yet the cause and the form of the acts were similar. A strange inner call led both to a radical transformation. The Syntagma man had discovered an unknown and awesome ability to speak in public. The taxi-driver had committed what was for him a major sin. In different circumstances both had become men of resistance.

In an interview towards the end of his life, Michel Foucault commented that 'politics has existed since the nineteenth century because of the revolution'. Now that revolution has disappeared, he continued, 'there is a risk that politics will disappear' unless one invents another form or substitute for it'. Against the models of the Greek sage, the Jewish prophet and the Roman legislator, Foucault imagines a type of intellectual who would pose the question 'whether the revolution is worth the trouble, and if so which revolution and what trouble?'[2] If the revolution has ended, what is the politics after the revolution?

Does the recent wave of resistances and Syriza's victory mark the emergence of a new post-revolutionary politics? There is no doubt that they have brought a long period of left defeat and retreat to a temporary end. Radical philosophers, however, have responded with a sense of embarrassment, almost disbelief. It is as if the lull that followed the emptying of the squares came as a relief, allowing the theorists to return to well-known reservations about the crowd, democratic politics, the Left. The Syriza victory increased the embarrassment. It was clearly a victory for resistance. Syriza won because people who resisted the right-wing government at every turn adopted the Left and brought it to power. The victory confirmed the ability of resistance to move to institutional politics and even win elections. It obliged radical philosophers to take a view towards the Syriza government.

The encounter with Syriza has not been the happiest. Let us have a brief survey. Jacques Rancière's argument that politics is the emergence of the excluded 'part of no part' is perhaps closest to recent events. However Rancière himself admitted somewhat ironically that 'I have nothing in particular to say about Greece, or about the revolutionary strategy that should be adopted so that Greece triumphs and Europe goes on to become Communist.'[3] Antonio Negri and Michael Hardt, the theorists of multitude, conclude in their *Declaration* that 'we need to empty the churches of the Left even more, and bar their doors, and burn them down!'[4] From a different perspective, Howard Caygill's book *On Resistance* shares the pessimism. Its concluding sentences refer to contemporary insurrections without much hope. 'Resistance is engaged in defiant delegitimization of existing and potential domination but without any prospect of a final outcome in the guise of a revolutionary or reformist result or solution…The politics of resistance is disillusioned and without end.'[5] Finally, Slavoj Žižek. He called 2011 'the year of *dreaming* dangerously'. 'Now, [in 2013]', he added, 'every day brings new evidence of how fragile and inconsistent that awakening [of radical emancipatory politics] was.'[6] Žižek kept telling audiences around the world that he did not appreciate the carnivalesque explosion of the street. The key question for him was not how to get to the radical change but what to do the day after. He did not trust the Left to win elections or to succeed as a government. I demurred. 'The day after should be the same as the day before', I argued in various debates with Zizek.[7] Getting to victory after decades of defeat is hard. The best guarantee of success for the Left is to build a close relationship with social movements and working people. Once in. power, strengthen the collaboration and develop policies in conjunction with people and movements. After two years of Syriza government, it is clear that policy drawbacks are often a result of abandoning the people or policies that brought the victory. Zizek came to Athens before the 2012 elections and spoke at a rally with Alexis Tsipras and this author. After the 2015 coup, however, he distanced himself from the 'defeated' Syriza government.

Alain Badiou is the philosopher who has most consistently tried to answer Foucault's question. He is the last representative of the French philosophical renaissance of the 1960s. Politics is a type of thinking, he argues; its 'truth' emerges in political action. Philosophy takes this truth and universalizes it. But when he turned to recent resistances and the Syriza victory, he had the greatest reservations. His theory of the event has been particularly influential among young radicals who have used it to analyse the recent uprisings. Not the Master. At a conference about the 'Greek symptom' in January 2013, this author shared a panel with Badiou. After my upbeat presentation of resistances in the Mediterranean, Badiou responded: 'I certainly admire the eloquence of my friend and comrade Costas Douzinas, who has buttressed his avowed optimist with precise references to what he takes to be the political novelties of the peoples' resistance in Greece, where he has even discerned the emergence of a new political subject.' When I heard the next sentence I thought I had misunderstood: while the courage and inventiveness of the resistance is a cause of enthusiasm, it is neither novel nor effective. The same things happened in May '68, in Tahrir Square and even 'in the times of Spartacus or Thomas Munzer'.[8]

Badiou returned to his musings in a newspaper interview. The 'Left' is part of a 'structural imposture' he claimed. It has abandoned its commitment to radical change and promotes the myth that parliamentary elections can be used for 'revolutionary' purposes. The interview was taken a few days before the crucial 2014 European elections, which Syriza was hoping to win – as it did. The interviewer tried to distinguish between social democracy and the Left. Badiou had none of it. The radical Left differs only in 'nuance and detail, a minimal further redistribution without any foundational changes in the dominant capitalist logic'. The present author is a 'useful enemy' because, despite his links with emancipatory movements, he offers a 'beautified and limited' picture of the situation and does not realize that we must begin from scratch, following the example of the 1840 revolutionaries in 'ideology, political criticism, types of mass action, organization. We must rethink everything and experiment.'[9]

I plead guilty to the indictment of 'avowed optimism'. New forms, strategies and subjects of resistance appear regularly without guidance from Badiou, Zizek or Negri. We have entered an age of resistance. The Syriza victory, prepared by the Greek resistance, was the first major success of the age. As resistances spread around the world from the austerity-hit countries to Turkey and Brazil, the former poster boys of neoliberalism and later to Britain and the USA, philosophy has the responsibility to explore the contemporary return of protest, insurrection and direct democracy and to reflect on Syriza's lessons for the Left. There is an additional reason for 'strategic' optimism. In his late political essays, Kant advocated a kind of philosophical public relations *avant la lettre*. In Kant's philosophy of history, nature guarantees the eventual civil union of humanity in a cosmopolitan future. Theoretical certainly does not release the philosopher from the duty to preach the inevitability of cosmopolitanism, offering a helping hand to nature. Similarly, after the repeated claims about the 'end of history', the 'end of ideology' and the like, the Left must proclaim that radical change has returned to the historical agenda and little Greece is leading the way.

What causes the pessimism of radical philosophers? It looks as though Hegel's 'owl of Minerva' has not left its nest. Is this because we are not at 'dusk' yet? In other words, philosophy cannot respond to the uprisings and the victory of the Left because they are still too recent and raw? Or, is this enduring melancholy the result of a certain theoretical and political sclerosis? Failure, defeat, persecution and the accompanying paranoia have marked the Left. It is true that it has lost a lot: a unified theory, the working class as political subject, the promised inexorable forward movement of history, the planned economy as alternative to capitalism. The falling masonry of the Berlin Wall hit Western socialists more than old Stalinists who relatively easily morphed into post-soviet oligarchs. Following Wendy Brown, we can call 'left melancholy' the attitude of the militant who is so attached to his theoretical love object despite its repeated failures that he is unwilling to abandon it.[10] Left melancholy betrays the world for the sake of old certainties.

Radical philosophy has returned to a particular type of 'grand narrative', which combines an obsession with the explanation of life, the universe and everything with the 'anxiety of influence' the previous generation of greats – Sartre, Althusser, Foucault, Deleuze, Derrida – generates for their successors. There is much to learn from contemporary radical theory. However, contemporary philosophers differ from their Marxist predecessors. Reacting to the economism and statism of the Left, they steer clear of socio-economic analysis and, with a few exceptions, despise the state. In Badiou's term, they advocate a 'subtraction' from state politics. They prefer the lecture hall and the art gallery to the street or the party and have little participation in politics. Syriza dirtied its hands. It fought and lost an asymmetrical battle but is still there, bloodied but fighting. The Greek people recognize that.

There is nothing inherently wrong with grand theory, except when it paraphrases Brecht's dictum that if the people have chosen wrongly the rulers will elect another people:

if the facts disprove the theory, so much the worse for the facts. Cases that cannot be seamlessly inserted into the theoretical edifice – Greece, Spain, the youth insurrections, the Syriza victory – are downplayed or rejected. It may feel better for some on the Left to lose gloriously than to win even with some pragmatic compromises along the way. Repeated defeats do not help the millions whose lives have been devastated by neoliberalism. What the Left needs is not a new model party or an all-encompassing brilliant theory. It needs to learn from the popular resistances that broke out without leaders, parties or common ideology and to build on the energy, imagination and novel institutions created. Ordinary people created the historical opportunity by being well ahead of theory and party.

The Syriza victory was a direct effect of Greek resistances. It could become the catalyst for radical change elsewhere. For this to happen the European leftists would have to abandon its fixation with rapid and ultra radical and exotic but unrealistic solutions. Many are happy to celebrate Fidel, the late Chavez, Morales or Correa. They carry out politics by proxy and theory by association dismissing the indigenous Left as irrelevant or misguided. This could be justified in the 1990s and 2000s, the years of the defeat of the Left and the rise of radical Latin America. It has changed now. Greece has given the first victory to the European Left. One reason for the July 2015 retreat was the absence of a strong solidarity movement by the European Left and Social-Democracy. The Syriza government fought and is still fighting a David and Goliath battle. The responsibility of European democrats is to support the Gaul village still resisting.

4

A Philosophy of Resistance

When does resistance rise, how does it work, can it ever succeed? Can we generalize the new forms of resistance and its links with state power? Michel Foucault started the analytics of power. Françoise Proust, following Foucault's pioneering work, continued with an analytics of resistance.[1] This chapter follows and updates Proust's project offering seven theses on resistance. They could help build the New Left for the twenty-first century.

Thesis 1. Resistance is a physical law of being, affecting every relationship

Resistance is physical: every force affected by another provokes an action, which thwarts the first without stopping it. Wherever there is power, in an intimate relationship or family, in a university, company, political party or state, there is resistance. 'This would be the transcendental of every resistance, whatever kind it be: resistance to power, to the state of things, to history; resistance to destruction, to death, to war; resistance to stupidity, to peace, to bare life.'[2] The resisting force accompanies the force it resists, but also confronts, destabilizes and redirects it. Resistance is therefore inescapable, immanent to every relation. From the moment being takes form and figure or a balance of forces stabilizes itself, it encounters resistances, which irreversibly turn, twist and fissure it. As the mirror of power, resistance is a relationship, a series of interactions among people and things. It keeps changing the balance of forces, disturbing power asymmetries, continuously re-defining and amending the position of the participants. Resistance is therefore the condition of existence of every power relationship and not a transcendent force or violence that befalls its site of intervention from outside. It is in this sense that Gilles Deleuze commenting on Foucault writes 'the final word on power is that *resistance comes first*'.[3]

Thesis 2. Resistances are situated, local, concrete and multiform

Resistance emerges in a concrete situation and reacts against a unique balance of forces. Resistances are local, arising on a specific site and a singular conjuncture. It is therefore difficult to develop universal principles of resistance, even though common trends in different sites of power may lead to similar reactions. Every situation and age creates new forms, strategies and subjects. Resistance reacts to the concrete circumstances it finds itself in; it breaks down the basic constituents of the power constellation, analyses and puts them again together in a different new edifice that opposes or reroutes the earlier combination. This process feeds into power too. The new dissident configurations may be taken on by the counter-resisting dominant force and transfer from resistant to ruling positions.

This parochial operation is evident in most cases of political resistance. In early modernity, the breaking of machines and sabotage by Luddites and Diggers among others responded to the capitalist destruction of traditional skills and crafts. Today the huge movement of populations in and across continents leads to demands for free travel and a guaranteed minimum income. Excessive indebtedness of individuals, companies and states leads to repayment strikes and calls for debt haircuts. Their dependence on the operations of power is evident in recent resistances. The new forms of resistance emerge within and against the circuits of power, reacting and rearranging its operations. As we will argue below, they react to postfordist capitalism, the operation of power on life, the decay of parliamentary democracy and the effects of these developments on law. This is the reason why a presentation of the state we are in must necessarily precede any attempt to understand the specificities of forms of resistance.

Thesis 3.   Resistance is a mixture of reaction and action, negation and affirmation

Resistance is local and situated, it responds to a situation or reacts to an event. Reaction may turn into reply, retort, renewal. Reactive resistance conserves or restores a state of things power has disturbed. Active resistance deconstructs the adversary's arms and borrows, mimics or subverts their components. Using the enemy's rules, it invents new rules and institutions and occupies the space reactive resistance has cleared. When power promotes privatization of public assets, resistance deconstructs the private/public dichotomy and promotes new forms of property, such as the commons. When power creates unemployment, resistance constructs new cooperative, self-ruling forms of work and social activity.

In the current state of Europe, resistance against austerity is necessarily negative and reactive. It tries to protect the remnants of the social state and to reassert the right of citizens to a minimum dignified standard of life. This struggle could bring together radical, social-democratic, centre-left, liberal and even centre-right political forces which reject the neoliberal obsessions and perversions of the European elites. It would be a defensive alliance aiming to return in part to the post-Second World War social contract. The travails of the Greek people and Syriza's opposition to austerity allowed a large part of European social-democracy to re-examine its position. The creation of an anti-austerity alliance friendly to Syriza looked improbable in 2015. In early 2017, things have changed. Italian, German and French social-democrats have moved to the anti-austerity pole scared by the punishments meted out to Greece and the scary rise of the extreme Right. For Syriza and the Left, such an alliance can only be temporary and preparatory for the next active and creative steps.

Thesis 4. Resistance changes subjectivities and constructs new identities

Individual and collective subjectivities emerge in the interstices of relations of power. Subjects are always subjected, subjugated to the dominant forces in order to become free.[4] Resistances unpick and re-direct the subject. At the individual level, revolt lies at the foundation of self. For Freud, happiness exists at the price of revolt. There is no pleasure without obstacles, prohibitions and interdictions, without law, injunctions and sanctions. The pleasure principle calls on the self to conform, to obey the law, to fit in the social order. But this accommodation to the world is followed as day by night by the transgression of prohibitions, the Oedipal revolt against the principle of power symbolized by father, sovereign and law. The autonomy of the individual emerges at the price of revolt. Legal and social prohibitions and injunctions open the route of revolt, allowing the self to reach autonomous maturity. Revolt forms an integral part of the pleasure principle. But it is also part of the darker timeless drive beyond the pleasure principle. The return of the repressed trauma is integral to part of the repertory of resistance.

Individual and collective dissident identities emerge out of acts of resistance. The tension between symbolic differentiations and hierarchies on the one hand and imaginary idealizations on the other disarticulates the psychic sense of normality. We become new subjects, the 'stranger in me' emerges because my existence has misfired. When an unemployed youth realizes that his condition is a symptom of the disease of the socio-economic system and not his own failure; when a *sans papiers* immigrant realizes that her predicament is the symptom of a political and juridical system that divides and excludes; when a lesbian realizes that the suppression of her sexuality is a symptom of a system of disciplining and controlling bodies; at that point subjects of resistance emerge. The negation following the failure of routine identities opens the road to the universality of resistance. It involves risk and perseverance, resistance is the courage of freedom.

This means, however, that one cannot become a subject of resistance simply through education or ideological training.

Love and revolution come unannounced, like a miracle or an earthquake. One is hit on the head, like the blow of a *coup de foudre*; after that nothing remains the same. Joining the uprising or the occupation, irrespective of ideological commitment, is more important than ideological pedagogy or indoctrination. A Turkish protester told me that the first time she found herself in Gezi Park, Istanbul, with her little daughter during a riot-police attack she was paralysed with fear. Then people pulled both mother and child back and gave them water and protective masks for the tear gas. Her first reaction was to push them away, unused to the caring touch of strangers. But once she realized that people were trying to help and felt the force of solidarity, the fear left her; she came back to the occupation every evening.

If, according to Louis Althusser, ideology 'interpellates' the obedient subject, in the political baptism of resistance, subjectivity is 'interpellated' by the event. The call does not come from Althusser's proverbial policeman but from what one may call the 'normativity of the real'.[5] Resisting subjectivity emerges when this initial call of refusal perseveres in the care of self with others. It is about behaviour not language, bodies not ideas, courage not theorizing. As Foucault puts it, 'There is after all no first or final point of resistance to political power other than in the relationship one has to oneself.'[6] Resisting subjectivity is the change of one's relationship to oneself, to the pleasure principle and the death drive. 'I resist therefore I am', as Daniel Bensaid put it.[7]

These elliptical theoretical notes have developed out of the experience of recent forms, strategies and subjectivities of resistance. Three forms of political subjectivity or subjectivization have emerged reacting to the current modes of subjection: the expendable humans or *homines sacri*, the bio-politically excluded, finally, the democratically disenfranchised.

The resistance of the contemporary *homines sacri* takes the form of exodus or martyrdom. Suicide, self-mutilation, hunger strikes, boarding the floating coffins that daily sink in the Mediterranean are characteristic responses of those treated as expendable, redundant, economically useless. The Arab Spring started with the self-immolation of Muhammad

Boazizzi in Tunisia. The uprisings of pupils, students and marginalized youth in Paris 2005, Athens 2008, London 2012, Ferguson, Missouri in 2014 and elsewhere reacted to the biopolitical combination of the injunction to consumer satisfaction and police repression. Here the form is the spontaneous insurrection and riot, which often involves violence against property and looting. It arises after a violent event such as the killing of Alexis Grigoropoulos in Athens, Mark Duggan in London or Michael Brown in Ferguson after a long series of humiliations that exhausts moral patience. The insurgents are people who exist socially but not politically. As their interests are rarely heard, accounted or represented, they must perform their existence, through the absolute negation of what exists. They did not demand anything specific using Roman Jacobson's 'phatic expression': they simply said 'enough is enough, 'here we stand against'. We do not claim this or that right, but the 'right to have rights', the right to resistance.[8] This is politics at degree zero, a first but inadequate political baptism in the emergence of political subjectivity. Caught between the demands of insatiable desire and brutal repression, they performed the absolute freedom of acting out. When negation and affirmation, reaction and action cannot be synthesized they remain opposed, with violence the link.

Finally, democratic experimentation is carried out in occupations and encampments as well as in other forms of direct democracy. Citizens have been disenfranchised by the decay of parliamentary democracy and the disappearance of serious alternatives in the rush of right-wing and social democratic parties to the mythical centre. The principle of popular sovereignty that forms the foundation of many constitutions has turned into a legitimation myth as democratic government increasingly mutates into technocratic governance. Occupations and encampments reject corrupt politics and post-democratic governance, abandon representation and the mandating of parliamentary politics and experiment with new arrangements of political space and time. The localization in a square creates a new fluid and open spacing of political power, while the intensity of bodily and emotional proximity, created by a common political desire, acquires the characteristics of an emergent constituent power.

The Syntagma multitude was the material coming together of people in public with a common political desire: radical political change. The demos returned to its original meaning as the *plethos* in assembly. The Syntagma occupiers were not the suffering and victimized population of media coverage. They were a resisting and active people who put into practice direct democracy and prefigured the necessary institutional reforms of a democracy to come.

Thesis 5. Resistance is a fact not an obligation, is *not* ought

Resistance does not simply apply values and principles and does not have a predictable point of condensation and explosion. We don't resist in the name of something. It is not the idea of communism or the theory of justice that makes us take to the streets. Resistance is the bodily reaction to an overwhelming sense of injustice, the almost irrepressible response to hurt, hunger, despair. Resistance may involve a vision of justice but this is not necessary, certainly not at the beginning.

Ideals are not the cause but the result of resistance. The ideas of justice, equality or communism are maintained or lost as a result of the existence and extent of resistance. Principles and values emerge in specific contexts as part of a resisting response to a particular configuration of power and only later claim universal validity. For Nietzsche, morality is the absolutization of a temporary balance of forces. In classical Greece, the *logos* was initially a philosophical weapon against the claims of elders and priests to power and authority. Christ's teachings started as part of the Jewish resistance against the Roman Empire. Early Christianity was a small and persecuted sect before turning into a global religion assuming the character of empire. Human rights started as political claims of citizens excluded from political rule before becoming universal principles of legality and morality. Today they are paradoxically both the ideology of late capitalist empire and the cry of the dissident. All normative claims start life as particular strategies of resisting a local configuration of power in a particular place and time. Parochial provenance and local encumbrance are entombed in their foundations and carry the seeds of their dissolution.

Universal values and their expression in rights exist not in some ethereal normative space of law-books and international treaties. It is only when people resist power and defend themselves that an actual conception of right comes to existence. It is not the existence of rights and law that makes people stand up. It is because people have stood up, and still do, to defend their dignity that rights have been created and power minimally respects them. For the ordinary person, disobedience is the deeply moral decision to break the law. It is a 'dangerous freedom'. In normal circumstances, morality and legality represent two different types of overlapping but not identical duty: the external duty to obey the law (in formal terms a heteronomous duty) and the internal moral responsibility that binds the self to a conception of the good (autonomy). Conflicts are usually solved in favour of the law. In disobedience, the duties collide and morality takes over.[9]

Thesis 6.   Resistance and its subject emerge through the exercise of the right to resist

While resistance is a fact not an obligation, the right to resist is the oldest, indeed the only natural, right. A legal right is justified and enforceable individual will. Whether private or public, the right to property or to vote, it appears as one, in-dividual, undivided. It claims a single source, the subject's will, a single justification, law's recognition, a single effect, the will's ability to act and shape the world. The modelling of political rights on property, however, contaminated their operation. As Hegel realized and Marx emphasized, a yawning gap separates the normative weight from empirical operation.[10] Formal right, the legal subject's capacity to will, is theoretically limitless. But real people are embedded and embodied in the world of particularity. Property and normalized propriety act as quasi-transcendental preconditions, bridging the divide between formal right (the universal recognition of will) and its effective realization in the world. We are all legally free and nominally equal, unless of course we are improper 'men', in other words men of no property, women, colonials, of the wrong colour, religion or sexuality.

At that point, will, the source of right, splits into two between that accepted and justified by law and a second, adopted by the dominated and the oppressed for whom right is not about law and judges, a game they can scarcely play. It happens when men act against a system that, while claiming to represent the common good, has become an alien essence. Secondly, when an inner rebellion reacts to the widening chasm between universal vocation and particular belonging and prepares the resisting subjectivity. The split in will and right is replicated in the resisting subject, who sees his inner rebellion not as a personal inadequacy or failure but as the symptom of the disease of the social order and its law. Right now becomes a battle-cry, the subjective factor in a struggle, which asks to be raised to the level of the universal. It is the claim of the dissident against the abuses of power or the revolutionary against the existing order.

Right has therefore two metaphysical sources. As a claim accepted or seeking admission to the law, right is a publicly recognized will, which finds itself at peace with the world, a world made in its image and for its service. Secondly, right is a will that wills what does not exist, a will that finds its force in itself and its effect in a world not yet determined all the way to the end. This second right is founded *contra fatum*, in the perspective of an open cosmos that cannot be fully determined by (financial, political or military) might. 'All the forms of freedom that are acquired or demanded, all the rights that are claimed, even concerning the things that seem to be of least importance, probably have a lost point of anchor here... [in a man who prefers the risk of death over the certainty of having to obey]... more solid and experiential than "natural rights".'[11] This drive to resist eventually confronts domination and oppression, including those instituted and tolerated by the first legalized will. These two conceptions of right, or of the universal, manifest the confrontation of the death drive against desire and the pleasure principle. On one side, an acceptance of the order of things raised to the dignity of general will, dresses the dominant particular with the mantle of the universal. The second universality is founded on a will created by a diagonal division of the social world separating rulers from the ruled and the excluded. It forms an agonistic universality emerging from the struggle of the excluded from social distribution and political representation. The excluded and disenfranchised are the only universal today in a legal and social system that proclaims incessantly its fake egalitarian credentials.

Thesis 7.   Collective resistance becomes political and may succeed when it condenses different causes, struggles and complaints

Resistance to power exists everywhere and keeps transforming relations between power and subjectivities. Uprisings go beyond their situated, regional operation and limited effectiveness, however, when they are compressed in their demands and concentrated in their appearance. Michel Foucault, commenting on the Iranian revolution, stated that 'it is a fact that people rise up, and it is through this that a subjectivity (not that of great men, but that of everyone) introduces itself into history and gives it its life...It is precisely because there are such [uprisings] that human time does not take the form of evolution, but that of "history"'.[12] As long as the protesters ask for this or that reform, this or that concession, the state can accommodate them. What the state fears is the fundamental challenge to its power by a force that can transform the relations of law and present itself as having a 'right to law'. In such cases, politics becomes the 'prescription of a possibility in rupture with what exists'.[13] After a long period when markets and pliant governments claimed that smooth uninterrupted evolution was the future of humanity, we have entered again a time of history. The world Occupy insurrection in 2011–12 did not lead to a significant rise of the Left. Only Syriza moved from militant opposition to government mansion. Only in Greece and Portugal did the resisting multitudes adopt left parties in order to transfer the demands of the street into the bowels of institutions. Discontent, anger, indignation survived and increased all over advanced capitalism. The 2011 insurrection was followed therefore, as expected, by a second wave of popular revolts. In 2016, the people of Britain, the USA, Italy, Austria, France and elsewhere turned to the populist and nationalist Right. The convergence of centre-right and centre-left into the 'extreme centre' was comprehensively defeated everywhere. Tony Blair, David Cameron, Hillary Clinton and Matteo Renzi were the victims of this popular insurrection.

The Left, besides Greece and Portugal, has not been able to capture and express the anti-systemic popular mood. Syriza, despite its compromise and defeats, has paved the path for a revival of the Left. Whether the alternative it offers catches on depends on the European Left's ability to learn from recent experience and build on popular resistances.

Part II
Syriza Agonistes

5

A Very European Coup

5.1 A crazy economics

The remarkable rise of Syriza, a small protest party hovering around the three per cent entry to Parliament threshold, is a story combining historic necessity, good fortune and a large dose of popular wisdom. In 2011, in a *Guardian* article entitled the 'Greek Spring', I argued that the resignation of the Papandreou government, hot on the heels of the Arab Spring, should remind Western governments that they too can fall 'if they abandon basic principles of democracy, social justice and independence'.[1] The article, published at the height of attacks on Greeks for corruption, laziness and cheating, attracted an avalanche of negative comment, including suggestions that I should resign my academic post. I persevered. Just before the May 2012 general elections, which Syriza lost to the right-wing New Democracy with the smallest of margins, I suggested that the election was the 'start of the European Spring'.[2] The penultimate step in the inexorable rise of the radical left came at the 2014 European elections. Syriza was four per cent ahead of the New Democracy governing party, giving a clear warning to those concentrating exclusively on fiscal deficits and bond prices that a major political earthquake was about to hit Greece.[3]

The Syriza victory in January 2015 and the formation of the first radical left government in Europe was the result of a strong trend that started in the 2011 hard winter of resistance. Greece was turned into a guinea pig for testing the most stringent austerity in Europe. The 2010 first bailout loan and its accompanying memorandum imposed tough recessionary policies and regressive public and private sector reforms. They were carried out on two fronts: fiscal austerity and internal devaluation. Austerity, aimed at reducing the 15 per cent deficit, was pursued through the reduction of public spending, the privatization of key state assets and the increase of tax revenues. Large numbers of civil servants were sacked or made to resign, social services were slashed, with health and education in particular unable to meet basic needs. ERT, the Public Television and Radio Corporation, was shut without warning in June 2013. Three national TV channels and many national and local radio stations were closed and two thousand five hundred journalists, technicians, administrators and musicians were dismissed. Repeated tax increases, including a regressive tax on real estate, took the bleeding of the economy to unprecedented levels. The humanitarian crisis that followed is well documented. The creditors hoped that their policies would generate primary budget surpluses,[4] which would be used to repay the escalating debt. The New Democracy and Pasok coalition government that preceded Syriza had agreed to create annual surpluses of up to 5 per cent of GDP between 2016 and 2022, something that no government since Ceauşescu's Romania has attempted or achieved.

The internal devaluation was carried out through the repeated reduction of private sector salaries, including the minimum wage, and the abolition of the bulk of labour law protections such as collective bargaining, the minimum wage and trade-union privileges. The impoverishment of working people alongside the deregulation of professions and trade, the IMF argument goes, would improve competitiveness and help economic growth. But the result was abject economic failure. The IMF admitted in 2013 that it had undercalculated the adverse effect of austerity on the economy – the so-called fiscal multiplier – by a factor of three. They believed that every euro taken from the economy would lead

to a fifty cents recession. In reality, national wealth shrank
by one euro fifty cents. A report by the Independent Evaluation Office of the IMF, published in 2016, offers the most
serious critique of the Fund's participation in the 2010 and
2012 programmes. It details a series of errors and reveals
that the Fund's involvement was the result of intense 'political pressures' by European governments and the EU. Despite
the IMF's view that the programme could only work if the
country's debt was substantially reduced, no serious attempt
was made to evaluate the viability of the debt or to insist
on its easing. The Europeans had decided to rescue Greece
from bankruptcy but were virulently opposed to a haircut or
restructuring of the debt, the larger part of which was held
by German and French banks. The Papandreou government,
desperate to get the loan, removed the reduction of the debt
burden from the negotiations. Even after the first bailout
loan was agreed, the report continues, the IMF participation
was not functional, lacked flexibility and violated its own
rules and procedures. The Europeans feared that the Greek
crisis would be exported and contaminate the Eurozone. As
a result, IMF staff were under permanent political pressure.
In a telling aside, the report admits that the IMF did not
appreciate until much later that the interests of the Greek
establishment would create unsurpassable obstacles. The IMF
'overestimated the administrative capacity of the Greek government and underestimated the opposition that structural
reforms would face from vested interests. In was in response
to the apparent lack of administrative capacity and political
will that structural measures proliferated at each successive
review.'[5] As Ambrose Evans-Pritchard commented, 'the harsh
truth is that the bail-out sacrificed Greece in a "holding
action" to save the Euro and north European banks. Greece
endured the traditional IMF shock of austerity, without the
offsetting IMF cure of debt relief and devaluation to restore
viability.'[6] He adds that the 'International Monetary Fund's
top staff misled their own board, made a series of calamitous
misjudgments in Greece, became euphoric cheerleaders for the
Euro project, ignored warning signs of impending crisis, and
collectively failed to grasp an elemental concept of currency
theory.' The combination of IMF repeated errors, absence
of political will of pre-2015 governments and resistance by

vested interests created the toxic environment in which the Syriza government now has to navigate.

The IMF *mea culpa* came too late. Salaries and pensions were slashed, the state silver was sold at bargain basement prices, a weak welfare state was starved of funds. After five years of economic and social devastation, the economy had shrank by 25 per cent, unemployment was at 27 per cent and the income and standard of living of the population had declined by 40 per cent on average. Private sector salaries were reduced by 25 per cent and the labour cost unit by 14 per cent in the hope of improving competitiveness. Most economists told the austerity governments and the IMF that salary levels make little or no contribution to the economy's competitiveness to no avail. The World Economic Forum reported in 2016 that in the period of salary cuts labour market efficiency plummeted placing Greece 116th out of 140 countries.[7] More than three million people were on or below the poverty line. More than 90 per cent of the 'bailout' loans were used to repay previous debt. The debt was €300 billion and 120 per cent of GDP in 2009 but had grown to €320 billion and 183 per cent in 2016. It is a crazy economics, resembling the medieval 'treatment' of using leeches to bleed people dry to cure them from all kinds of maladies. The therapy is worse than the disease. If undergraduate students of economics had made such basic errors in an exam paper, they would have failed the exams. In the Greek case, a whole people were condemned to failure as a result of the technocrats' abject mistakes.

5.2   A brief account of Syriza's rise

The Greeks resisted longer and more intensely than any other austerity-hit nation.[8] National and sectional strikes, protests and demonstrations came to a peak in the 2011 occupation of Syntagma, the central Athens square.[9] Over a three-month period, the occupiers experimented with direct democracy in daily assemblies. Specialist working groups provided efficiently many of the services usually offered by a functioning state. When the squares emptied following police attacks, people returned to towns and neighbourhoods and developed an elaborate network of solidarity and social economy initiatives. The ERT open initiative by the journalists, technicians and musicians who had been sacked when the government closed down the ERT Public Broadcasting Corporation in June 2013 offered the most pluralistic and free programming seen on Greek TV. The cooperative *Efimerida Syntakton* (Newspaper of Journalists), founded by sacked journalists and technicians after a major newspaper went bankrupt, fast became the largest selling paper on the centre-left. Thousands of solidarity initiatives offered basic services to Greeks and immigrants, from food and health care to clothing, education and legal advice. Three governments, that of Pasok under George Papandreou, the technocratic under banker Loucas Papadimos and the New Democracy-Pasok coalition under Antonis Samaras, resigned partly as a result of acts of resistance. In the national and European elections that followed, Syriza gradually climbed from four per cent of the vote in 2009 to 37 per cent in September 2015. It was a rare textbook case of a system of power collapsing.

Syriza is a small party hailing from the 'Eurocommunist' tradition. Initially it was a coalition or federation of smaller parties and groups on the Left. It eventually unified into a single party in 2013. Its tendencies and factions represent a wide spectrum of ideas and organizations aiming to renew and modernize the Left after the demise of Soviet communism. The rainbow colours – green for ecology, purple for human rights, pink for LGBT, red for class struggle and the movement against globalization capitalism and austerity, were added to the 'Eurocommunist' moniker of the 1970s and 1980s. Syriza members participated fully in the resistances and occupations without attempting to lead or impose their ideas on the multitude. Well before the crisis, the party had abandoned the Leninist tradition of democratic centralism and had adopted internal pluralism and democracy. Syriza is the only Western European party which managed to overcome in part the splits and internecine war on the Left. Acceptance of minority views created problems however. The so-called Left Platform of ex-Communists, operated as a party within the party using Syriza as a host in the tradition of Trotskyist entryism. The Platform secured positions in the party leadership, funds from the party coffers and a number of ministries in the 2015 government. Factional loyalty put Platform interests above those of party and state. After the July retreat, Platform members defected and created the left Unity splinter group. Syriza reassembled after the split. It still allows tendencies to operate but not organized factions. This helps create a climate of debate on principle and policy. Occasionally this leads to a confusing polyphony. The many shades of the Left cohabiting in party and government were and still are Syriza's great strength.

The encounter between the Greeks and Syriza was serendipitous. Just before the 2012 elections, Alexis Tsipras was asked on live TV about the party's plans. In an unprecedented and insolent display of youthful audacity, he replied that Syriza was ready and prepared to take power. Coming from the leader of a party that had received four per cent in the previous elections, it veered between the ironic and the ridiculous. It showed a new determination on the Left and is now considered as a key moment in the rise of Syriza. The Left had accepted its marginal political position in the past. For the first time, it declared that this acquiescence was over; Syriza was putting an end to a long period of defeat and marginalization.

5.3   The Syriza manifesto

During the hard years of austerity, the people massively deserted New Democracy and Pasok, parties that had dominated the *metapolitefsi*, the post-dictatorship political landscape. Syriza offered a new set of values and a highly educated political personnel (many graduates of British universities) unsoiled by endemic elite corruption, clientelism and cronyism. It promised to end the economic and social madness of escalating debt and catastrophic austerity within the EU's institutional framework. Its policies would hopefully enable progressives all over Europe to stand up to austerity and, if successful, return the EU to its founding principles of prosperity, democracy and solidarity. Alexis Tsipras called for a 'European New Deal' to restructure the debt burden for the whole of Europe and help initiate a period of growth. Citing the 1953 London Debt Agreement, which wrote down

German debt by half and linked repayment to the country's ability to pay, the government promised to seek a substantial 'haircut' of the debt's nominal value. A development clause would peg repayments to economic growth. This would allow the funding of a number of socially progressive measures: the easing of the huge tax burden imposed by the austerity governments, particularly of the hated real estate tax; pensions slashed by up to 50 per cent would see a moderate increase; public investment would help ease unemployment. This was the class foundation of the Syriza manifesto. It linked the easing of austerity and debt forgiveness to development priorities that would help the unemployed and poorer members of society.

Another cluster of manifesto promises related to identity politics and Syriza's powerful rights culture. It included citizenship for immigrants, cancelling the high security C-type prisons programme, reducing the prison population, introducing a number of laws protecting minorities from hate speech and crime and legalizing homosexual civil unions. Economic and social policies would not work, however, without a root and branch reform of the state and public administration. Corruption, cronyism, scandalous intertwining of banks, business, media and political elites are endemic and have contributed greatly to the country's malaise. It was widely known that public tendering was often a facade with major contracts given to government friends in advance of the bidding. It was widely known that citizens had to pay a fee to meet civil servants or ministers; investors, including foreign businessmen, had to advance a large bribe to various regulators and middlemen before receiving the necessary licenses and certificates. Professional football was riddled with corruption, fixed results and referee bribes. A colloquial 'shed' was the centre for fixing the winner of the league and non-cooperating referees or officials were brutally attacked forcing FIFA to intervene and suspend the premiership. Large kickbacks to political parties and politicians accompanied arms procurement and the fixing or the price of medicines. Tax evasion and avoidance was rife and was considered as normal practice with tax revenues consistently below those of other European states. Various lists of large and unjustified deposits of Greek citizens in Swiss banks and other tax havens were given to the

Greek government but were 'forgotten' and not acted upon. A relative of mine was told by the tax inspector that if she paid a large sum he would substantially reduce the valuation of an estate she had inherited and slash the inheritance tax. When she refused, she was told that people like her were 'a danger to our well-functioning system'. The infamous *fakelaki* or little envelope, a bribe offered to doctors in order to expedite tests or surgery, is part of the Greek lore. Legislators aware and often benefiting from such practices had passed laws giving immunity from prosecution to MPs and bankers and short limitation periods for ministers' criminal offences making their prosecution almost impossible. Corruption had become the normal state of affairs, universally known and widely tolerated.

The third pillar of the Syriza manifesto therefore promised zero tolerance towards large-scale and micro-corruption, the streamlining of red tape and a strict application of the rule of law ensuring that the state becomes the servant and not the oppressor of the people. Public tendering would become transparent; corrupt public contracts and outsourcing would be prosecuted. A Syriza government would upgrade the civil service, apply meritocratic criteria in appointments and promotions and abolish the practice of filling ministries and public utilities with political advisers and party apparatchiks. Private television stations, which had been broadcasting without licence or standard company and auditing practices for decades, would have to bid for a licence, pay an appropriate fee and comply with company and media law. Tax evasion and avoidance and a large black economy had played a major role in the perilous condition of state revenues. The party promised to pursue tax thieves and those who siphon their capital to tax havens and offshore companies.

The enumeration of the ills and failings of the Greek state in the Syriza manifesto reveals the enormity of the task facing the new government. The strict application of law in the public sector and respect for labour rights in the private, administrative efficiency and intolerance for corruption and cronyism are taken for granted in Europe. Improvements in these areas would give a clear sign that Greek politics has entered a new era. The first priority of the Syriza government, however, was to reverse the humanitarian crisis. It was the emergency corollary of the three policy directions. No civilized country can allow its people to go without food, heating, proper accommodation and a living income. Syriza promised free electricity, food, health care and help with the accommodation of the poorest members of society. It would stop the repossession of family homes for loan arrears and create a special bank to deal with the enormous household and enterprise debt. None of these policies was socialist in nature. They reflected the sorry state of austerity Greece.

In the January 2015 elections, the people adopted Syriza as the anti-austerity party closest to the ideals of democracy and solidarity that had dominated the protest movements.[10] Syriza had to deliver on its hard historic mission. The party did not manage an outright majority and its government was and still is in coalition with the anti-austerity right-wing Independent Greeks (AnEll). As people said in the street, they would be happy if a Syriza government delivered a tenth of its promises. They were not wrong. It soon became clear that Syriza was not fully prepared for governing in such hard conditions. The manifesto promises had not been accurately costed. The party sections had not prepared detailed policy plans for key ministries. Party personnel was not well equipped for the tasks ahead. Many ministers did not have a good understanding of their portfolio. Some who were appointed from outside party ranks were opposed to key policy directions developed over many years.

The Syriza government had to deal with many predictable shortcomings and own goals. But even a government of angels with Teutonic discipline, the wisdom of Athena, the cunning of Odysseus and the prudence of Nestor, would have been defeated by the concerted power, the vitriolic hatred and the black arts at the disposal of its opponents.

5.4   A very European coup

The novel *A Very British Coup* was written by the Labour MP Chris Mullin in 1982.[11] Inspired by Tony Benn's candidacy to become Deputy Leader, it has Harry Perkins, a working-class left-wing leader of Labour, winning the 1991 elections. The Labour manifesto promises to break up media monopolies, withdraw from NATO and the EU, remove American military bases, abolish the House of Lords and public schools and introduce true open government. To avoid taking IMF money and the accompanying austerity conditions, the government agrees a loan with the Soviet Union. Media magnates, top civil servants, the financial world, the MI5 and the CIA – indeed, the whole fearful establishment – conspire to stop the government. The stock market and the pound fall dramatically, firms close, factories and companies relocate overseas, a bank run is orchestrated. Extramarital affairs and youthful misdemeanors of ministers are excavated and are publicized all over the papers. Eventually, after an accident in a nuclear plant, probably engineered by the conspirators, the government resigned.

A real putsch that became known as the 'postmodern coup' took place in Turkey, in 1997. The Turkish Security Council published a statement on the Army website telling the government to change its mild Islamic policies. Within a couple of days the Erbakan political Islamist government resigned and his party was dissolved. Resentment against the Army and the deep state led eventually to the repeated victories of Erdogan, Erbakan's political heir. It was a conspiracy that turned against the conspirators. The real postmodern coup, however, was that of July 2016 against President Erdogan. It showed that taking over state television and a few barracks is not enough in a postmodern society. Widespread networking, social media and a plethora of broadcast and online news outlets have changed the rules and have neutralized the army's power to overthrow the government with a few clinical strikes on central targets.

The negotiations over the future of Greece in 2015 and 2016 amounted to a third kind of a 'very European coup'. It combined the steps of the English novel and the Turkish putsch. The huge power gap between the two parties made the negotiations brutally asymmetrical. 'Banks' was the advice God gave to Hitler for conquering the world, according to the joke, but he misheard and thought that the Almighty had said 'tanks'. The Greek negotiations were an attempt at 'regime change' using banks and the ECB's printing presses instead of tanks. It all started in 2012. Just before the elections, which marked the beginning of the Syriza ascent, *Forbes*, the magazine of the rich, published an article by Bill Frezza entitled 'Give the Greeks what they Deserve: Communism'.[12] The world needs a new communism in action and there is no better candidate than Greece, he argued, bullishly stating, 'Kick them out of the EU, cut the flow of free euros, sit back comfortably and enjoy the destruction of the Left for a generation.' It was the first published example of what became known as the 'left interval', a prescription for the overthrow of the government. Let them get into power, *Forbes* argued, make sure they fail and, by the same token, kill off the Left in Europe. Whether intentionally or not, the Frezza plan was put into action well before the Syriza victory. The outgoing government did everything in its power to make life impossible for the new people. They were expecting that Syriza would resign within three months of their victory.

When Syriza took over, in January 2015, the country was still in the second bailout programme; a final installment of €7 billion was due. The trap was set from the start. The Europeans set tight time limits for agreement on the incoming government. The Syriza government had to reach a deal about the existing loan within a couple of weeks of assuming office. The outgoing government had prepared the ground. Last-minute profligacy meant that Syriza found a €516 million hole in the state accounts. Former Premier Antonis Samaras admitted in 2016 that he did not complete the final review of the second programme and refused to have it extended for six months in order to deprive the incoming government of breathing space. In a later interview, he claimed that it was the creditors' decision not to advance the last €7.2 million installment of the second bailout in December 2014 because they knew that Syriza would win the coming elections and they did not want to 'risk' having the funds end up in the hands of the new government. It is clear that both the European and domestic troikas acted in concord.[13] Their shared aim was to accelerate the asphyxiation of the Syriza government by making sure that it would soon run out of money for salaries and pensions.

The Greek response and negotiating strategy was developed by Finance Minister Yanis Varoufakis and his team. It was unveiled when Varoufakis signed an agreement with the creditors on February 25. Its terms were characterized by a 'creative vagueness' that would be cleared in later negotiations. A number of Syriza policies were jettisoned with Varoufakis claiming, to astonishment on the Left, that '70 per cent of the [earlier] memorandum was acceptable'. The deal extended the loan term till the end of June by which point the post-2015 financing should be agreed. The government accepted not to take any unilateral action with fiscal consequences and to suspend its demand for a 'haircut' of the debt. It was not enough. Immediately afterwards, German Finance Minister Wolfgang Schäuble started issuing increasingly hostile ultimatums. The Greek proposals were naive, he declared, they were a 'Trojan horse'; beware of Greeks bearing gifts. The government was told that if there was a liquidity problem they should not pay salaries and pensions for a couple of months. The attacks soon took on a nasty personal character. Varoufakis was attacked for the way he dressed, for his academicism and didacticism, for his bad manners. He was said to be 'foolishly naive'; he should be replaced – giving rise to a diplomatic incident when the Greek ambassador in Berlin lodged a formal complaint. The CEO of the Frankfurt Stock Exchange called Tsipras and Varoufakis 'Taliban', while *Spiegel* claimed that Varoufakis displayed symptoms of psychosis. Like a schizophrenic, he believes in a parallel reality in which the villain is not Syriza but capitalism.

Following the German lead, the black arts of threat, blackmail and misinformation were put into overdrive. Daily anonymous briefings and hostile press commentary were accompanied by official threats about a pending 'Grexit'. Selected newspaper editors were told that the Greeks were 'uncooperative, confrontational, stubborn' and the patience of the Europeans was running out. Newspaper reporting on the confidential negotiations often sounded like the syndicated republication of a single source. Brussels had become a large *pissoir*: damning and often inaccurate information about the Greek position was leaked daily by commission officials to friendly journalists and was then widely repeated as fact. The Greeks did not reciprocate.

The threats were followed by punitive measures, described by Varoufakis as 'fiscal strangulation' and 'liquidity waterboarding'. The list is long. The European Central Bank (ECB) did not return to Greece the €9 billion profit made on Greek bonds as promised. It did not advance any part of the last installment of €7.2 billion from the second bailout loan despite the extension of its term. The ECB is legally obliged to offer liquidity to the Eurozone commercial banks. It piled on the pressure, however, by stopping the normal credit lines to high street banks and capping the mandatory Emergency Liquidity Assisntance lending. A drip-drip approach was adopted, offering small sums to the banks and keeping them begging for cash on a weekly basis. As Greece was still in the second bailout programme, this practice was probably illegal. Greece may receive some of the funds owed, Mario Draghi, the 'neutral' ECB President stated, if the government continues with the airport privatization programme started by the previous government. The threats and blackmails were self-fulfilling. People started removing their savings creating the beginnings of a bank run. No major panic followed, however. Bars and tavernas remained busy throughout 2015. After five years of catastrophic policies, dignity had returned. The European hostility was met in the streets with stoicism and a 'what do you expect?' reaction.

The European blackmail meant that the government had to give up the power of every sovereign state to implement governmental policies. It has to submit for approval its economic policies to the lenders, who insist on inspecting even non-fiscally sensitive legislation. As a result, several manifesto promises had to be abandoned. The first to go were fiscally sensitive class-related measures on tax, minimum wage and pensions. The policy emphasis moved from economic measures to easing the humanitarian crisis and improving the rights of minorities. Three hundred thousand families received free electricity, food vouchers and subsidies for rent. Close to four million families and small businesses were given the chance to pay tax, social security and other debt arrears in one hundred installments. Finally, the seizure of family homes for non-serviced loans was banned. People backed the strong negotiation strategy and the commitment to social justice. Syriza's dignified negotiations, after five years of continuous and voluntary government submission, compensated for the abandonment of economic promises. The watering down of promises to ease the tax burden and improve private sector

wages and pensions, however, started giving rise to popular
unease.

5.5   Get Syriza

No other interpretation can explain the emerging domestic and European establishment position except 'Get Syriza'.
Either overthrow the government or make it accept such
humiliating conditions that it would lose popular support
and split the party. How did the government respond? The
best guide for the early Greek negotiations strategy is Carl
von Clausevitz's theory of war.[14] Unlike Kant and Hegel,
Clausevitz believed that the metaphysical principle of modernity is enmity and war not freedom. Humanity is insecure,
surrounded by foes and persecuted by bad luck. Its existential priorities are therefore resistance and self-protection.
In an asymmetrical combat, the weaker force aims to preserve its power and to attack the enemy's weak points. It
avoids all-out war and uses guerrilla tactics, quick forays and
retreats, skirmishes and ceasefires. The inequality of material
arms makes the use of moral and symbolic resources central.
Furthermore the weaker side needs to gain time in order to
prepare its next steps and to secure space, safe zones for
supplies and lines of flight for retreat. The strategy aims to
maintain capacity while avoiding an escalation that could
lead to certain defeat.

The Greek government fought a metaphorical guerrilla war.
Material weapons and hard negotiating chips were scarce.
Greece had to resort to soft power and to moral and symbolic
arguments. The aim was to buy time and gain space through
the politicization and triangulation of the negotiations. Talks
were conducted as far as possible away from unaccountable technocrats in political institutions, such as EU Council
meetings and summits. The hope was that unlike recalcitrant
number crunchers, even hostile politicians would appreciate the significance of Syriza's popular support. Buying time
was necessary in order to gain some control of the hostile
state machinery, prepare negotiating positions and implement
a few manifesto promises. Inexperienced politicians had to
learn the rules of ruling from scratch. The government needed

time in order to communicate its unorthodox positions and start building alliances. Time won would allow the moving of the negotiations terrain towards friendlier territory. This was achieved in the first few months of negotiations.

Third parties or issues were directly or indirectly introduced into the negotiations in the hope that the huge power imbalance between the principals could improve. The visits by Premier Alexis Tsipras and senior ministers to Russia, USA, China and Latin America moved in this direction. The government communicated internationally that the fate of Greece had serious economic, geopolitical and security implications. The country is in the middle of a geographical crescent in flames from Ukraine to Syria, Iraq, the Middle East and North Africa. The response of foreign governments was friendly but reserved. No financial help was forthcoming nor were major powers prepared to antagonize Germany and the EU. The warnings and fears were confirmed in 2016. The escalating wars in the area, the huge refugee flows into Greece, the terrorist attacks and instability in Turkey turned Greece into the only stable country in the Eastern Mediterranean.

The next Syriza task was to consolidate the home front. Successful guerrilla depends on the support or toleration of a sympathetic public. Containing and reversing the humanitarian catastrophe helped retain the support of the population. In the first part of 2015, up to 60 per cent of Greeks approved the hard negotiating position. Tsipras had an unprecedented approval rating close to 80 per cent, despite extreme hostility from establishment media. It made sense. A feeling of national dignity and honour returned after five years of ritual humiliation. The humanitarian crisis had an international dimension too. Recent crises were triggered by natural causes, such as earthquakes or tsunamis. By insisting on the humanitarian effects of austerity, the government highlighted its man-made nature. Austerity was castigated as a moral wrong. Its authors have moral and perhaps legal responsibility. The parallel reactivation of the old claim for reparations for Nazi atrocities, closely linked to the concept of crimes against humanity, strengthened the moral argument. When Jerun Dijsselbloem, the Eurogroup president, and Declan Costello, a EU emissary, tried to stop the humanitarian crisis bill going through parliament because it violated the 'no unilateral action' condition, the government persevered and the lenders under public pressure had eventually to concede.

Moral and symbolic arguments must be communicated to the Greek and European public in order to work. Those who donated funds for the relief of Ethiopian, Pakistani or Indonesian victims of natural disasters are more receptive to moral than to economic arguments. Stories of great suffering are more effective than the recitation of deficit and debt figures. The negotiating strategy had to play to the European gallery and not just to the 'suits' in the conference room. The Greeks were addressing the European publics above the heads of the hostile Berlin, Brussels and Frankfurt establishments. They had to tailor their message for multiple audiences. Stopping home repossessions and reconnecting electricity was of importance to the Spaniards; stopping water and other public utility privatizations to the Italian and the Irish; giving good arguments about the catastrophic effects of austerity to the British. The Greeks were telling people in London, Madrid and Dublin that elections matter and that democratically elected governments have greater legitimacy, if not greater power, than financial markets. The hope was that the European publics would put pressure on their own governments to reach an honest compromise. Immanuel Kant argued in his late political essays that the moral progress of humanity was confirmed by the European public's celebration of the French revolution. Supporting the Greeks in their asymmetrical negotiation would similarly confirm popular commitment to democracy and solidarity.

Getting the public involved exposes the protagonists to great acclaim and even greater vituperation. The theatrical aspect of the negotiations attracted interest in the persons involved. Varoufakis performed brilliantly as an actor and became a European celebrity. The German government and the EU demanded his removal from the Finance Ministry. It was a clear indication that Varoufakis was succeeding in the communication, if not negotiation, stakes. How did the early successes of the Varoufakis' negotiation turn to the defeat of the third memorandum? The enthusiasm created by the polished public performance concealed problems that became clearer as time passed. The path to the July 2015 defeat was opened by the February deal. The vagueness of its terms extended to a newcomer's basic mistake. Varoufakis expected and – according to other versions – was promised that the substantial sum of money outstanding from the second loan would be paid to Greece on signing the 'creatively vague' deal. When the government claimed the money, the Europeans responded that no written agreement existed, except for an equally 'vague' oral promise, and they refused to pay. The story is symbolic of the negotiations. On the blue side, the aggressive and 'perfidious' Europeans were assisted by an army of advisers; on the red, the naive Greeks were good at presenting the wide picture but without much preparation and detailed technical understanding or support. Used to heated and highly sophisticated debates in student union assemblies, they believed that logical and theoretical argumentation would persuade people determined to impose harsh terms as a *quid pro quo* for the loan. When funds started running out the government faced great difficulty in paying salaries, pensions and maturing bonds. It had to ask local authorities and public sector Pension Funds to transfer their contingency funds to the state in April, opening a front between the government, civil society and Quangos. The noose was gradually tightening around Greece's neck.

The second error was to drag the negotiations out after April in the belief that the Europeans would cease worrying about the implications of Grexit on the Eurozone. It was a reasonable assumption sustained by many, mainly American, economists and think-tanks, who predicted an economic Armageddon if Greece left the Euro. 'Chicken', 'dare' or 'hawk-dove' are popular applications of 'game' theory. The player in a duel assesses the opponent's willingness to go all the way or to blink first and acts accordingly. It is the poor man's version of the Hegelian master-and-slave dialectic. The EU and the ECB, unlike the Greek government, however, started taking precautions. The limited use of the 'chicken' tactic became apparent in late May when Athens delayed the scheduled payment of a maturing IMF bond. The Greeks expected a major crash of stock markets and a worsening of the credit rating of vulnerable countries such as Spain, Portugal and Italy. However, the quantitative easing introduced by Mario Draghi as part of a series of fire-prevention measures meant that the fears of the financial markets were contained.

Furthermore, German and French banks had offloaded their Greek bonds. Greek debt was now held by European institutions, governments and the IMF. The ECB had built a fortress around the Eurozone and had neutralized the main Greek weapon.

Time started working against Greece. The existing second bailout agreement was ending in June, allowing the ECB to stop the financial drip that was keeping the banks afloat. The time bought had changed the perception of European public opinion towards Greece. But now the government had no time left and should have concentrated on gaining space in the form of clear concessions in return for the unavoidable third bailout loan and the accompanying austerity conditionalities. Varoufakis continued playing dare, not appreciating that the goalposts had moved. It was even worse. In early May, Greek negotiators learnt that the German authorities were preparing a plan to exclude Greece from the Eurozone. Schäuble's plan, revealed fully during the July negotiations, had reached full operational level. Greece would be expelled from the Eurozone, initially for a five-year period and some financial assistance would be offered to mitigate the resulting humanitarian catastrophe. The government's negotiating strategy was in tatters. Not only did the Germans not fear any adverse effects, Grexit had become their preferred solution. Varoufakis' main chip in the poker game was stolen by the opposition. Grexit turned into a powerful weapon against Greece. The miscalculation was made possible by the negotiators' inexperience and was aided by a second mistake. The Left aims to carry out a concrete analysis of the concrete situation taking full account of the balance of forces. Liberal cosmopolitans, on the other hand, believe that good arguments, reasoned positions, and the Enlightenment values can carry the day against materially superior opponents and their aggressive political and ideological interests. It is the Habermasian illusion: the belief that an 'ideal speech situation' exists in politics, which allows reason and good will to prevail. Like all bargaining positions relying exclusively on argument, moral value and high principle, the strategy was doomed to fail.

The political stakes were – and still are – huge for Greece but not insignificant for the Europeans. Syriza's victory had opened the possibility of anti-austerity ideas taking hold in other Southern states. The dream of Spain, Portugal or Italy going left was the stuff of German and Dutch nightmares. The Greeks had to be stopped for political not economic reasons; the left contagion had to be contained in the Eastern Mediterranean. The capitulation of Cyprus under a nominally Communist government was seen as a model for the disciplining of Greece. The July retreat was a result of a combination of factors: the overwhelming anti-left balance of forces, the overestimation of European fears about Syriza's contamination effect, liberal naiveté and a lack of alternative strategies. Varoufakis had to go. His performance started on a high but wilted with the passage of time. His mark-sheet is mixed. His early strategy was excellent. He took his opponents by surprise and spoke to the European public with a combination of academic gravitas and theatrical panache. But his inability to change strategy once the early plan backfired undermined the government's attempt at an honourable compromise. Hubris is the combination of excessive voluntarism, unrealistic rationalism and unbridled self-belief. Voroufakis had all three. His departure was inevitable. It finally came when the government changed negotiation strategy. It was understandably seen as a capitulation to the Germans.

5.6   The endgame

Strategy and tactics have to be tested against results. By May, after three months of delaying tactics, it became clear that the Europeans had decided to engage the heavy artillery. Every time the Greek government presented a proposal to solve the long-term problem of debt viability, it was asked to have it reviewed and evaluated by the technocrats. Every time Greek authorities returned with detailed cost calculations of the new austerity programme, the creditors challenged the political framework behind it. The IMF insisted on internal devaluation through further reductions in private sector salaries, weakened labour law protections and deregulation of professional activities. But it also kept asking for debt reduction to make it viable. The European Socialists were more sensitive to Syriza's democratic mandate but unwilling to negotiate the easing of debt. Caught between the rock of a permanently increasing debt burden, with new loans used to pay the earlier debt, and the hard place of escalating recession, Syriza ran out of negotiating room.

The endgame brought out fully the players' power imbalance. On Thursday 18 June, while Tsipras was in Russia, Reuters reported a leak from a member of the ECB Board, according to which the high-street banks might not open the following Monday. It was a clear call to people to withdraw their savings on Friday – a self-fulfilling prophecy that could amount to a criminal offence. I was having dinner with senior government members in Athens when the news broke. I was surprised and delighted by their response. They decided not to give much emphasis to the leak and to play down the continuing attacks in order to contain its adverse effects. There was no bank run on Friday morning. Savings of up to half of GDP had already fled in 2014 and 2015 to foreign banks or were hidden under mattresses. The Europeans had finally decided on an all-out attack. Unusually for such an emotional people, the Greeks were keeping calm.

Greece submitted a new set of fully costed proposals in late June. They were a major retreat from the Syriza manifesto and went a long way towards the creditors' demands. The government accepted further fiscal discipline by cutting public spending and increasing taxes to a total of €7.9 billion. The new burden was distributed in a more just way. Seventy per cent of the new taxes were placed on the shoulders of the rich by increasing the corporate tax rate from 26 to 29 per cent and imposing a one-off tax on corporations with profits of over half a million. For the first time, the proposals were received well by the lenders, who stated that they formed a basis for agreement. Immediately afterwards, four days before the end of the second bailout programme, the lenders increased the amount demanded to over € 11 billion and reversed distributional priorities. The bulk of the new burden would hit the poorer part of society through a reduction of pensions and increases in VAT. Angela Merkel called the deal 'generous'. Donald Tusk, the President of the European Council, said that it was a final 'take it or leave it' proposal. 'The game is over'. It became clear that the 'negotiations' would conclude only if the government capitulated to the blackmail. Against this background, late on 28 June, Alexis Tsipras called a referendum asking the people to reject the creditors' proposal.

The 61.3 per cent 'No' in the referendum changed the political landscape. Chapter 15 discusses the referendum in detail. After his victory, Tsipras went back to Brussels to negotiate, with the full support of opposition leaders. He was hoping that the popular mandate would allow him to reach a better deal in return for a third bailout loan. He was wrong. The weekend negotiations were 'the most fateful days in the history of the beleaguered single currency' and probably in the history of the EU before Brexit.[15] He faced an unprecedented blackmail that became known worldwide with the Twitter hashtag 'this is a coup'. Tsipras was offered a third €84 billion loan, accompanied by a series of harsh austerity prerequisites. The alternative was an exit from the Eurozone. Capitulation or Grexit were the two equally bad prospects. Tsipras did not have a choice between good and bad but between worse and worst. He could neither accept nor reject the blackmail without jeopardizing Syriza's political identity or the survival of the country. This kind of desperate dilemma is well known to the Greeks. Classical tragedy is built on such non-negotiable dilemmas, from Oedipus and Antigone to Medea and Phaedra. Two obligatory laws clash; the human will err and will be punished whichever he obeys. Alexis Tsipras' referendum call was an attempt to divert this typical *aporia*, this impossible passage between the gaping mouth of Scylla or the aggressive claws of Charybdis, towards a more manageable question: do the people back the government's rejection of aggressive austerity while accepting its commitment to keep the country in the Eurozone? On Monday 15 July, after seventeen hours of talks with the European leaders through the night, Tsipras isolated and exhausted conceded. He accepted a deal that, while much better than that offered the previous week, continued the neoliberal agenda and further abandoned the class-based promises of the manifesto.

Grexit, solidly rejected by the Greeks in repeated opinion polls, would have been disastrous. Even its staunchest supporters agreed that its immediate impact would have further deteriorated the economic situation of a country that had already suffered such economic catastrophe. Unlike Argentina,

Greece could not foster its recovery by exporting commodities. Its negative trade balance is dominated by the import of oil, food and pharmaceuticals, the retail price of which would have skyrocketed in the wake of the devaluation of the post-euro national currency. It is not possible to calculate in advance how long the post-Grexit recession would last. Rationing fuel and heating oil, milk, meat and basic medicines would have been the left government's short suicide note.[16] The middle-class' pots and pans protests against President Allende in Chile, or the repeated military and civilian attempts to oust President Chavez were chilling reminders of the limited powers of a government that has acted against entrenched class interests.

Tsipras admitted that the blackmail and the calamity of Grexit made him concede. He compared the agreement positively with that of the previous New Democracy-Pasok government or that offered to him before the referendum. He presented the deal to parliament in August. The main opposition parties backed it; the pro-Grexit Syriza MPs opposed it, depriving the government of its majority and bringing it down. In early September, Tsipras called new elections. The electorate was given a full prospectus of the July capitulation and still voted for Syriza with a percentage close to that of January. It was clear that the strong relationship between leader and people, forged at the referendum a few months earlier, had weathered the problematic outcome of the negotiations. Faced with the third memorandum, the Greeks chose Tsipras, who promised a cautious and socially just distribution of the new burdens, against the New Democracy opposition, which is ideologically committed to neoliberalism and austerity. It was the third Syriza victory in nine months and a confirmation that the radical Left still had a popular mandate. But the relationship had changed: the powerful January love affair was turning into an ordinary marriage. Tsipras was no longer the indisputable love object of the Greeks, someone who could give them back both dignity and prosperity; he was gradually turning into another normal political leader.

The blackmail and the defeat in the July negotiations was inflicted in order to make the Greeks consider Syriza turncoats at worse or hypocrites at best. It was the final part in the 'Get Tsipras' strategy. Did the coup succeed? Yes and no. The overall strategy succeeded but not fully. Syriza was split; the government fell. Twenty-five deputies, many of them senior government ministers, and many party members left Syriza and created the Popular Unity pro-Grexit party. The ex-communist old-timers chose to abandon the responsibility of running the country in order to keep their hands pure and their souls beautiful. They have introduced two innovations into the pantheon of radical strategy: the juridical and the monetary road to socialism. Zoe Constantopoulou, the parliament speaker who left Syriza, treats the law as a sacrosanct entity that through its strict application can bring about socialism. Popular Unity leaders on the other hand claim that Grexit is the only path to a radical future. Their hubris was punished by the ultimate nemesis of not receiving the three per cent threshold necessary for entering Parliament. Against the hopes of Greek and European elites, Syriza survived and is likely to become a dominant political pole in Greece, replacing the rump Pasok party. Greece's overall success or failure depends on the fortunes of the Syriza government elected in September.

6

Contradiction is the Name of the Governing Left

The Left in power? Four enticing words. The question mark at the end is most important though. What does the Left mean today as ideology and vision, as organization and party, as movement and government? No simple answer exists. We have no recipe or textbook to pick from the shelf, adjust to the Greek situation and apply. The theoretical and political uncertainties become harder when the Left gets into power – or, more to the point, when the Left is elected into government. After all, power and government are not synonymous. The Greek power structure has hardly noticed the Syriza government. The first Syriza government (January–August 2015) gave at times the impression of a rabbit frozen by the powerful beams of the incoming juggernaut of the troika, recently upgraded to a quartet with the inclusion of the European Stability Fund. It forms a powerful holy alliance of creditors. In return for loans, it has imposed stringent austerity and structural reform measures similar to those catastrophically tested in Africa and Latin America. Greece is a country with limited sovereignty, a quasi-protectorate.

Ministers report that they often feel like a 'government in exile' with the creditors' emissaries acting as colonial viceroys. The lenders have used the weak power of the country to increase their vetting powers by stealth over almost every governmental policy even if it does not have fiscal implications. Education is a case in point. The creditors in apparent close collaboration with previous ministers have tried to block reforms extending basic labour protections to private school teachers and insisting that private universities should be allowed against the clear constitutional provision. But the government has also to deal with the 'domestic' troika. Banks, big capital, establishment media and politicians launched on election day a campaign of support for the anti-Syriza coup. The greatest difficulty is encountered in the public sector. Senior civil servants opposed to the government's existing or feared policies and junior officials accustomed to minimal effort hold ministers hostage. Ministers were (and still are) thwarted by public officials who believe or plan the downfall of the government and the return to right-wing dominance. Senior officials are not the Permanent Secretaries of 'Yes Minister' repute, who kowtowed to arrogant and ignorant politicians on the surface, while pursuing their own policies. In the short period between the two 2012 elections, when the hitherto absurdity of a left government became a possibility, Syriza members visited various ministries and were briefed by civil servants. After the polite briefing at one of the key ministries, the delegation was told that when the government changes from one party to the other seven thousand civil servants and advisers are replaced by members of the incoming party. Syriza had fewer members at that point. It resolved not to follow that highly inefficient and problematic practice. Syriza ministers have kept to the pledge through principle and necessity. The number of political advisers has been radically reduced and trust has been placed on existing officials. The civil service has not reciprocated. Built over forty years by the *ancien régime* it has attached its loyalties firmly to the colours of its political sponsors. Wrecking tactics have a single purpose: to frustrate their political 'masters' and expedite their departure. Ministers recite stories of impotence and frustration. They were and still are denied files and data necessary for the development of policy; policies have repeatedly failed because officials are unwilling to implement them; anonymous briefings and leaks alert the press about the planning of a radical policy. As Ian Traynor put it, Schauble's finance ministry in Berlin has been 'the most promiscuous leaker of documents in Greece'.[1] The Syriza government has been operating in a minefield.

These difficulties could have been predicted. As Michalis Spourdalakis, a leading Syriza academic, put it, 'no attempt at radically transforming society has ever been anything but a painful marathon with numerous retreats, defeats, diversions, and short-term disappointments'.[2] The core contradiction is this: when a radical left party takes charge of the state, it encounters a hostile institution organized to prevent its ascendancy and frustrate its plans. Marxist political and legal theory has considered state and law antagonistic to the Left in content and form. For critical jurisprudence, legal personality, rights and property are the forms necessary for the operation of capitalism.[3] A fundamental function of the state is to ensure that the class struggle is contained and the small victories of the working class do not jeopardize capitalist domination.[4] The claim that the law will 'wither away' in communism follows from these premises. The Greek state's long history of repression and persecution of the left has made the hostility even stronger. From the end of the civil war to 1974, state employment and various benefits depended on the existence of a 'certificate of correct social beliefs' issued by the police and denied to left-wingers and their families. The relationship between the Left and state institutions has been frosty at best and antagonistic at worst.

The old left strategies for taking over the state have become irrelevant for some time. The reform or revolution dilemma no longer applies. Power cannot be taken by charging the Bastille or the Winter Palace. The 'transitional' government strategy was developed in an age of liberal democracy with developed constitutional guarantees. It is of little help in neoliberal capitalism. Gramsci's 'war of attrition' and Berlinguer's 'historical compromise' opened new ways for the Left in advanced capitalist states. It was Nikos Poulantzas, a member of the Eurocommunist precursor of Syriza, who came closest to developing a strategy for a democratic road to socialism. The Left has to be both in and against the state, it must take it over and act against its institutional constraints, strategic choices and ideological direction. For the late Poulantzas, the state is not an entity or instrument but 'like "capital", it is rather a relationship of forces, or

more precisely the material condensation of such a relationship among classes and class fractions, such as this is
expressed within the State in a necessarily specific form.'[5]
As the material condensation of the class struggle, the state
both organizes the unity of the dominant bloc and serves the
overall legitimacy of the social order by managing popular
consent. State institutions, typically the law and the civil
service, normalize and solidify the balance of social forces.
State power selects strategically its areas of intervention in
order to maintain class domination. According to Bob Jessop,
these strategic choices serve class or fractional interests and
operate through the selective filtering of information, the
systematic lack of action on class sensitive issues, the pursuit
of mutually contradictory priorities and counter-priorities,
the uneven implementation of measures and the pursuit of
ad hoc and uncoordinated policies.[6] At the same time, the
struggles of the working people both in and outside the state
re-direct institutional priorities and score occasional political
victories, which register the intensity of the class struggle. For
Poulantzas, 'centres of resistance' emerge in the state. They
are represented by personnel coming from the popular classes
and are manifested in institutional decisions that promote the
interests of working people without jeopardizing the overall
balance of forces.

This analysis helps us understand the predicament of the
Syriza government. The Greek state and its top personnel
have consistently helped stabilize the relationship between
capital, politicians and the media. Its strategic choices and
institutional structures serve to maintain the balance of class
forces. In the recent period, state intervention promoted the
interests of finance and banking and downplayed those of
industry and construction. State practice has consistently
mobilized corruption and favoritism for pacifying dominant class tensions and micro-delinquency for keeping the
people at bay. State 'delinquency' generates a modicum of
consistency and continuity and mediates class and personal
interests. Rogue practices guarantee class domination and
popular acquiescence. Thus Syriza inherited a public sector
which combines traditional anti-left bias with a distorted
view of strategic selectivity. Civil servants resisting institutional reforms or progressive policies express both their class

position and deeply embedded vested interests. Faced with such recalcitrance, the government should have removed top civil servants as soon as it realized that resistance to change is a structural characteristic supported by a sense of personal entitlement. The class orientation and ability of public sector workers should have become the main criterion for posts with policy or implementation responsibility. This did not happen in the first period giving the impression that the government was not bold enough in its fight against corrupt or inefficient practices and encouraging their more discreet continuation. If class domination is inscribed in the organization and institutions of the state, the Left must facilitate popular advances in the public sector and encourage social movements to keep putting pressure from outside. Secondly, when it became clear that fiscal constraints would block class policies, Syriza should have concentrated on institutional reform. Popular participation in micro-corruption does not prevent a widespread clamor for a more efficient and honest state. The Left has the responsibility to move towards a normal public administration while at the same time introducing policies that change the persistent class bias of Western state rationality. If Syriza cannot succeed in its class policies, it should at least claim the mantle of the great reforming power. It could be its greatest legacy if the combined forces of the European and domestic troikas succeed in overthrowing it. Finally, the strategic selectivity, so successfully used by the dominant class, should be adopted by the Left too. The key sectors that would help transfer resource and power from capital to working people and from state to citizens should be identified, priorities and tasks should be set with ministers and institutions charged with their time-limited and reviewable delivery. It would be a delightful irony if the methods and disciplines of a well-functioning administration were to be introduced for the first time by a left government intent on frustrating the capitalist state's strategic aims. Those considerations mean that the extension and deepening of democracy in state and society are of prime importance. Socialism will be democratic or it will not be.

The specifically Greek problems have been exaggerated by changes in the international environment, which have removed or weakened state competences and have built protective fences around capital. The former political 'heights', state government parliament, no longer have adequate control of social and economic life. The balance of power has moved towards financial capital. Globally, the financial system has become almost free of state regulation. International and transnational bodies such as the World Trade Organization, the World Bank, the IMF and the Basel Committee on Banking Standards, as well as various forms of private ordering, have undermined the national–international law divide, creating a hybrid regulatory system that stands above domestic law. Neoliberal policies have entered all areas of international economic law, seriously restricting national freedom of movement.[7] The German demand that fiscal discipline and debt breaks must become constitutional provisions in Eurozone countries is one part only of the wider constitutionalization of a particular economic dogma. Domestically too public administration has been structured in a way that limits political control. The separation of powers has atrophied, the executive has become all-powerful, parliamentary control of the executive has become a perfunctory ritual; administrative functions have been divided into small, highly independent units, regulators and Quangos have proliferated and have been insulated from political oversight; development mechanisms and financial tools have been given to non-political agencies. Finally, a legal wall has been built around capital, making the exercise of non-orthodox economic policy almost impossible.

These complicating factors and the hostile environment make the left project especially hard and full of paradoxes. Contradiction, negotiating a way between and overcoming opposed and even incompatible demands, is the name of the governing Left. The general contradiction between state and Left takes a particular form in Syriza led Greece. The austerity memorandum signed by Alexis Tsipras is the effect and cause of the inherent and unsolvable tension between capital and state on one side and working people and the Left on the other. Although the agreement was better than the first two and a clear improvement on that offered to Tsipras in June, it includes a set of recessionary measures. It reduced the burden on the economy by €20 billion, shrinking the primary surplus the country must achieve by 2018 from the five per cent agreed by the previous government to 3.5 per cent. Compared with the Syriza manifesto, however, it was a clear retreat and a partial acceptance of neoliberal policies. The debt was treated once more as a liquidity problem; the new loan will be used to repay the maturing debt and recapitalize the ailing banks. As with previous deals, the loan is predicated on a number of 'prior actions'. They include a rearrangement of the pension system to reduce its cost, increased taxation, including hikes of the regressive VAT, and the creation of a super-fund charged with the exploitation and partial privatization of public assets. The implementation of these measures in 2016 led to popular discontent and to a crescendo of attacks from the opposition. The people's reaction was understandable. They voted for Syriza in September 2015 knowing that further austerity measures would follow. They preferred a party that disagrees with neoliberalism to manage the new conditionalities instead of those who ideologically support them. They had not realized, however, the full nature of the measures agreed, which was now becoming painfully clear. The attacks by opposition parties on the other hand are typical of political hypocrisy. These parties had voted the July 2015 compromise. They had put pressure on the government to concede and accept harsher conditions than those eventually agreed. In the referendum they had argued against the government's defiance of the troika and threatened people that if the 'No' wins, European Union membership would be jeopardized. They had displayed the kind of blind Europhilia that has been roundly defeated in the Brexit referendum and the rise of anti-elite parties around Europe.

There is no doubt, however, that Syriza was defeated. As Athena Athanassiou noted soon afterwards, party and government must acknowledge defeat in the July battle and prepare for a long campaign. It must turn defeat into victory.[8] Slavoj Žižek has similarly argued that 'the true courage is not to imagine an alternative, but to accept the consequences of the fact that there is no clearly discernible alternative: the dream of an alternative is a sign of theoretical cowardice, it functions as a fetish which prevents us thinking to the end the deadlock of our predicament'.[9] This is a necessary first step. Yet, the claim that the left interval was completed, that Syriza 'betrayed', 'sold out' or accepted the neoliberal orthodoxy, is absurd. Those on the left of Syriza claim that the 'short' road to socialism should have started immediately after the elections. Negotiations and compromise with the creditors is tantamount to apostasy and treason. For the Right, small victories for the unemployed, the poor and the workers, achieved within the memoranda straitjacket, prove the government's Communist leanings. They are both wrong.

All governments, whatever their colour or ideology, have to govern. A left government is not accountable solely to party members, social movements or its electorate. It is accountable to the whole population first, then to its voters and, finally, to its own party members. Syriza is a government of all Greeks and bears responsibility for the whole country, not just a part of it. It must negotiate a passage between state continuity and commitment to ideology. This is why the party must remain separate and independent of the government in order to debate and develop theoretical tools and policies, which can be used to correct and re-direct the necessary compromises. The question remains, however. Can Syriza govern in a radical way after the July agreement? Only time will tell whether the defeat turned Syriza towards the social-democratic 'third way' or forced it into a temporary retreat. Let me repeat: we don't have a textbook definition of what 'radical Left' means in the twenty-first century and, similarly, what 'left governmentality' is. Planning for a socialist future is a conundrum that could tax the brightest minds and the fieriest hearts. And we have to deal with it here and now.

6.1   A litany of contradictions

The most general contradiction facing Syriza is that between left ideology and the austerity policies imposed by the creditors. The measures implementing the deal are the material recognition of defeat. The contradiction takes a number of concrete forms. It appears when the ideology of ministers clashes with the specific policies they have to implement. Several ministers have stated publicly, for example, their disagreement with the privatization of public assets. The ministers of Maritime Affairs and Energy have repeatedly railed against the privatization fund and have expressed strong disagreement with the forced sale of the ports of Piraeus and Thessaloniki, provincial airports, the land of the former Hellenicon airport, or a large part of the Public Electricity Corporation. The ministers responsible for these sales have negotiated a better deal for the Exchequer and local populations than that agreed by the previous government. Still, as James Galbraith comments, the sale of the port of Piraeus to the Chinese company Cosco 'had the interesting postmodern twist of a left-wing government in a capitalist society imposing labour standards on a right-wing company from a Communist country'.[10]

These sales go against Syriza's clear opposition to privatizations. Perplexed opposition politicians and mainstream media use ministerial reserves as proof of its inability to govern. It is further evidence of its hypocritical or 'schizophrenic' behaviour. The role of the governing party, they believe, is to support ministers, popularize policies and distribute patronage. Yet a left party is not a job centre, a lobby group for big interests or a cheerleader for its government. It must keep a distance from the state, acting as a socially embedded critical ally. It must condemn policies that depart from ideological commitments. The party and its ideology form the main insurance against the attractions of power and gradual capitulation. As Stathis Gourgouris has noted, the denunciation of austerity by ministers and party manifests the agonistic nature of left governmentality in a capitalist society.[11] Nothing is more radical and scandalous than a government that proclaims its disagreement with the policies it has to implement and calls them the result of blackmail. This condemnation would not be enough, however, if it was not accompanied by policies and programmes mitigating the effects of austerity. The government has been consistently developing such programmes. They fully justify Syriza's claim that it remains a radical party.

The tension extends to relations between the government and the party. It takes two forms. The party has repeatedly called its members to participate in strikes against austerity and has marched alongside protesters. The party youth has condemned the use of police to evict long-standing occupations and squats in Thessaloniki, police brutality against refugees and the teargasing of pensioners. Local party branches are the party-in-community, limbs and manifestations of a collective intellect. They gauge problems, anxieties and expectations and try to resolve them locally. If this proves impossible, they pass them to on to MPs and ministers. Unlike previous practice, however, party and government should not promise or offer personal favours. Party intercessions with ministers should only take place when general principles are at stake or a large number of people is unfairly affected by law or policy. The role of a left party has to be redefined when it gains power and Syriza has responded well to the new duties.

There is a second more problematic tension however. Some leading ministers sidelined the party after the January victory. They misinterpreted the change in government as regime change and tried to appease establishment figures, while neglecting their own constituency. According to Spourdalakis, 'joined or at least supported by political figures with roots in a wide range of old and new political parties ranging from right-wing to centre-left modernizers, the leadership became alienated from Syriza's radical physiognomy as a party'.[12] As a result, party members are rarely invited to participate in planning governmental policies and are often ignorant of legislative initiatives. The danger of becoming too enamored with power and its accoutrements is ever present. The party's role is to keep ministers on the ideological straight.

These tensions extend to the relationship between government and party on one side and social movements on the other. Syriza's victory was built on resistance and activism. After the elections social mobilization declined. The reasons are many. The election of a government broadly supporting the social movements demands has a calming effect. Voting soothes the street; electoral victory crowns the resistance and sends people home. The first Obama campaign mobilized a large number of politically inactive African-Americans and Latinos. Once the White House was won, however, activists were told to return home, creating a political lacuna later filled by the Tea Party and the Bernie Sanders campaign. Something similar happened after the January 2015 Syriza victory. People had been exhausted after five years of austerity and incessant activism. They were happy to mandate a government rhetorically committed to their demands and celebrate a rare popular victory. In the first half of 2015, support for the government remained exceptionally high despite the difficult negotiations. It was evident at a Syntagma rally in February, which, unlike previous events, was called not against but in support of the government and its negotiating position. This initially strong approval started receding when it became clear that manifesto promises, including the return to the pre-crisis minimum wage and pension levels and the abolition of the hated real estate tax, could not be implemented. Disappointment grew stronger after the July agreement seen by many as a reversal of the referendum result, turning the popular 'No' into a 'Yes'. When the second Syriza government started legislating the agreed measures, the reaction of those excluded from the new dispensation grew. Right and extreme left-wing protesters started targeting individual ministers and deputies. Early in 2016, heckling, attacks on Syriza offices and disruption of public events became common. Lengthy strikes by privileged groups, such as lawyers and rich farmers, indicated that the motivation was loss of influence and decrease of privileges rather than indignation at injustice. In the absence of a credible opposition or alternative programme, these protests did not escalate into an existential threat for the government. This however should not comfort party and government. Resistance, militancy and social movements were crucial for Syriza's victory. It would be a bitter irony if they were to contribute to its downfall.

A final tension exists between the different and often opposing programmes and policies that government, MPs and party have to pursue simultaneously. Party and government develop policies and adopt measures in order to ameliorate the effects of the July agreement. It is necessary for the weaker members of society initially, eventually for all. These measures include offering free health care to two million uninsured people; free meals to school children and a minimum solidarity income for the poor; a stop of family home repossessions and a restructuring of non-serviced loans. This 'parallel' programme, as it became known, both complements and undermines memorandum policies. It is a proper Derridean 'supplement'. Without the parallel programme the principle is incomplete; but when the principle is implemented the parallel undermines it.

The enemies of the Left and the ultra leftists claim that these contradictions will inevitably lead to Syriza's downfall. For dialectics, however, contradiction is not a debilitating condition, nor does it lead to stasis. On the contrary, contradictions allow a living organism to renew itself. The Left has to work with and out of contradiction as it always did. They are manifestations of deep social tensions and class conflicts. Being in contradiction and negotiating a way out offers a dialectical opportunity. According to a standard presentation, Hegelian dialectics works when contradictions and conflicts become synthesized or 'sublated' at a higher level, which transcends the antagonists while maintaining their tension. This is a limited understanding. Dialectics operates when the subject intervenes into the object, when social consciousness confronts social being. In this confrontation, subjective intervention separates a universal dimension from its negative part. The universal is not a pre-existing abstract and empty notion – like the Cartesian cogito – or a fully-formed normative substance – such as human rights – confronting the particular. On the contrary, the universal emerges when the political intervention splits the particular, raising one part into universality and rejecting the other. The renunciation of austerity, which the Left has to implement, splits governmental action into a negative neoliberal part and its opposing 'parallel' programme. The question is which will become the universal dimension of the situation. This is what is at stake as the government enters the second half of its life. Dialectics helps us understand the treatment of refugees too. Their popular welcoming started as a humanitarian and philanthropic response to suffering. But as the government started settling the refugees in towns and cities all over the country, what appeared initially as a local humanitarian response turned into a social justice strategy and a catalyst for solidarity activism. People mobilized massively to help those arriving into the islands. The content of this new activism was different from the earlier resistances but the form similar. People took a major problem into their hands and acted in a manner that was not planned or directed from above. While the popular dynamic of the 2010s has subsided, it is still there as a *potentia* and finds new ways of manifesting itself.

The political version of the contradictions is somewhat different. Syriza achieved a number of electoral victories without ideological hegemony. Aligning the two is the greatest challenge facing the party. The simple answer to the ultra-leftist claims that Syriza betrayed its values is that people did not vote for it when it was a small radical left party. Before 2012, when full-bloodied left ideology, rhetoric and personnel were intact, Syriza received at most five per cent in elections. In January 2015, Syriza's vote was 37 per cent, in September 2015 36 per cent, in the referendum the 'Oxi' received 61.3 per cent. These successive victories in a short nine-month period were unprecedented and cannot be attributed exclusively to Syriza's radical credentials. Electoral victory did not emerge out of but against the ideological hegemony of the right-wing and Pasok parties, against persistent anti-left institutional biases and state strategies and without the support of any major electronic or print medium. The vote for Syriza was negative: a guilty verdict for the *ancien régime* instead of a positive adoption of socialist ideals. This anomaly was evident in the 2014 European and local elections held on the same day. Syriza won the Euro-elections comfortably but lost most Town Halls. Defeat in local and trade-union elections is a result of Syriza's lack of extensive involvement in civil society and societal institutions. Decades of New Democracy and Pasok domination at the local level could not be overturned. Mayors and councillors are socially embedded; they have extensive networks for outsourcing contracts and distributing local favours. Unravelling these networks and the associated petty corruption takes determination and time. It is more about a change of mentality rather than the replacement of a few mayors and councillors. Syriza's radical reform programme depends crucially on a change of institutional sloth and popular toleration of under-the-table dealings. Can Syriza succeed? It is uncertain but clearly no other party from the old power system can.

Syriza's political future depends on analysing the causes and limitations of its national victories and local defeats. It has to turn winning votes into capturing hearts and minds. A good starting point is to go back to the source of its success and combine again parliament and street, the ballot box and social mobilization. Greeks share a strong family and friendship tradition with an equally unmitigated suspicion of the state. The Left must promote a new democratic communitarianism while putting the state at the service of citizens. It is a tough mission.

Contradiction is the name of a left government held captive in a sea of neoliberalism. In this sense, the Syriza government is a problem, a scandal. It is scandalous, unacceptable, beyond the bounds of reason of European elites. In a theological sense, Syriza is a *skandalon*, a miracle-like event that has the opportunity to influence the route of history. This can only happen if both during the implementation and immediately after the completion of the austerity measures the government starts pursuing a programme of social transformation. It is a question of time management, radical determination and clear political priorities.

6.2   Political temporalities

The dramatic developments in 2015 and 2016 made people claim that political time is dense, fast, 'pregnant' with unprecedented events. But time has also been elongated. In July 2016, when the first anniversary of the 'Oxi' vote coincided with the Brexit referendum, its memories had started fading and interpretations of the result differed widely. Many felt that 2015 was a year that lasted ten; others that it went like a flash. If we follow the logic of contracted or extended temporality, 2015 was the longest, slowest, toughest and most fascinating year of our political lives. Time fast or slow, long or slow, constitutes the dimension in which the left wager will be won or lost.

We think of time as a linear sequence of points, a succession of 'nows'. Time is the present while the past is no longer a now and the future not yet a now. Yet this temporality of clocks does not meet our experience. Phenomenologically, time is neither united nor uniform; we live simultaneously in several overlapping temporal cycles – some short and dense, others long and slow. Take a political act or an artistic performance. It does not happen in a series of 'now' points. The act has duration; it unravels and comes into presence over time moving towards its end. Without this temporal and teleological integrity the act cannot be carried out or understood. The present in which the act happens brings with it what is no longer present and opens towards what is not yet present. Time is therefore fragmented and multidimensional. Take someone preparing for next month's exams, training for a swimming competition in a year's time and writing a novel over a period of many years. She lives simultaneously in three temporal cycles, some short, others longer, each with its own project. They all place demands on the subject. When overlapping temporalities and projects are potentially in conflict we have to prioritize their demands. In the month before the exams, she will concentrate on revision, go to the pool rarely and leave the novel to one side. Yet these two activities, while suspended, give the person the necessary motivation to continue with the unpleasant examination preparation. Our temporal horizons are continuously framed and embedded into each other. This way every temporal cycle is directly related to the previous and helps unravel the future one, bringing the three cycles into overlap and co-existence. The reciprocal relationship, the constraints and openings between past and future horizons bring about the present. Present activity acquires its meaning and significance when immersed in the past, while anticipating and preparing the future.

Syriza members, deputies and government ministers live simultaneously in three concentric cycles or temporal durations, each committed to different but related projects. The inner and shortest cycle takes us to the conclusion of the compliance review of the third bailout loan and completion of its 'prior actions' at the end of 2017. The second is the four-year period from 2015 to 2019. It is the time of left governmentality and the start of social transformation. Finally, the third cycle is the long and slow time of socialism or *isodemocracy*. It started in 2015 and moves forward into the future with no discernible terminal point or conclusion. Government, MPs and Syriza members share all three overlapping temporalities. What happened (the austerity memorandum) and what is to come (the idea of communism or isodemocracy) create the positivity of what is taking place in the present. The intertwining of the temporal cycles leads to tensions and contradictions but also prepares the ground for their overcoming.

2016 and 2017 are the toughest years. Syriza ministers and MPs have to legislate and apply the July 2015 agreement. It is a 'dense' and hard time for those asked to implement measures they fought against. It is the time the creditors assess the implementation of the third memorandum measures. These compliance reviews are preconditions for the release of the loan installments. The lenders examine policies and legislation and can veto those they disagree with. Only the successful completion of these reviews and the government's release from the position of hostage and supplicant will allow the unraveling of the full social transformation programme.

The difficulties the government faces until the end of the reviews have offered a last-ditch opportunity to the opposition. The *ancien régime* hopes that the government will resign under pressure from the lenders and popular dissatisfaction before the end of its term in 2019. The plan started a few months after the September elections. The right-wing opposition orchestrated an Allende-type 'pots and pans' campaign calling for immediate elections under the slogan 'Resign'. It was a bizarre request. New Democracy had just changed leader and had not prepared a government programme. If new elections were called at that point there was every chance that Syriza would win comfortably.

As the pressure from the creditors increased in late 2016, the opposition turned the government's resignation and new elections into its main policy. Those keen to see the government fall have gone into overdrive, creating a scene of political panic and personal hysteria. The media are full of conspiracies, intrigue, potential apostasies. A fake state of emergency has been constructed with Syriza ministers, deputies and members targeted for all kinds of crimes and misdemeanors. The bombardment has been relentless. Instant gratification has become instant catastrophe, a political infantilism that functions through the multiplication of false rumours and unfounded attacks. Right-wing politicians project their past failure onto their opponents, unconcerned about the damage they inflict on the negotiating position of the country and the integrity of the political system. The systemic forces have adopted the Samson strategy: they try to take Syriza down with them as they decay. When the latest accusation is proved a lie, a retraction in small print covers the legal position and the attack moves to the next victim. The strategy is clear. Government, party and movement were at their weakest in 2016. The necessary reform of the pension system, which was close to collapse, a basic taxation of farmers, who had paid little tax in the past and the increase of VAT had created a febrile atmosphere. The opposition hoped that Syriza's parliamentary majority of three could be undone through external pressure and internal dissent. It is a question of resilience for the Syriza deputies. If they hold until the end of the compliance reviews when the social transformation programme starts in earnest, the party is likely to win the next set of elections.

Nonetheless, the existential problems faced by Syriza ministers and deputies cannot go away. Party loyalty and expectation of economic improvement can only soothe them. Resilience depends on the contemporaneous unravelling of two other temporalities, which exist in the present only as weak traces. The second cycle is slower and longer. It involves a medium-term plan of two to four years, when governance starts moving towards left governmentality. This is the time of the 'parallel' programme, the first phase of a wider social transformation. The 'parallel' mitigates the effects of austerity and prepares the left turn. Its early part tackled the humanitarian crisis and implemented reforms emerging out of the rights and identities agenda. They include citizenship for immigrants, gay and lesbian civil union, ending the persecution of conscientious objectors and draft evaders, offering a dignified life to refugees and a host of economic policies supporting the unemployed and poorer parts of the population.

But is there a 'left' way of doing government, a left 'governmentality'? It is a hard question not only because we don't have an answer, but also because we don't even have a fully worked out set of problems. There is no precedent; this makes Greece an important experiment for the Left. Returning from London, I was shocked by the huge disparities in the work and efficiency of civil servants. Many are dedicated and work overtime, despite big salary reductions. But there is also a minority for whom the civil service is a sinecure. As argued above, systemic parties used the state as a power base and a holder and distributor of favours. The government has to reform institutions and change long-established mentalities by learning from the organizational principles and structures of Western Europe. The reform agenda starts with the full application of the rule of law: expediting the judicial process, enforcing court decisions against the state and major corporations and ensuring that the judiciary is free of political influence. The civil service should learn how to set clear tasks, review their delivery and assess the efficiency of officials. Syriza's unique responsibility is to reform Greek institutions while under attack from their foreign counterparts. Left governmentality has a second democratic component. Syriza MPs are often informed about legislative initiatives on the eve of their introduction. This leads to insufficient preparation and last-minute reversals. Left policies and statutes should be the outcome of the greatest possible deliberation. They should be developed in close contact with Syriza MPs, the party and, when appropriate, social movements. Syriza is a political not a technocratic government; it should therefore back its policies with the greatest amount of research and scientific expertise. Reforming the state and democratizing the operation of government is a first step and a revolutionary task.

Do we have a test of radicalism that could inform government planning? The main criterion of left governmentality is whether individual policies and legislation form an integral part of the plan for social transformation. Major policies and bills should aim to change the balance of forces by moving resource, opportunities and power from capital to working people and from the state to citizens. Has it happened? Only partially. Some ministers have pursued personal agendas without a medium or long-term plan and without informing or consulting the party. The arrogant and aggressive style of others has hurt the left ethos. At times, it looks as if the government will fail through a series of self-inflicted wounds. But the alternative is atrocious. Letting into the scions of the old regime, those who brought Greece to its knees, will be a major dereliction of duty. Government and party must persevere, clean their act and start the wider planning for social transformation. Every policy should be a rupture in the old regime; every successful measure should immediately lead to the next step, every successful law to the next break with the old. Every reform is a station in the wider journey of successive waves of radicalization. The balancing point between rupture and assimilation will be achieved when every policy and law is inspired by and leads to the horizon of *isodemocracy*.

6.3   *Isodemocracy* or democratic socialism in the twenty-first century

The third cycle of the radical left vision is the longest. It began with the January 2015 elections and extends into the indeterminate future. Its weak trace, faintly manifest in the present, operates in and against the imposed policies. It is the time of the ideal, of a socialist vision that has no visible or predictable end. This is the longest and slowest time of a programme that must constantly mobilize popular approval and legitimacy. Using the Lacanian topography, the memorandum is the symbolic order of Syriza, left governmentality its imaginary, while the real is the socialist rupture. The implementation of the memorandum distributes government, deputies and party members into positions of unwilling agents in the matrix of capital accumulation. The 'parallel' programme allows us to keep adopting measures that first reverse the humanitarian crisis and then lead to economic and social transformation. Finally, the third cycle of the socialist horizon mitigates the difficulties of the present and inspires future policies. We believe and act now in the name of a future 'not yet' and still 'to come'. It redefines our current predicament as the necessary precursor of a democratic and socialist future.

Syriza needs resilience and endurance as the three cycles progress in different velocities and their projects often clash. It will reach the second temporality of left governance and the third of socialist vision only by continuously and simultaneously implementing and undermining the memorandum. Only when the third temporality starts unfolding fully, freed from the neoliberal lambast, will the programme of the Left emerge. As the real of the situation, it lurks behind now time pushing it forward. It is the kernel in the midst of present time, a void in which the past disappears and the future emerges. This way, the Left escapes into the future, acting now from the perspective of a future perfect, of what will have been. In this sense, the future becomes an active contributor to our present predicament. For Marx, communism appears in history as a political movement or an idea. The communist horizon, as a combination of the two, transcends and politicizes its own historical expressions, abandoning teleological aspirations. It interpellates political subjects, over-determines social relations and promises a radical humanism that brings people together in harmony with nature. Syriza's long-term vision is to move towards the democratic socialism of the twenty-first century.

The cycle of the left vision, which lurks in the other two, is a journey towards the horizon of equality and democracy. We call this horizon *isodemocracy*, paraphrasing and developing Etienne Balibar's *Equaliberty*.[13] As a horizon, *isodemocracy* is a dividing line, an arc that moves back and away as we approach it. This is not because *isodemocracy* is a future utopia or a non-realizable ideal. A horizon remains open and unreachable but is integrated as a lighthouse beam into everyday practice. It is a kind of Kantian regulative idea. Every application or instantiation opens up to further extension and deepening, changing both strategic task and political subject. *Isodemocracy* is therefore not a telos, a terminal station or the purpose of historical teleology. We will not cry out at some future point, 'here we are', 'we reached our destination'. On the contrary, the horizon exists here and now, embodied in every relationship and struggle, in every victory but also in our defeats. We failed, we will try again, we will fail better. Because we failed better we are now perhaps on the threshold of success. If horizon is the form, its content is double: equality and democracy.

First, the axiom of equality or better the struggle for the reduction of inequality. While freedom is open to all kinds of incompatible interpretations (such as freedom of choice, autonomy or license) the foundation of the equality claim is simple. Everyone counts one and no one for more than one. What matters is not equality of opportunities but equality of results; policies leading to the material equalization of peoples' lives. A left government concretizes the axiom and makes it operational. Deepening equality leads to freedom as existential autonomy. There is no freedom without equality and no equality without freedom. But as we know, equality on its own does not lead to a change in the balance of power. We need therefore, secondly, the deepening and extension of democracy. Neoliberalism subjects politics to economics, government to governance, democratic debate and agon to scientific 'truth'. Democracy becomes impoverished and representative institutions anaemic servants of greedy capitalism. In this context, *isodemocracy* means the re-politicization of politics and the democratization of society. The Left introduces the institutional manifestations of direct democracy such as national and local referenda, the recall of MPs and other elected officers as well as gender and race quotas. When these institutional reforms succeed, it becomes clear that formal democratization is not enough. Democracy from formal procedure and method of vote aggregation has to become a form of life. It passes from central politics into the economic, social and cultural fields and into everyday life. Democracy too is a horizon that as we approach keeps moving and changing. The general principle becomes concretized and transformed, the horizon takes on the colours and tints of the rainbow. We advance from strengthening a formal method that has been hollowed out to the recognition that the principle itself has limited purchase. It needs to be universalized and deepened. In this process of extension and deepening, institutional democracy is supplemented by direct and non-representative forms. Services and powers are gradually subtracted from state power and transferred to the deliberations and decision-making of citizens. Workers' councils are given executive powers, cooperatives and social economy initiatives are supported materially, young entrepreneurs are offered loans, tax breaks and legal advice by the state. This is how the balance of forces changes gradually and power passes from the elites to citizens.

The radical Left needs unwavering loyalty to the horizon of equality and democracy. Take social policies. A task such as reversing the humanitarian crisis is set. If achieved, success leads immediately to the next step. The equality axiom gives shape to policies that gradually close the gap and introduce those who escape the poverty trap into progressive ideas. Every demand, every success becomes a step in a long march and a precondition for the next, more radical task.

The horizon moves away and again gives the direction for the following chapter, the next step, deeper radicalization. In this struggle, both the task and the subject keep changing, transforming themselves along the way. Stasis and immobility, on the other hand, lead inexorably to assimilation. Or, consider the rule of law. Developing a modern rule of law state is a radical demand in Greece and the prerequisite for democratic socialism. The legal system must deliver on its promises. Existing rights and entitlements must be fully enforced, normativity and actuality must gradually come closer. But as soon as the basic legalistic requirements are achieved, it becomes clear that formalism, proceduralism and individualized rights cannot deliver substantive equality. The law must move from equality of opportunity at the entry point to equality of outcome. This way, equality and democracy become deeper and richer and *isodemocracy* operates as the dialectical method of reality.

Socialism and radical change is nothing more than perseverance in our initial decision to commit ourselves to the axiom of equality and democracy. From the perspective of the future, our original commitment will appear well founded and foundational, although in reality it is as much necessary as it is contingent. This is how great love affairs and revolutions happen. After the fact, they are considered necessary, predetermined, and indispensable. But if you get to the rendezvous a few minutes late, or if you delegate the change to others, to politicians, experts, insiders, then what was predestined turns into a lost opportunity, a love affair you will never experience. The political and moral duty of the Left is to meet our object of desire.

Is Syriza ready? Can it succeed? There are acts you prepare for and others that hit you on the head, like a miracle or an earthquake. Syriza has been adopted as the subject of radical change and it can only accept the challenge. It is an historic wager; its outcome is not given.

Part III

Reflections on Life as a Politician

7

Welcome to the Desert
of Disorderly Order

When I entered Parliament with another 143 Syriza deputies in September 2015, I was shocked by the surprise and disbelief of those who had ruled Greece for the last forty years. They were indignant that Syriza with its army of provincial lawyers, teachers, engineers, farmers, pensioners and veterans of the resistance movements had invaded Parliament again. They had hoped that after the traumatic events of 2015 Syriza would lose its majority and return to its marginal postion. In the past the Left was tolerated as long as it stayed in the political periphery. The Communist party, in particular, with its eschatological ideology and rejection of anything it does not control ('we don't want socialist isles in a capitalist society') is praised for its steadfastness a.k.a. verbally militant acquiescence. Now that the Left finally acquired a modicum of power, it became the devil incarnate. The right-wing and Pasok MPs showed in every way possible how they despised the *sans culottes* who had entered their temple, sanctuary and playground. As an academic in London, I did not fall into that category. My career fitted the model 'modenizers' proffer as a corrective for the 'backward-looking' oriental proclivities of Greece. 'How come', asked a prominent right-wing deputy, 'that someone like you is a Syriza MP? You are a London professor. Your Syriza comrades do not speak foreign languages and have not travelled outside the country. They have no manners and don't know how to choose a good bottle of wine.' 'They are honest, hard-working people', I replied. 'They did not join the Left because they expected to become deputies or ministers. In fact, being on the Left had badly affected their careers. And how could you', I added, 'a good bourgeois, share life and ruling all these years with people on the fringes of the extreme racist right-wing?'

And **that** was the end of that conversation.

Perplexity towards someone who does not fit the establishment's stereotype of a leftie soon turned into hostility. A professional failure or secret plan must lie behind my unnatural conversion from academic to politician. The anger reached a tragicomic crescendo when I started curating 'Theory at the Megaron', a series of lectures at the Megaron Mous-ikis, the Athens Concert Hall. The series, inspired by the activities of the Birkbeck Institute for the Humanities which I founded and directed for ten years until 2015, brings to Athens some of the most influential critical theorists to debate topical issues with the Athenian public. It is part of a wider effort to invigorate the intellectual scene with a progressive agenda that speaks to the younger genera-tion. Nothing similar existed and the series was welcome. The lecture hall filled with people who had not entered the Megaron before. Its high-brow programme and expensive ticketing regime had alienated everyone but the self-identified owners of culture. As a result, the Megaron had failed badly, running a debt of €300 million. The media barons, who had helped found it and ran it for cultural aggrandisement, were not able to service the debt; they had to accept its nationalization. Taking the Megaron into public ownership was going against the grain of privatizations the country's creditors demand. Still, many Syriza members opposed it. It had become a huge white elephant that had surpassed any similar institution in profligacy and lack of interest in the *hoi polloi*.

The first speakers in the series were Etienne Balibar, Judith Butler, this author, Jacqueline Rose, Marina Warner, Joanna

Bourke, Georges Didi-Huberman and David Harvey. After Balibar's lecture, an elderly lady embraced me in tears clutching the ticket with the lecture title *The Idea of Revolution: Yesterday, Today, Tomorrow.* 'I will keep it as a memento. I never expected to see such a title in a Megaron lecture', she explained. The second lecture was one of the most successful ever in the Megaron. Judith Butler spoke to seven hundred people, mostly young women and men, creating a festival atmosphere, with another few hundred following the lecture through a video link. It was a rave with ideas. The keepers of the political order were furious by the unprecedented success. They chose the curator as the target of their indignation. The media corporation associated with the foundation and bankruptcy of the Megaron led the attack. In an article entitled 'Douzinas in the Megaron', To Vima newspaper claimed that my life's aspiration was to invade the 'temple of bourgeois consecration' and mourned the entry of plebs into the hall. Ta Nea newspaper published an academic profile accusing me both of irrationalist postmodernism and diehard communism. I was a continuation of the 'French May', I had published bizarre books with titles such as *Nomos and Aesthetics* and, pièce de résistance, I 'have seduced many brilliant young minds into the gay science of antisystemic theory'. It was an accusation of such delightful insight that became the title of my next newspaper column. Kathimerini, the competitor newspaper on the Right, claimed that I had been appointed President of the Megaron (wrong); that the series was the morsel given to me because I had not been appointed minister; that I started the series after the Megaron was nationalized in order to promote Syriza (wrong, I had agreed with the director appointed by the previous government well before nationalization); that I was inviting only Syriza members to speak (wrong, I was the only Greek among the first twelve speakers). I replied with a polite letter refuting the lies. It was not published. It was a tough baptism of fire into propaganda journalism and the febrile atmosphere of public debate.

The keepers of order treated me with respect in Parliament and with derision outside. One part cancelled the other out. Mirth more than mire was my response. Academic life is a continuous process of judging and being judged. Every lecture, every article, every book is thrown out into the world and becomes the target of criticism, praise or condemnation. Usually both. Evaluation, assessment, testing is an intrinsic, uncomfortable, yet welcome part of academic life. In the case of critical academics, being a target of attack by the mainstream becomes a *modus vivendi*. When I started contributing articles to the *Guardian* newspaper and website supporting the Greek resistance, the racism of 'below the line' opprobrium was hurtful but limited to the anonymity of the web. Was my 'accidental' introduction into political life worth it? Some friends had warned me that the relative public immunity of the academic would disappear. It was much worse than that. I was unprepared for the brutality and dissembling of the Greek attacks. They were written by elite commentators but were false and irrational. They were penned by successful journalists but were full of lies. They were spiteful *ad hominem* attacks by people who had never met me. The fact that a London academic had been elected a Syriza MP was so extravagantly counterintuitive that it had clouded whatever sense of balance they still had. The keepers of systemic order were acting in the most disorderly manner.

The allegation about the ministerial post was particularly interesting. Early in my political career, I had been asked on live TV why I had not been appointed Education Secretary, as had been mooted in the media. I replied that accepting such a position at that point would have been the shortest suicide note. I had been away for forty years, I had little knowledge of the issues or the key people involved in one of the most fractious areas of public life. I needed to learn how things work. I repeatedly stated publicly afterwards that I was not interested in a ministerial position. But this goes against the grain of political commonsense. The politician's ideal ego is a government minister. Most deputies' imaginary order is held together by the expectation of a junior ministerial position. There are exceptions; for some Syriza politicians, power is not their love object. As they came to prominence unexpectedly, they will easily go back home if they cannot implement ideas they fought for all their lives. Nevertheless, a politician who is not interested in power is a strange phenomenon.

The keepers of political order and public decorum concluded that I had a devious secret plan. That I have no grand plan or ambition, that I am in Athens to help promote values and ideas, that I am an observer and ethnographer of an historic moment, that I keep body and soul together by commuting regularly in order to teach could not enter their minds. Either way I should be preemptively attacked. It inspired the title of my political career. 'Welcome to the desert of disorderly order.'

8

Learning from Ideology

8.1 The Right

Louis Althusser has famously argued that ideology is the imaginary way subjects relate to their real conditions of existence. Ideologies are not descriptions of how the world is or how it should become; they are not a species of true or false consciousness. Ideology works for the individual in a highly structured and highly individualized way. It tells people how to fit in the world. It prepares us for our role in social reproduction by teaching ways of living and life practices. Ideologies are not therefore just a bunch of words, ideas or ideals. They are sets of material practices that slot people into pre-existing social roles, (male) boss or (female) secretary, landlord or tenant, shopkeeper or consumer. For example, if I pursue relentlessly my interests and use other people as means or hurdles to my plans, I will tend to believe that the market is the natural way of life. If I prioritize friendship and collective endeavour, I will value care for others and solidarity over my strict personal interest. Wider ideas and political ideologies – socialism, capitalism or liberalism – are shaped by daily practices and routine thinking. They may or may not emerge in a fully formed and articulate manner. We become subjects by being admitted into a matrix of differentiated, interlocking and overlapping positions, which a particular ideology then confirms.

How do formal political ideas contribute to this picture? The ideology of a party is a set of values and aims that define its mission, identity and purpose, the way it presents itself and wants to be seen by the people. It is not always easy to discover party ideologies in their programme or manifesto. These are often vague and contradictory or extremely detailed and uninformative. Consistency is not a main characteristic of political life. It is used mostly in order to attack failures of opponents instead of defending one's own positions. After the July 2015 agreement, for example, New Democracy attacked Syriza from the 'Left' for abandoning its ideology. The right wing had relentlessly pressurized the government to accept any agreement whatsoever to ensure the country stays in Europe. When the referendum and Tsipras' negotiations delivered a better deal than that of the previous government, New Democracy and Pasok voted for it and commended the government retreat with clenched teeth. Soon afterwards they changed tack. The agreement was conceding too much, it was bad for the poor; the Left had abandoned its long-standing commitments. This ideological seesaw was confusing. Parties were not playing to the score assigned to them. From my perch at the back of the Parliament chamber, I concluded that the best way to divine ideology is to observe the conduct of deputies and ministers. Their actions, behaviour and words would help me perhaps to understand political values and beliefs.

I had come to politics expecting to witness the historic rise of the radical Left. I soon realized that just as important was an ethnography of the decline and fall of the ruling elite. Shouting, screaming and swearing by opposition at Syriza MPs was my first unexpected and unwelcome experience. Parliament is not a sacred place where MPs should behave as if they were in church. Class, ideology and interests divide society; these conflicts should be represented loudly and clearly. Their verbal dramatization introduces a theatrical element and expresses emotion and passion, indignation and anger, those deeply ethical reactions according to Spinoza. Shouting and screaming interrupt the often boring debates or the parallel monologues of MPs who often repeat party memoranda and press releases. However the exchange of banter, repartee and forceful gesticulation (a Greek renown) often escalates into verbal and occasionally physical abuse. The leftists, with a few exceptions, are polite; the right-wing and Pasok MPs, however, collectively heckle and shout down Syriza speakers, often forcing them to stop their address. The abuse is massive, co-ordinated and follows the protocols of football teraces. The refrain of those bad-tempered incidents remains the same: 'You are not entitled to govern. You are in Parliament by mistake. Resign, your place is in the streets.' Grown men and some women act like children who have had their toys taken away. It is an effective strategy for politicians whose only connecting link is power or money. Ideologies and manifestos are not the stuff of parties and people of power. As a young New Democracy MP told me, he had already been best man and godfather at more than one hundred weddings and christenings. 'Pressing the flesh' the Greek way is to lead 'Isaiah's dance' (a central part of the Orthodox wedding ceremony) and to push babies down the baptismal font.

The most shocking experience, however, is the way opposition parties target ministers and MPs, accusing them falsely of criminal, corrupt or immoral acts. Scurrilous campaigns, usually initiated by right-wing media and obscure websites, are then picked up and disseminated by opposition politicians. Alexis Tsipras was accused of acquiring his modest flat in an auction of repossessed homes (false, he inherited it from his father). George Katrougalos, the Minister of Labour, was accused of acting as lawyer and adviser for civil servants sacked by the previous government and receiving hefty commissions if he managed to reinstate them (he did not). The Foreign Secretary, Nikos Kotzias, was attacked for hiding the fact that he had studied in East Germany and of falsely claiming that he held academic posts at major Western universities (he did not). Nikos Pappas, the Minister in charge of Media and Communications, was accused of setting up an office to offer services and favours for a fee (he had not). They all denied vigorously the allegations, to no avail; those who sued for libel, won. However this did not stop websites and journalists repeating the defamatory statements. Court decisions have become victims of the wider disrespect for state institutions. No contempt of court law exists; it is obvious why.

An incident in August 2106 shows the size of the problem. In a tragic accident near the island of Aegina, a speedboat impaled a tourist caique. Four people died and some twenty were injured. The speedboat passengers did not stop to help the victims and surrendered to the police a few hours later. By coincidence, a number of Syriza members have holiday homes in Aegina. Right-wing media and journalists linked these unrelated facts and claimed that three ministers were on board the boat that caused the accident and fled the scene in order to protect themselves. The accusation was bizarre but was repeated and became a front-page news item. In the frantic atmosphere of 2016, the 'no smoke without fire' cliché fuelled conspiracy theories for weeks. A second incident illustrates the wider sexism that still characterizes the ruling elites. Efi Ahtsioglu, a brilliant woman, who had led the government team negotiating labour relations was appointed Minister for Employment in late 2016. Immediately afterwards, right-wing newspapers and websites began a sinister campaign of sexual innuendo and personal humiliation. She is 'only thirty-one years old'; she is 'good-looking' (therefore) she has 'slept her way to the top'; she is involved in 'pervert' sexuality. The false and sexist accusations proliferated. The obscenity of the invective was inversely proportionate to the ample qualifications and universally acknowledged abilities of the Minister. The attacks showed a level of toleration of sexual harassment and bullying that would be unacceptable elsewhere. Greece entered the post-truth and fake news era well before Donald Trump.

This is not normal political fare. Motives deeper than ideology are involved. Political behaviour is closely articulated with the unconscious part of the psychic economy. Ideological and political analysis needs the assistance of psychoanalytical theory. The rise of Syriza, the collapse of the establishment parties and the sense of an ending have left the habitual rulers deeply traumatized. Their decline is partly the result of maladministration and corruption in their forty years of domination and, more recently, the six years of austerity. The assertion that they will rescue Greece from the consequences of their own mistakes is not credible. Politicians do not own up to failure; instead they fall back into standard psychological defences.

Two types of defence are used to bandage psychic disturbance, denial and displacement. The subject denies the trauma or it projects its causes, symptoms and effects onto an outsider. Displacement, first. If the personal failure is in reality the work of someone else, if the decay of the power base is the result of the enemy's perfidy and lies, the real culprits are not guilty. This is why the attacks on Syriza, Tsipras and his ministers are so vitriolic. They are criminals and liars; they have set out to destroy the nation. These personalized attacks make the accusers conclude that only the removal of Syriza will allow Greece to return to normality. Belief in the existence of a common national interest is a well-known motif of right-wing ideology. Perversely, however, opposition MPs do not accept that they are purveyors of ideology or promoters of personal interests. Ideological delusions belong to the Left; the Right is beyond ideology. Their concern to save the country is above ideology and politics. The claim not to have an ideology is the most aggressive ideology of our age. As national harmony and ideology cannot co-exist, 'ideological' Syriza is not a normal party playing by the rules of the game; it is an existential adversary and a threat to the nation. The political stage will be cleansed and peace will return only if Syriza is removed from government. Why such hatred with a ferocity unknown to European politics? It can only be explained by an unconscious belief that Syriza has stolen the rightists' enjoyment and entitlements. The Left has usurped the habitual rulers' *jouissance* and has spoilt their way of life. It must be destroyed therefore before enjoyment returns. Externalizing the trauma and blaming some other is the psychological answer to personal failure and guilt.

The second defence strategy is to deny the trauma. The tiresomely repeated demand that the government resigns is the psychological cover for the unconscious belief that New Democracy has not lost power. It is all a bad dream; soon the country will wake from the nightmare. The 'short left interval' claim is the surface appearance of this belief and desire. This strategy is not available to the rump Pasok and its deputies. For the erstwhile social-democrats, denial of defeat is impossible. The term 'Pasokization', the dramatic collapse of support for a previously dominant party, has entered the international political lexicon. For Pasok diehards, trauma externalization takes the form of extreme hatred and *ressentiment* against the Left. The shrill shouting, incoherent screaming and swearing at Syriza ministers and MPs by a handful of Pasok deputies forms an integral and sad part of the 'socialist' presence in Parliament. It is the sign of a political force in its death throes, an impotent acting out, a 'kicking against the pricks'. The perverted logic behind it joins the right-wing strategy of displacement *ad extremis*: the Greek tragedy is not the work of those who ruled the country for forty years; it is the doing of others, of aliens, the *indignados*, the leftists. In a weird hall of mirrors, the sins of those who until 2015 had nothing to do with power are victimizing the perennial and innocent establishment. Parliament is a thick institution and power a strong addictive. They socialize and discipline people. For long-standing deputies, losing power, departing the parliamentary chamber is like expulsion from the family home. Only subliminal fears and irrational hatred can explain the extreme behaviour of opposition MPs.

8.2   Golden Dawn's postmodern racism

I faced my toughest moment in Parliament in February 2016. I was chairing a meeting of the Standing Committee on National Defence and Foreign Affairs in which the Minister of Defence would brief MPs about NATO's participation in stemming refugee flows to Greece. The leadership of the armed forces was in attendance. The session would take place in camera because of the sensitivity of the issues. From the start, Golden Dawn MPs started swearing and cursing first me and then the Minister and the officers. The refugees were 'bogus immigrants' contaminating Greece; the Greek top brass were acting like 'Filipino maids serving the Muslim immigrants'. The fascist MPs were behaving as if they enjoyed total impunity. I asked them repeatedly to stop without success. I sought the advice of officials, who told me that I have the power to expel MPs refusing to comply with a formal reprimand. I again asked the deputies to withdraw the slanders and apologize. They refused; their extreme swearing was about to turn into a physical brawl with Syriza MPs. I called a recess and signed an ejection order. When they refused to leave again, I asked the parliamentary guard to intervene. It transpired that the incident was planned for publicity. A Golden Dawn MP had illegally filmed the confrontation and placed it on social media. I was later told that this was the first time the power to restore order by expelling misbehaving fascist MPs was used. My ignorance and relative naiveté had led me do something unheard of. I had done what lawyers are supposed to do: I had enforced the rulebook. Had I been more experienced, I would have known that the relevant rule had atrophied. Acting as an innocent abroad, I had highlighted a problematic tolerance of hate speech.

The racist insults combine two superficially opposed claims. The refugees are inferior 'illegals' on the one hand and 'tourists with maids' on the other. How can we explain the fact that refugees are both 'sub-human' invaders and superior 'visitors' having fun in Greece? Austerity, recession and unemployment have led to the rise of racism and xenophobia throughout Europe. Postmodern racism comes in many forms. High unemployment in Spain did not lead to the rise of fascism; low unemployment in France did. In the Netherlands, France and Great Britain, the extreme Right is targeting Muslims and Islam. In Hungary, Jews, gays and Roma. Fascism targets a weak and vulnerable 'other,' who is presented as the root of all evil. In the twentieth century, anti-Semitism united European racists. Contemporary racism is more eclectic. It uses three different types of argument which soon slide into each other creating a toxic combination. First, the openly racist claim about superior nations and inhuman others contaminating our purity. Second, a utilitarian argument in various forms: the country is full (Britain), there is no work (Greece), social services cannot cope with the burden of immigrants (everywhere). Finally, cultural and religious identity comes into play. Christian nations cannot cohabit with Muslims. This eclectic racism targets a plethora of victims who keep changing. In Great Britain, the scapegoat figure has changed from the blacks and Indians of the 1960s and 1970s, to the 'scroungers' and 'bogus refugees' of the 1990s, to the 'illegal immigrants' and the Muslims today. New racism is networked, horizontal and mobile. It shares behaviour more than ideology. The incoherent 'theories' and horrifying murders of Norwegian killer Anders Breivik symbolize one type of new racism and Marine Le Pen the other.

Psychoanalytical theory can help explain the return of racism. We can trace two strategies. First, an incoherent effort to 'rationalize' the crisis and its symptoms. Racism discovers a common cause of our evils using a distorted version of the rationalist maxim *nihil sine ratione* (nothing exists without a reason). The list of traumas is long: the decline of state sovereignty, unemployment, economic hardship, political incompetence, social decadence, family dysfunction and moral decay among others. The same devil lurks behind the different public disasters and personal failures. In reality, the causes and reasons of national and personal misfortune are diverse and often unrelated. The strategy of irrational 'rationalization' however discovers an evil other – the Jew, the refugee, the Muslim – behind every problem. This malignant presence is responsible for all ills; it operates as the Lacanian *point de capiton*, the quilting piece that links together the parts of a patchwork or puzzle. The second strategy is the exact opposite. it is the belief that 'others' are stealing our enjoyment. They are taking our jobs, scrounging on our benefits, seducing our women. The lack and discontent that, according to Freud and Lacan, torment every human are the work of people who steal our jewels. The others – refugees, Muslims, gays – may be persecuted and suffering. Still they take our jobs and benefits, they have better music, food and sex, they enjoy strong communities and lovely children, the things 'we' have lost. The suffering refugees can thus be portrayed as 'tourists with maids' exploiting the Greeks. A similar interpretation explains the German tabloid slurs against the Greeks for laziness, easy-living and cheating. When resentment and envy become dominant emotions, the alleged inferiority and the imaginary superiority of the Other are confused. Hatred towards the 'inferiors' is a defensive strategy and a symptomatic reversal of the feeling that 'we,' the native and pure, are in fact inferior.

One more factor contributes to the appeal of racism. Young men feel alienated and threatened by unemployment, uncertainty, lack of opportunities. Families bring up young boys calling them 'princes' and telling them that the world is theirs. But women are now outperforming men academically and professionally; traditional gender expectations have started changing. Feelings of inadequacy – even hatred – towards oneself are defused in violent movies, heroic fantasies and online games of killing and torturing. Extreme Right organizations exploit male vulnerability. Many young people who follow Golden Dawn are not fascists or extreme nationalists. Polling shows that they know little about Nazism, the German occupation and the Greek resistance. The Golden Dawn offers the youth a community of rhetorically and physically violent men with easily scapegoated targets. Endemic feelings of failure are thus hidden behind comradely militancy and attacks on people who, as inferior, deserve contempt, but as superior, envy and hatred. The Left should not abandon these desperate young men who fall prey to fascism out of ignorance and failure.

The illegal filming and broadcast of the Parliament incident was meant to nurture sub-cultures of individual frustration and cultural impotence. The creeping social violence that features in crime, hooliganism and solitary fantasies finds in Greece a parliamentary guise. Traditional fascists are united with advocates of violence who have little political ideology. It is a national shame. The strict application of the law should expose the dual nature of the organization as a political party and criminal gang.

8.3   The Left (melancholy)

Recent debates about Greece in the international Left have been characterized by a somewhat infantile leftism. Grexit – a return to the drachma and even an exit from the EU – has turned into the litmus test of radicalism. A 'left-o-meter' has been invented and is rigorously applied. Whoever does not accept Grexit as the holy grail of left correctness is denounced as a 'traitor'. This kind of attack used to be standard fare of Marxism in the internecine struggles of the twentieth century. The repeated theoretical failures and political defeats of the last fifty years, however, should have taught the Left that, instead of quoting Marx or repeating soothing mantras, it is more important to work out what Marx would have said today in the difficult situation of contemporary Greece and Europe. This involves an analysis of the concrete situation, an understanding of the balance of forces and a correct assessment of the international environment.

The Grexit and 'rupture or assimilation' arguments are the contemporary form of the old reform or revolution debate. The only difference is that 'revolution' cannot mean today the storming of the Bastille or the taking of the Winter Palace. Power can no longer be approached as a substance held by a small group of capitalists and politicians; nor is it exercised from a grand centre, the conquest of which radically alters the situation. Power is decentred, plural and capillary, it operates at all levels of personal, social and political relations. It does not take hold of people formed outside its circuit in order to subjugate them. On the contrary, power produces subjects, including radical subjects, attitudes and behaviours. Behavioural discipline and control is more important, therefore, than old-style ideology critique. If someone follows the behavioural diktats of advanced capitalist economy – borrowing, consuming, competing for benefits and favours with others – she acts within the systemic parameters irrespective of ideological commitments. Radical change cannot take place, therefore, in an apocalyptic event or moment. It is a long and complex *peripeteia* full of successes and failures, advances and retreats, small victories intertwined with defeats.

The doctrinaire Left, Marxist or not, has been stuck to a centralized and outdated conception of power, despite its theoretical and tactical limitations. It chooses to speak to the converted. Whether in the university hall or in the public square, this type of Left has been repeating old beliefs and clichés. The academic Left avoids testing its arguments against those who disagree. The politically active ultra-Left, similarly, sets its unquestioned theoretical stall and judges reality accordingly. If the world does not follow the theoretical prescriptions, so bad for the world. It is as if the Left is not interested in power but in the purity of its beliefs. This leads to 'left melancholy' and the 'narcissism of small differences', attitudes characterizing those who brought the government down after the July 2015 agreement and then left to form the Popular Unity splinter group. Many had been senior ministers. They chose to abandon the responsibility of running the country in order to keep pure hearts and beautiful souls.

In psychoanalytical theory, mourning a love object is necessary and liberating; melancholy on the other hand is the result of a failed and incomplete period of grief. At the end of mourning, the libido withdraws from the lost object and is displaced onto another. In melancholy, it withdraws into the ego. This withdrawal serves to 'establish an *identification* of the ego with the abandoned object'.[1] Walter Benjamin has called 'left melancholy', the attitude of the militant who is attached more to a particular political analysis or ideal – and to the failure of that ideal – than to seizing possibilities for radical change in the present.[2] Benjamin asked the Left to grasp the 'time of the now', while for the melancholic, history is the 'empty time' of repetition.[3] Unfortunately, part of the Greek Left is narcissistically fixated on its lost object – revolution and its failure – with no obvious desire to abandon it. Left melancholy leads inexorably to the 'narcissism of small differences', the interminable conflicts, splits and vituperation among erstwhile comrades. Attacks on the closest ally, seen as a threatening double, can be more vicious than those on the enemy. For Jacques Lacan, the narcissism of the lost cause operates when the only way for a subject to believe in an ideal is by ensuring that it cannot be realized.[4] Lacan told the May '68 Paris students that they want a 'new master'. The pure left strategy is similar. They bombard Syriza with impossible demands (leave the Euro or/and the European Union, nationalize everything) hoping, like the hysteric, that the master will manage things somehow and save them from having to deal with their problems themselves. Left melancholy betrays the world for the sake of old and failed certainties.

The Greek Communist Party, perhaps the most orthodox in the world, is a different case. Greek communists are convinced that the arrival of socialism, seen as a variety of Soviet Communism, is scientifically or metaphysically guaranteed. They are not interested therefore in any type of programmatic or sectoral alliances with a Left that does not share their certainties or their nostalgia for Stalinism. The communist mission is to keep uncovering and denouncing the Syriza government as a capitalist stooge. This way they assist the right-wing opposition, frustrate government initiatives and support indirectly the capitalist establishment they rhetorically condemn. The communists are perhaps the most conservative, with a small c, political force. During the December 2008 Athens uprising, following the murder of Alexis Grigoropoulos, the party secretary denounced the Syriza leadership for 'caressing the ears of the anarchists' and condemned the limited attacks on luxury shops. 'Come socialism these properties will belong to the people', she added. 'We cannot condone acts damaging the future property of the people.' Greek communists resemble those evangelical Protestants who expect the Second Coming and prepare for the rapture and the Last Judgment. For the evangelicals, the end is nigh. The communists have interminably postponed the hour of reckoning and care only for the preservation of their corner shop.

Ideology is not a simple application of ideas. It works through practices and action, it moves the emotions and creates effects. Rational beliefs are often belied by irrational behaviour and conscious ideas by unconscious motivations. The Communist party is a textbook case for the dissonance between rhetoric and action. The best indication of ideology in action is when deeds disprove words. Performative contradiction is the name of the Greek communists.

8.4   Syriza

'I have never read a book in my life', boasted a fellow MP a couple of weeks after we joined Parliament. I have always believed that the Left is thinking in action, that theory and concrete analysis separates the Left from other political groups. In the 1970s and 1980s, it was necessary to quote from obscure texts by Marx or Lenin in order to win an argument in student and union assemblies. After the failures and defeats that followed, the Left became passive, introspective. It abandoned general theory – the 'grand narratives' of Jean- François Lyotard's postmodern condition – for local and identity-based campaigns. This theoretical parsimony came to an end in the 2000s. Grand theory returned with Tony Negri, Slavoj Zizek, Alain Badiou and Ernesto Laclau leading the line. The Greek Left did not follow. A large part stayed with the old ideas, embellished with a little Gramsci or Althusser, and dismissed new theoretical directions as 'postmodern'. The pedantic devotion to classical texts dissolved into its opposite: lack of interest in theory, pride in not reading books. Action without thinking leads to voluntarism, the belief that you can change the world through the sheer force of will. Thinking without action leads to Hegel's 'beautiful soul', someone who stays outside the political fray in order to preserve the purity of ideas. Many mishaps and failures of the Syriza government are consequences of these two maladies.

The ignorance or dislike of theory has not allowed Syriza's ideology to match the needs of government. The party's electoral victories were based on the anti-austerity strategy rehearsed in the five years of resistance. The attack on austerity split the social body into a popular and an elite pole. This division allowed classes, groups and professions with internal tensions and conflicts to unite around the rejection of austerity and the established political class. The 2015 elections and referendum expressed this denunciation of the old regime. Negative support, however, based on the rejection of the opponent is temporary and contingent, electoral rather than ideological. Syriza has won four elections but its ideas have not acquired wide acceptance.

This conundrum determines Syriza's ideological pronouncements. They move along two overlapping juxtapositions. First, that between a government of all Greeks and a class-based party representing the working class, the unemployed and the poor. Secondly, that between class policies and identity politics. The four sides converged in 2015 creating a temporary hegemonic division, which, while representing class interests and identity claims, could also express the universality of national interest. Once this alliance dissolved, Syriza was caught in the horns of the two dilemmas.

The Prime Minister regularly adopts the position of the national leader speaking domestically and internationally on behalf of the nation. The refugee crisis and foreign affairs give politicians the perfect opportunity to suspend political antagonism. This is obvious at the inter-parliamentary conferences I have to attend. The Greek delegation consists of Syriza and New Democracy deputies. The right-wing delegates give me *carte blanche* to represent the Greek position in the debates. On those occasions, I address the delegations on behalf of Greece. It is a moving experience for the expatriate academic. As soon as the meeting closes, however, political tensions return and the bonhomie of the conference room disappears.

Speaking for the country is the government's prerogative. At the same time, ministers and the party keep raising class issues. A strategy becomes hegemonic if it can turn particular interests or demands into universal aspirations. The government wants to occupy this position – turning class interests into expressions of the common good. The opposition, aware of the danger, tries to prevent this transfer. Ridding the country of corruption, for example, has been a main promise of the Left. Corruption in banking, the media and football is intrinsically linked with big capital and elite politicians. The attempt to clean the country is therefore both an assault on class privilege and a claim to moral universalism. Moral probity is a trump card for the Left. It can be weakened by sporadic or incidental violations of a strict but under-defined moral code. Similarly, the attempt to combine speaking for the nation and championing the class is not always possible. The translation of class politics into moral claims, necessary as it is, often confuses the issues. The resulting ideological seesaw, occasionally unavoidable, has slowed down the hegemonic mission.

The second dualism between class and identity politics unravels in the space opened by the first. Syriza's history is steeped in working-class politics. Identity politics, social movements and human rights campaigns were added to the party's core ideology relatively late by a younger cosmopolitan generation. The two sides have co-habited happily. When the government was unable to deliver on its class promises, identity and human rights became a privileged site of intervention. On a couple of occasions, however, class and rights diverged. The EU–Turkey agreement obliges Turkey to stop the flow of refugees to Greece and provides for the return of failed asylum seekers and economic migrants. If refugees are returned before their asylum applications are examined, human rights would be violated. This has not happened, even though the processing of asylum applications has been snail-like. Greece did not have the requisite numbers of qualified officials for the task. The EU promised to help with asylum experts but has not delivered. Despite the huge reduction of arrivals from Turkey and the difficulties Greek authorities face, the human rights contingent has loudly condemned the agreement; a Syriza deputy resigned. Class analysis and political sensitivity lead to a different conclusion. In the autumn of 2016, some 60,000 refugees were trapped in Greece. If Turkey allows another 100,000 to come to the islands, the government would probably fall and the extreme Right's agenda would dominate politics. After the fall of Communism, human rights enjoy global approval without much consideration for their provenance and concrete operation.[5] For some, rights have become the last utopia and have replaced class politics and social justice.[6] For the Left, however, the interests of class and political considerations are at least as important as those of the abstract human that human rights treaties protect. An unthinking prioritization of rights and law over competing claims by politics threatens to harm both law and politics.

Before 2012, Syriza's parliamentary group hovered around ten MPs. It is now 144. This huge jump meant that most MPs had no preparation or knowledge of parliamentary etiquette. Unexpected elevation to Parliament and the difficult conditions they face under constant personal and political attack have formed a group of people both determined and confused. The ideological and theoretical tensions divide Syriza MPs into three categories: the honest and idealistic majority, the complacent few and, finally, the power-crazy. The first group is by far the largest. Its members tend to come from provincial cities and towns; they do not belong to tendencies or factions and are fiercely independent. Many have flourishing careers and do not aspire to become professional politicians. They are not particularly versed in political philosophy or left doctrine; they live by their conscience and carry the burden of the government's compromise. They experience existential difficulties when voting austerity measures into law and suffer when party or government misfires. Their speeches and actions support general principles and values; they keep away from anything that smacks of cronyism or favouritism. They are the Left's salt of the earth, the fertilizer for a future society of justice.

Secondly, the complacent few. They often belong to a party tendency or grouping. The ideological veneer of these factions differs but their main function is to secure party positions and influence for their members. Many come from a communist past and value discipline more than independence. Early in 2016, a number of unattached MPs launched the 'Ideas Lab': a fortnightly university-type seminar for deputies. It aims to build a shared understanding on key ideological and theoretical issues and to foster a collective and comradely spirit. In the absence of regular parliamentary group meetings, the Lab became the main forum for debate, socialization and friendly group therapy. The Left has always been the application of theory in practice. This old principle has been sidelined under the pressure of events. Many errors and failures can be attributed to this neglect for the insights of theory and philosophy. Returning to a more reflective practice will help party and government address the difficulties they face.

Finally, the seekers after power. They are often betrayed by their 'diagonal focus syndrome'. While speaking with someone in Parliament, their eyes are wandering about. As soon as a senior minister enters the viewing field, they abandon the conversation in mid-sentence and rush to accost him (senior ministers are all men). They isolate ministers in order to have their uninterrupted attention and press on them personal and constituency requests. Most of them come from Pasok and differ from the majority in ethos and style. They have their own private 'political offices' separate from the local Syriza headquarters, a practice the party disapproves. They are obsessively chasing a ministerial post and are in mourning after every 'barren' government reshuffle. They use fully the privileges offered by Parliament – up to five assistants, a car and two policemen to go with it, free travel. For them, politics is not a vocation but a full-time profession and a quest for aggrandizement. There is nothing wrong of course with a politician's ambition to ascend the ladder of power. This is the *raison d' être* and *modus operandi* of most professional politicians. But Syriza did not come to government to distribute favours or to promote the careers of individuals.

This group minimizes the distance between the old parties and Syriza.

Syriza's balance sheet has been mixed. Most ministers have stuck to their ideology and values. A few have followed the old practice of planning, legislating and acting without consulting with the party or MPs. Some speak and act in a style incompatible with left ethos. Some have been accused of replacing the old corrupt 'magic circle' with a left circuit of favours, privileges and protections. Very little credible evidence for these accusations exists. But the allegations, repeated *ad nauseam* by the systemic media, hurt the government. The Left, as collective intellectual, differs from mainstream parties. A Syriza government ought to develop ideas, policies and legislation in a continuous debate with party members, who represent popular interests and concerns, and with MPs, who mediate between government and the people.

My own half-term report has a few successes and a number of disappointments. Perhaps I was too naive. I came to Greece inspired by ideals and hopes expecting to see critical theories and radical conjectures translate into policies and transform the political landscape. It has not happened yet. Perhaps I was too innocent. I expected to see the ethics and aesthetics of the Left in every party and government action. The signs are there but so are people and attitudes that hurt left ideals. A life in the university does not prepare for the boredom, lack of effectiveness and small-mindedness of politics. Still, Syriza is a last hope for Greece. Only this unconventional government of hopefully incorruptible semi-professionals can get the country out of its recent acute and perennial crisis. Only this amateurish bunch of young people can prepare Greece for the challenges of the twenty-first century. If they fail, the return of the old will condemn the country for a generation. Success depends largely on protecting the moral advantage and the institutional reformism of the Left.

9

The Curious Incident of the Missing TV Licences

On 10 November 2016, and after five failed attempts, the conference of Parliamentary Presidents elected the nine Commissioners of the National Radio and Television Commission (ESR in Greek), the Greek Ofcom. The ESR saga dominated the news for many months with meetings of the conference broadcast live on TV. The story offers a microcosm of everything that is wrong with modern Greece: the strong link between political elites, banks and electronic media; the judiciary's political role and malfunction; the electronic media's consistent violation of the law; sex, scandal and corruption; finally, the opposition's attempt to use its own and its patrons' anomie in order overthrow the government. If the record of Syriza's tenuous occupation of power was lost but the ESR saga was saved, future historians would be able to reconstruct everything that went wrong in Greek life. They would also be able to reconstruct the lengths to which the elites go to prevent Syriza from carrying out its promises.

The Commission was established in 1989. Under Article 15 of the Constitution, 'Radio and television shall be under the immediate control of the state and shall aim at the objective transmission, on equal terms, of information and news reports.' A 2001 amendment delegated state control to the ESR. The Commission has legislative executive and disciplinary powers. It has issued a number of codes of practice about

the content and quality of programmes, journalistic deontol-
ogy and advertising standards. It oversees media compliance
with legal duties and codes of practice and can impose fines
and even suspend the licence of media seriously violating their
conditions of operation. A key power of media regulators is
to license private radio and TV stations for a fee. Except that
the licensing power was never exercised by the ESR.

The first private radio station was established illegally in
1986; the first TV channel in 1989. From that point until
2016, major print-media corporations and entrepreneurs
started setting up TV channels and radio stations without
permission. They were given temporary licences after their
launch renewed annually through legislative amendments. It
was a good example of the principle that (unlawful) possession is the best road to (legal) ownership. There is nothing
more permanent than the temporary, states a Greek maxim;
the licensing regime fully confirms it. No procedure for
issuing licences was established or followed and no fee was
paid for the use of the publicly owned frequencies. Some
right-wing politicians expressed concern about the practice.
The government of Kostas Karamanlis attempted in 2005 to
contain cronyism and corruption by making it incompatible
for major public works contractors to own TV channels.
The 'pimps', as the right-wing PM called them echoing John
Major's 'bastards', ganged up and fought back. The European
Commission, under the pretext of free competition, rejected
Karamanlis' law and forced the government to repeal it. As a
result, electronic media remained unlicensed for twenty-seven
years. Television ownership stayed in the hands of large corporations and major construction companies.

Over that period, eight national TV channels operated,
with two going bankrupt as advertising revenues collapsed.
The rest survived through bank loans, most of which are not
serviced. According to evidence offered to a parliamentary
committee examining the debt of media and parties, media
companies have over one billion euros debt in 2016, €800
million of which will not be repaid; it will be borne by the
taxpayers through the repeated recapitalization of banks. The
CEO of the largest but seriously indebted media empire was
asked what security he offered for receiving further loans
and replied 'air'. Hot air, political support for friends and

blackmailing opponents is the capital of the media. Their huge and growing debt forms the bridge linking politicians, banks and major public contracts. Establishment politicians put pressure on banks to give loans to the media, which reciprocate by promoting their policies. It is a deep and strong bond that could only be broken by people outside the magic circle of the 'three hundred families' running the country.

Syriza's destiny is to (try to) break this circle. It is proving hard, almost impossible. The totality of the print and electronic media campaigned vigorously against the party in the 2014 and 2015 elections and acted as propagandist-in-chief for the 'Yes' campaign in the 2016 referendum. The objective and neutral news and current affairs reporting, prescribed in the Constitution, became a dead letter in a media landscape resembling Greece under the Colonels. The latest chapter of the saga began with the Syriza government. The party had promised to introduce legislation for licensing and regulating the media. Soon after the September election, a bill was passed providing that national free-to-air high-definition TV channels should be licensed through a public tender and auction to be organized by the ESR. To ensure that the successful channels would not depend on loans and politicians' favours, the law limited their number to four, following recommendations of a report by a European University Institute research team – Britain has three private channels of this kind. Finally, the law creates for the first time a European-type regulatory framework, which provides for a minimum number of properly employed staff and sets strict technical and administrative conditions for their operation. For the first time, television would be licensed properly, operate lawfully and contribute a fair fee to the depleted public coffers.

The reaction of the tight knot of politicians, media and industrialists was vitriolic. The media barons hated the law and opposition politicians resolved to frustrate its operation. A strange coincidence came in handy. The ESR stopped being operational in 2015, when the term of its commissioners came to an end. Under the law establishing the regulator, later repeated in the Constitution, the ESR commissioners are elected by a four fifths majority of Parliament's Conference of Presidents.[1] To reach this increased majority at least four parties must consent. In early 2016, the then temporary leader of New Democracy indicated that he was prepared to collaborate with the government and meet the constitutional obligation to create a fully functioning ESR. Kyriakos Mitsotakis, the new leader, stated on the day of his election that his party would not help elect the ESR members until the government repealed its media law. It was clear that the lack of licensing and the illegal operation of television and radio would continue indefinitely.

At that point, Nikos Pappas, the minister in charge of media policy, amended the law, giving the power to organize the first public auction to the government's General Secretariat for Communications. The TV channels reacted with indignation. They turned up their anti-government propaganda to maximum, participating at the same time in the ensuing auction for licences. The process was strictly organized and policed with the bidding representatives of TV channels confined for three days in closed offices without contact with the outside world. Two existing channels and two new companies secured licences for an unexpectedly high total fee of €240 million.

While the auction was going on, a number of channels petitioned the Council of State (STE in Greek) to review the constitutionality of the tender and the law on which it was based. The Council had repeatedly ruled in the past that the constitutional duty to license TV stations is pressing and should be fulfilled at the earliest opportunity. The channels, on the other hand, argued that licensing could only be carried out by the ESR, forgetting the fact that for twenty-seven years, the Commission had failed to start the process. It was a typical case of conflict between two equally valid constitutional provisions. In the past, the Council, like most superior courts, had avoided involvement in such hard political disputes by invoking the 'law of necessity'. Necessity, like so-called 'political questions' in the USA and the royal prerogative in Britain, ensures that courts leave politically controversial decisions with no clear legal answer to the politicians. Under that doctrine, the Council of State had accepted the constitutionality of the first memorandum conditionalities signed by the Pasok government. The 'necessity' to deal with the country's debt made the measures acceptable,

despite the serious violations of most constitutionally protected economic and social rights.

A febrile atmosphere accompanied the STE hearings.
Newspapers and TV channels kept threatening the judges if
they decided for the government. The STE President, who had
indicated that he was not opposed to the government's position, was repeatedly heckled and attacked in central Athens.
An opposition politician revealed that one of the STE judges
had an affair with a young lawyer who was applying to
become a junior judge and was given the entry exams questions. The government had been informed about the content
of the illegally obtained communications between the two
protagonists a few months earlier but had not taken any
action, as the evidential material was the fruit of an unlawful
invasion of private life. After the publication of the revelations,
however, the Minister of Justice ordered the investigation of
the serious allegations. The judge involved was reputed to be
on the anti-government side, giving the opposition and media
the opportunity to attack the government for its 'threatening'
action. Rumour, gossip, leaks and counter-leaks dominated
public life as if all other pressing problems had been frozen
in the wait for the STE decision. The future of the country
was being negotiated with the creditors; all TV news bulletins
cared about, however, were the political proclivities, sexual
adventures and voting intentions of the judges.

The denouement was farcical. The most anti-Syriza TV
channel announced on 26 October that the twenty-four STE
judges had decided with a 14 to 11 majority that the law was
unconstitutional. At the time of writing, no official statement
has been issued by the court; the scope and reasoning of the
ruling is unknown, as are the parts of the law that have been
ruled unconstitutional. It was a political decision confirming
the pro-establishment proclivities of the court. The attempt to
create a 'perfect' market by shutting away senior businessmen
for three days and extracting large fees for their licences was
in tatters. The government immediately admitted defeat. It
revoked the licences issued after the auction, repealed those
parts of the law that had been the basis of judicial review
and transferred the power to organize a new auction back
to the ESR. It accepted that the number of channels could be
more than four with the exact number to be agreed by the

regulator. It was the first occasion, to my knowledge, that an important policy was reversed on the basis of journalistic information about an unknown judicial decision. It showed the government's respect for the rule of law (or its desire to cut its losses) against the repeated failure of the former rulers to comply with the constitutional obligations.

The opposition had won and the regulator was back in business. Only that no regulator existed. Syriza parliamentarians continued the attempts to populate and restart the ESR. Over the course of five meetings, lists of nominees for the nine ESR positions had been circulated and were found with some changes generally acceptable. But New Democracy continued its objections, even though the prerequisites for cooperation kept changing. Before the court case was launched, the right-wing insisted that the government should 'repeal the law'. Before the judgment became 'known', they claimed that 'we should wait until the court decides'. After the court's decision was leaked, New Democracy went back to the demand that the law be repealed. The 'law-abiding' right-wing bourgeoisie was pursuing a double-pronged policy of anomie. First, they defended the lawlessness and licenceless of their media friends. Secondly, using the coincidence of the absence of a properly constituted regulator and the absurd requirement of a four fifths majority of Presidents, they kept blocking the operation of the law. As the two matters were unrelated, this was a new type of 'creative' resistance. It could be used to block any government bill before accepting and giving its consent to the appointment of commissioners. New Democracy was indicating that they would veto the constitution of the ESR until the government falls and they return to power.

This became clear after the leak of the court judgment. The minor opposition parties, whose vote was necessary for reaching the four fifths majority, celebrated the court decision and negotiated the membership of the regulator, eventually voting for the compromise list. It was not enough. The impasse was broken after a major opposition mistake. While insisting on the repeal of the law, they also put forward a former President of the Supreme Court as a potential President of the ESR. The Syriza members, keen to bring anomie to an end, gratefully adopted the nomination and presented a new list of members at the 10 November conference. New

Democracy was caught by surprise, tried to wiggle out but eventually had to accept the final list of nominees with their own man at the top. After a long period of political shenanigans, the ESR was constituted and a new process of licensing TV channels will commence under its oversight.

The saga represents the ills of Greek life. News and current affairs on Greek TV are so one-sided and uninformative that people were fully behind the attempt to regulate the field. The close links between politicians, media and banks had been repeatedly castigated. The ESR incident brought the golden triangle fully into view. Yet, it was also characteristic of ministerial inexperience and failure of style. Syriza had a just cause and huge popular support to start with but the public was left with the feeling that the government mishandled the case. The insistence on issuing just four licences while fully justified gave the impression that the government wanted to control broadcasting. Statements from ministers and officials at the height of the controversy sounded autocratic and arrogant. The threat of immediate closure of the channels that would not succeed in the auction was presented as a vindictive act against ideological opponents. Finally, the licensing of two new companies, owned by controversial owners of popular football clubs, was used to attack the government for an attempt to create pro-Syriza media. There were convincing answers to these allegations. But their continuous repetition, the occasionally insensitive responses by ministers as well as the judicial reversal created the impression of a government own goal.

The mishandling of an affair that was the first step in the combatting of corruption was a lost opportunity. However, the main lesson from the TV licensing saga is that forces outside Parliament and government continue to dominate public life. The government has only touched the outer layer of the power network. The 'left interval' is still the opposition's preferred plan. They are determined to overthrow Syriza and stop its attempt to clean the Augean stables. If they succeed, through their own undiminished power and Syriza's mistakes, the future of the country is bleak.

Part IV

The Moral Advantage
of the Left

10

The Ethos of the Left

The Greek Left could not and did not distribute favours and benefits. This was the privilege of the habitual owners of the state. The leftists are not weighed down therefore by corruption, cronyism and nepotism, the baggage that condemned Pasok to extinction and the right-wing to near permanent opposition. Morality is the trump card of the Left, a mark of honesty and of commitment to values. People appreciate this moral advantage, which bestows a certain haughtiness on leftists. The opposition cannot hide its problematic record on that front and tries to paint the Left in the same colours. Morality has therefore become a strongly contested ideological site. Its opponents try to show that the Left has adopted the same corrupt practices – non-transparent deals with the business world, favouritism and nepotism towards friends and voters.

The majority of Greeks agree that the advantage is still with the Left. Politicians are not 'all the same', as the opposition accuses Syriza, nor did we 'eat it all together'.[1] Very little, almost nothing, links the long-standing managers of power and state and those on the Left who, until the 1970s, could not get the certificate of 'social right-thinking' necessary for employment. The moral advantage of the Left is not limited, however, to the persecution and sacrifice of the past or its clean hands and blameless record. People join political parties to get employment or other benefits – the 'government-as-job-centre' and the 'state-as-loot-and-voter-service' mentality. People join the Left for simple values and complex ideas: social justice, equality, hopes for a better world. They read abstract and obscure theories – Marx, Lenin, Benjamin, Freud, Bloch, Adorno, Foucault, Derrida – and hone their skills in long and intense debates, in political and ideological struggles. I know of no one who joined the Left because he expected the kingdom of heaven on earth or, more pragmatically, a job in a public hospital. Politics is split between those for whom ruling is a hereditary entitlement and profitable profession and, the likes of Syriza MPs Nikos Manios, Thodoris Dritsas, Tassia Christodoulopoulou or Makis Balaouras. They represent the successive generations of resistance and have given their lives to the values of the Left without expecting any reward.

Yet, morality is not just the absence of corruption; nor does it consist in a small number of dos and donts. Moral and legal norms are part of what could be called the 'Greek ethos', what it means to be Greek. But morality is only one aspect of ethics. Concentrating on rules and norms misses the wider import of ethos and the practices it captures. *Ethos* is the classical Greek word for personal or collective character. A collectivity's ethos is a largely tacit order which facilitates social coexistence. It contains personal skills and habits such as care for others, rules of politeness and etiquette; a knowledge and understanding of the environment and its codes; finally, general values and moral norms regulating our relations with others. The Greek word *ethikos/ethike* was translated into Romance languages with two words: 'ethics' and 'morality': two distinct aspects of social co-existence, the largely practical and the predominantly normative. The Greek ethos has wisely preserved a strong link between practices and values, habits and rules.

We are introduced to the communal ethos at the start of life. The first sense of value, habit and understanding of the world is acquired in family, school and neighbourhood. We learn these skills in a mostly informal way, through imitation, repetition and apprenticeship. They constitute a moral and conceptual substratum, not always explicit or fully conscious. Georg Gadamer calls this preparatory set of skills and values, pre-judgments or pre-conceptions.[2] They are the ground understandings and values that will allow us later in life to make judgments about right and wrong, good and bad, beautiful and ugly. Moral attitudes, life choices and ideological preferences emerge out of that initial orientation towards the world. Our mature ethos develops in a constant dialogue between the known and familiar and the alien and universal. At home, we learn love, care and obedience to natural and cultural powers; at school, the universality of concepts and the significance of equality; at work or university, the power of knowledge to undermine unfounded beliefs, to fit in and control our environment. General values, concepts and ideas challenge parochial beliefs and orient them towards a more abstract level. A similar process takes place in our encounters with others. Our identity is constantly in motion, in a dialogue and a struggle for recognition with intimates and friends as well as colleagues, acquaintances and strangers. Our personal ethos evolves in a continuous debate between the particular and the universal and in the reciprocal desire and mutual recognition of others.

10.1   The three friendships

Augustine said that he cannot define time but he knows when it passes. Equally, we cannot fully define the Greek ethos but we know that it has been under coordinated attack. First, by the false and failed modernization of the early 2000s, later, by austerity policies. I learnt parts of this indefinable ethos in the neighbourhoods of Piraeus in the 1950s and 1960s. It had three elements: *filia* (friendship), *filotimo* (love and pride in honour), *filoxenia* (hospitality). Anthropologist friends claim that I have a memory of non-existing things. Perhaps they are right; perhaps my long time overseas made me nostalgic for lost entities or fantastic feelings. Still, I believe that the three *filias*, now hidden under the current state of exception, are the most important resource for the restart of society and economy.

Filia is the foundation of sociality, the opening to the other in a shared world. It acknowledges practically that identity develops in a struggle for recognition and builds characters for whom the other is part of self and self part of the other. In the years of austerity, however, *filia* retreated and was replaced by indifference towards others and withdrawal from public life and collectivities. *Filotimo* is the aesthetic aspect of ethics. It is to try your best and get pleasure from the effort and perfection of the work and its fruit: a tasty meal, a beautifully painted wall, a well composed sonnet. For the *filotimos*, work has autotelic value, it is as an end in itself. I am proud and enjoy what I create beyond its monetary value. In the years of plenty, this love for life and work was transformed into possessive individualism and aggressive consumerism. When austerity struck, individualism became fearful and defensive and was adjusted to the misery of the age.

Finally, *filoxenia*. When a *xenos* (foreigner) arrives for work or a visit, our first reaction is to welcome her. Hospitality acknowledges the finitude of the world and our dependence on proximate and distant others. As Immanuel Kant argued, the nature of the world as a globe creates the significance of hospitality. If we keep travelling around it, we will return to our point of departure having encountered every race on earth. In the age of austerity, the extrovert patriotism of *filoxenia* has been transformed into xenophobia, a turning away and even revulsion towards others. Under the right-wing government, the police carried out indiscriminate pogroms against 'illegal immigrants' in central Athens arresting foreign-looking visitors. Overseas professors invited by Greek colleagues and tourists were among the many people arrested. The Syriza government stopped this unacceptable behaviour. The xenophobic mentality was shaken by the massive arrival of refugees. The fearful response to the stranger, propagated by the right-wing, was replaced by a display of solidarity, *filoxenia*, a care for the suffering other that has always been central to the Greek ethos.

The three filias recognize our dependence on the other. The stranger is already inside us: the other's recognition and desire carves my own identity. Furthermore, the unconscious, 'the stranger in me', is an uninvited, demanding and controlling guest. The attempt to annihilate the other is doomed to undermine the integrity of self. This damage to the ego is evident in the followers of neo-Nazi *Chryssi Avgi*. Racist feelings of inferiority and humiliation are displaced into the idle claims of racial superiority. Severing the links with the other removes the anchor of self's existence.

10.2   Left values

The ethos of the three filias has returned in the resistance, the social movements, the solidarity for refugees. The baker of Kos, the shepherd of Lemnos, the grannies of Mytilini who saved and sheltered the suffering humanity in the face of the refugees are symbols of a new hospitality. It is organized by groups of friends, NGOs and ordinary people who take pride in the modesty of solidarity.

Ethos and ethics remain fundamental resources for social renewal. The moral responsibility of the Left is to reverse its long-term decline. Targeted policies should support all forms of family, empower collectivities, promote communal cultural and educational initiatives. Family, friendship and community remain the ground of ethos. The Left must help the creation of a new 'democratic communitarianism'. It accepts the centrality of groups, communities and individuals and strikes a balance between collectivity with its demands of loyalty and collaboration and individuality with its emphasis on autonomy. Its categorical imperative founds individual morality on the protection of the multitude of oppressed, exploited and excluded citizens. In a Kantian paraphrase, it reads: 'Act always according to a maxim that universalizes, attacks and cancels the symptoms and the causes which exclude and condemn to symbolic or natural death large parts of the population and dissolve communities.' This way, equality moves from economic doctrine into moral principle. Communities are revived and ethos survives – not in continuity with dead tradition but as complex encounters of unique selves created through and with others.

11

Greeks or Europeans?

The Greek culture wars have been fought between 'Orientals' and 'Westernizers' around the dilemma 'East or West?'; 'Does Greece belong to Europe or the Orient?' For the Orientals, a motley crowd of cosmopolitans, modernizers and Europhiles threaten 'authentic' Greek identity. On the opposite corner, cultural commentator Soti Triantafyllou believes that Greeks are characterized by 'ignorance, nationalism, conservatism, anti-Europeanism, anti-Westernism, pseudo-wisdom, arrogance, an inferiority complex and a persecution complex'.[1] It is quite a list and captures the high emotions generated by the debate.

Nationalists and Europhiles are two sides of the same coin. They both believe naively or hypocritically the idea of the 'elect' people and of the 'eternal' nation. For some, it is the highest value; for others, the worst but effective lie. The Orientals concentrate on a celebratory and often distorted version of Greek history and tradition. They emphasize the continuity and glory of the nation from classical times to post-modernism; the religious and cultural centrality of the Ortho-dox church with its Slav 'brothers'; finally, they denounce the relentless conspiracies and campaigns by assorted enemies to undermine the nation. The Orientals rallied to stop the northern neighbour from using the name Macedonia; they tried to stop the removal of references to Orthodox Christian-ity from identity cards; they use every opportunity to attack perfidious Turkey. The more extreme among them believe that the eternal traits of the Greek DNA are under attack. In this narrative, the population is sprayed with noxious fumes in order to undermine its will to resist austerity policies and so to weaken and enslave the nation.[2] The anonymity of social media and the internet have given conspiracy theories a boost. On the whole, however, these views rarely get a public hearing. The majority of the population believes little of all that. Greekness represents pride for ancient glories and a certain embarrassment for contemporary travails, a mild cultural religiosity, a love of family, distrust of authority and the three friendships discussed above.

The 'Europhiles' assert superior cultural knowledge and scientific expertise. They rely on 'facts' rather than feelings. But, as the quotation above indicates, they can be greater fanatics and victims of 'ignorance and pseudo-wisdom' than the Orientals. Their response to the dilemma 'West or East' is monotonously the same: 'Occident or Death' and, during the 2015 negotiations with the creditors, 'Occident and Death'. In the week of the referendum, they organized a 'We Remain in Europe' campaign and rally. They were asking the government to accept the European ultimatum at all costs. Their meeting coincided with the huge Syntagma No rally and was minuscule in comparison. It stays in the memory because of the high fashion of some participants and the white wine freely passing around. Unlike the Orientals, the Europhiles dominate the public sphere. A large number of opinion makers and social scientists subscribe to 'occidental-ism', a wide-eyed Eastern adoration of the West.

Many Greek academics import, copy and disseminate Western theories and ideas, viewing themselves as local correspondents of the Occident. Their ideology is cosmopolitanism, a faith created by three German philosophers after major German military defeats. Immanuel Kant, Hans Kelsen and Jürgen Habermas were the missionaries and emissaries of a world order to be ruled by law, the United Nations and Microsoft.[3] The high point of cosmopolitanism was in the early 2000s. It was soon buried under the debris of the Iraq and Afghanistan wars. The Greek cosmopolitans came late to the scene. The postal service is slow; intellectual missives take time to reach Athens. Delays in delivery

of Western dispatches and the sudden death of the cosmopolitan mission after the Iraq war meant that it did not take
roots in Greece. Constitutional patriotism, the honest but
doomed attempt by Jürgen Habermas to create a sense of
patriotism not based on blood and soil, made sense perhaps
in Hampstead, the sixteenth *arondissement* and Ekali. In
Keratsini, Tottenham and the Paris banlieues, young women
and men see Europe not as *patria* but as an alien, threatening force. The Greek cosmopolitans propagated a version of
'constitutional patriotism' in the mid-2000s, well after its
abandonment by its Western promoters. It was not taken
seriously. Craig Calhoun's apt definition, suitably adjusted,
defines cosmopolitanism as the class consciousness of the
frequent traveller with a mansion in Athens and a pad
in Brussels.

11.1   Nation and hybrid identities

Liberal Europhiles brag about their cultural superiority and
understanding of Western ways. However, they stopped
renewing their intellectual frequent-flyer cards in the 2000s.
The intense debates on identity, alterity and the postcolonial
condition escaped their attention. They seem to ignore the
fact that both 'Europe' and the 'East' are 'imagined communities', constructions of the *mission civilisatrice*, suitably
updated by orientalism. The strict juxtaposition between
Orient and Occident no longer exists. National and personal identities have become mobile, flexible and vulnerable.
As tradition and authenticity acquired monetary value, Big
Macs turned into MacSouvlaki for the Greeks and MacCurry
for the Indians. When a local cuisine or a religious festival
becomes part of the heritage industry, their connection with
a living community is loosened. Something celebrated and
sold as part of 'tradition' has stopped being a form of life.

The 'West' has been grafted onto the 'East'. Global access
to the internet and credit has undermined collective identities, turning them into folkloric remnants of a dead past. The
universal form of exchange value subverts all solid patriotic
content. Hollywood values, Facebook and electronic games
undermine the beliefs of the most orthodox nationalist. At the

opposite end, the 'Orient' is as much at home in London as in Lausanne and Larissa and has become an inextricable part of the 'West'. Eastern traces and hybrid East–West identities are found at the heart of every European metropolis, including Athens. The attacks on Madrid, London, Paris and Nice did not come from outside. The same applies to the fascists of *Chryssi Avgi* and the Breiviks of this world. Western jihadists and neo-Nazis have attended European schools, they have danced to rock and rap, they have been taught the Enlightenment values. Samuel Huntington's 'Clash of Civilizations' is not being fought solely in Syria and Libya. It is a part of everyday life in Europe. In Western Europe, jihadist terrorism is not the outcome of far-away wars but of repression and marginalization of minorities at the only place they can call 'home'. Against the doomsayers, however, the positive influence of the East is found everywhere. Southern friendship and solidarity, until recently ridiculed as backward, is now promoted as a bulwark against Northern individualism. As the social state retreats, the love and care of the Mediterranean or Asian family towards its weaker members is promoted as a progressive measure in Munich and Manchester.

The aspiration to create or protect a hedgehog-like national or personal identity is the noble dream for some and a nightmare for others. They are both equally wrong. The 'imagined community' of the nation is not a solid substance. People are not univocal creations of history and tradition. We are born into family, neighbourhood and nation. But this most fortuitous event of birth determines almost inescapably life's trajectory. We belong to a national community with its principles, values and prejudices but we are also in a constant dialogue with moral, ideological and epistemic principles and values. We do not enter life Robinson Crusoe-like as claimed by the liberals; nor are we weak-willed puppets, as imagined by the nationalists. Complex inclusions and interconnections create our unique self, which does not fit the old-fashioned polarity of either European or Greek. For some, the fundamental reference is the nation, for others gender, sexuality or Europe; for others still, all or none of the above. Identities are not static. Both the 'national' and the 'European' identity can be re-signified beyond the logic of the elect and inferior peoples, Occidentals and Orientals. Only the ideologues of nationalism and cosmopolitanism believe that the world is divided into clearly demarcated and mutually exclusive identities.

Personal identity looks like an inverted pyramid or globe, at the bottom of which stands the unique *I*. Each one is a cosmos, a node where different narrative lines and temporalities come together into an inimitable universe of facts and stories, persons and encounters, memories and fantasies, desires and fears. The singular *ego* is a unique constellation of meanings, events and people. Our irreplaceable cosmos is criss-crossed by the worlds of others, intimate or distant. The line between East and West is no longer a strictly policed border but a place of encounter and passage; identity is the outcome of traffic and trade between identity and alterity. The Left instinctively understands this position because it tallies with its internationalism and communal ethics. It has the task of using it in order to weaken the divide further and promote new opportunities for individuals and communities.

11.2   Left and responsibility

According to a *bon mot* credited both to George Bernard Shaw and Winston Churchill, America is the only country that went from barbarism to decadence without stopping at civilization. Similarly, Greece can become a country moving from traditional cronyist capitalism to postmodern democratic socialism without stopping at modernity in between. The modernizers adopted the European model of cheap credit and consumerism, leading eventually to the mountain of private and public debt. Those who wish to cleanse the errors of the past and build a progressive future should look beyond the banalities of the European fanatics. Greece needs a major public debate on identity. The idea of a glossy Western identity survives solely in the dreams of the eastern lovers of the West but not in the hybrid identities of Western citizens. Similarly, the idea of a pristine Greek identity is a delusion that leads both to idiotic arrogance and to pathological fears.

The moral and cultural rebirth of the country must be placed at the heart of politics. The exhaustive and exhausting debate on macroeconomics, austerity and debt was necessary. But the constant, tortuous and exclusive discussion of numbers, statistics and 'expert' opinion transformed the lives of Greeks into a TV financial noir. Its episodes, broadcast daily on the 9 o'clock news, give the impression that people are only material beings, bodies without spirit. The human is a symbolic animal, however. We are born in language, we live in meaning, we breathe values. This is why left principles and values should be heard louder and become more convincing. Only this way can governance become government and electoral victories ideological hegemony.

The word 'responsibility' is etymologically linked to response. You are responsible when you respond to a (moral) demand. The demand may be coming from power, orthodoxy and commonsense or from the Other. Responsibility cannot be moral when it consents to the demands of power. To be responsible is to welcome the refugee, the poor, the excluded. When this happens, the cosmos each one of us is becomes richer. The existential dilemma is not between East and West, therefore, but between those in East and West who live by values and those others who consider the Euro as the sole sacred and holy of our times.

12

The Euro, the Sacred and the Holy

In March 2014, Yiannis Stournaras, then Minister of Finance, repeated something Jean-Claude Trichet, a former Governor of the ECB, had first said. 'We do not play games with the Euro, we do not play games with the sacred and the holy.' The idea of the 'sacredness' of the currency brings to mind Descartes, who quipped that the English call unbelievers only the insolvent. The 'pious' minister hellenicized the statement, bravely publicizing the thought of establishment politicians. Remaining in the Eurozone is the ultimate moral and political value. I imagine that Mr Stournaras, later promoted to the Governorship of the Bank of Greece, must now feel like some kind of Cardinal, with ECB's President Mario Draghi as the Pope. Manolis Glezos, the man who lowered the Swastika from the Acropolis in 1941, responded to Stournaras in kind: 'Sacred and holy is solely the human being and its existence, human rights, freedom and dignity.' The Euro and humanity are our moral foundations. We move between moral valuelessnes and fullness of value, between the nihilism of exchange and the mythology of a shared common substance.[1] They constitute the fundamental pillars of a new 'political theology' in our 'post-secular' era. But is the Euro 'sacred'?

Money is a means of exchange, facilitating transactions and the operation of the economy. When the use of gold or silver coins ceased, the currency stopped having intrinsic value. Money translates the incalculable and incomparable needs and uses people have for objects, services and emotions into a common measure for buying and selling. In this sense, money cannot be sacred. Its function is to circulate, not to stay put on a pedestal or a reliquary. To be sure, money may be used to buy incense, holy icons and relics of saints, or even the remission of sins through the indulgences still issued by some priests. But that is another matter.

Does the Euro possess magical properties that other currencies do not? Does the European map printed on euro coins and banknotes carry the 'idea' of Europe? When holding a twenty-euro note, some people may feel that they have a certificate of European identity. The banknote acquires a dual existence resembling the medieval king's two bodies as Ernst Kantorowicz explained.[2] The King was human and transcendent, material and spiritual. Similarly, the banknote is credit for purchases and passport for escaping the Orient for the West of our dreams. I buy the few things that can be bought with a twenty-euro banknote. At the same time, I keep in my pocket a cultural ID and a moral value.

British banknotes carry the statement 'I promise to pay the bearer on demand the sum of twenty pounds' signed by the Chief Cashier of the Bank of England. When I was still a newcomer to London, I asked a bank clerk if the Chief Cashier himself could pay my meagre scholarship as he promises. The flustered cashier gave me a 'are you mad?' look. Worried that I might not get the money, I apologized telling him that I was conducting a research project on the use of rhetorical figures, metaphors and performative speech acts in everyday life. Friedrich Nietzsche has said that metaphors and metonymies are like ancient coins whose long usage has worn out and erased their engraved features. People forget their function and take them solely for useless metal. In the case of the Euro and its lovers, the opposite applies: its purchasing power constantly decreases but its transcendent spiritual value keeps growing.

12.1   Debt desire and value

Stournaras' statement is factually and morally wrong. Money only blasphemously could be regarded as sacred and holy when 'possessive individualism' and consumerism became the fundamental individual and social value. The desire for the possession of things turns at that point into an end in itself, making its tools morally valuable. The Greek 'modernization' of the 2000s was based on such a sacralization of finance. After the departure of the primary and secondary sectors of the economy to the developing world, growth was supposed to come from services fuelled by credit. Financial houses and banks in London and Athens used to offer credit cards, 'cheap' loans and their ubiquitous financial 'products' without any checks. Eventually the indebtedness of people, companies and states grew beyond any possibility of repayment. At that point, debt became a huge problem and debtors morphed into morally failing agents. In fact, debt is the lubricant of late capitalism. Without debt an economy of services cannot grow. Some time ago, Argentina wanted to pay the larger part of its debt to the IMF, but the Fund declined the offer. If the debt was paid off, the Fund would not be in the position to impose further structural reforms, privatizations and deregulation of work and professions. As Nietzsche explained, debt is a moral obligation and social relation that freezes time as it makes the debtor hostage to fear and the creditor. Only later debt became an economic relation and was accompanied by debt relief institutions such as the Jewish Jubilee and the Greek *Seisachtheia*.[3]

Psychoanalysis teaches that desire is always the desire of the other. I desire to find in the other what I lack, that 'something' I lost in the separation from the maternal body. The return to imaginary completeness is impossible, however, and the demand misses its target. The other is not able to give us what neither she nor I possess. Desire is therefore forced to produce imaginary scenaria moving from the other person to objects. I struggle and save for years in order to buy a used car. But the moment I buy it, I start dreaming of getting a Skoda. If I manage that, making all kinds of sacrifice, I start dreaming of a BMW, then a Mercedes, and so on. As real desire cannot be satisfied, the substitutes multiply; the desire for objects is insatiable. This way exchange value, the common denominator that measures the amounts of labour that produced the commodity, becomes the sole value. Then it is upgraded into the sacred and holy.

After the July 2015 blackmail and defeat, many leftists in Greece and Europe accused Alexis Tsipras of an almost fetishistic attachment to the Euro. Were they right? Has Eurozone membership become a Syriza obsession and Grexit a forbidden taboo? I believe not. No currency is sacred and holy. Its adoption or rejection is a matter of political and economic calculation. Eurozone entry under the Maastricht rules was a mistake not just for Greece but for a number of countries whose economies were lagging far behind Germany. The common currency and interest rates without a common budget, taxation or banking sector fuelled the Southern buying bonanza of Northern products and created a huge trade imbalance. German capital was looking for an exit in the sun; austerity measures, with privatization at the top, followed. All this is well documented.

But voluntary Grexit would be an even bigger mistake, a political suicide note. The memoranda have reduced the Greek standard of living by up to 40 per cent. A possible exit would further reduce Greek wealth by a little more than the devaluation of the new currency – 20, 30 or 50 per cent. James Galbraith, a liberal adviser to Yanis Varoufakis, thinks that 30 per cent is the right level.[4] But Grexit would not cut the debt. The government could try to reduce it unilaterally; it would be idle audacity. A real reduction would have to be negotiated with the creditors because the country would not be able to borrow from the markets in order to finance social and economic needs. The fact that the main trade partners of Greece are Europeans creates a further difficulty. Costas Lapavitsas, a dogmatic Grexiteer, has admitted that it would be necessary after exit to impose restrictions and even to ration food, medicines and fuel. Rationing was last used during the German occupation. How long would it take for the economy to start growing after the introduction of the new currency? Supporters of Grexit have been 'creatively vague'. It could take twelve months, perhaps eighteen, maybe thirty-six; no precise forecast exists. The precedent of Argentina – a country with many commodities for export – is not encouraging either. Under the precautionary principle, the government, unable to borrow, would have to prepare for a few years with capital controls and coupons for basic needs. It would be the perfect storm for a politically vulnerable government targeted by foreign and domestic powers.

The Left is existentially committed to social justice and democracy. External diktat cannot be allowed to cancel its foundational values. Faced with the July coup, the government temporarily conceded. Any further attempts to undermine core left values will be fiercely resisted and may lead to the government's resignation. Such eventuality would confirm that neoliberalism and democracy are incompatible. Following Brexit and the rise of Euroscepticism all over Europe, it would be the end of the idea of Europe and perhaps of the European Union. It would also be final proof that the currency is the sole sacred and holy entity for the political theologians of our age.

Part V
Left History

13

The Left and the Philosophy of History

A common view before the January 2015 elections held that Greece had a rendezvous with history. It was exaggerated perhaps for a small country and a tiny party that found itself in a strange love affair with the Greeks and the international Left. The people adopted Syriza and brought it to power. The world Left saw its victory as a sign of the beginning of the end of neoliberalism. But were Syria's four successive victories an historic event? Can we predict history? Does history 'teach' political lessons?

The belief that history moves in a known way is a secularization of Christian eschatology. Humanity progresses inexorably from lower to higher stages which follow each other until Christ's Second Coming. The theologian Joachim of Fiore was the first to conceive a historical periodization in three stages: the age of the Father (the time of the Old Testament before Christianity), of the Son (Christianity) and of the Holy Spirit (the epoch after the Last Judgment). In the secular version, the philosophy of history replaced eschatology. History moves to a predetermined end: Kant's cosmopolitanism, Hegel's ethical state (*sittlichkeit*) or Marx's communism. Philosophy offers a road map for the future of humanity. Immanuel Kant was the key link between theology and philosophy. He borrowed from Augustine the belief that divine providence predetermines the destiny of humanity and from Joachim the successive historical ages. In the Kantian version, humanity follows a secret plan put together by nature who, like a puppeteer, moves history's puppet. Human reason decodes the plan and discovers an irreversible march of progress behind contingent events and fortuitous turns. It will be completed with the *pax aeterna* and a world cosmopolitan federation. Contemporary cosmopolitans, like President George Bush and Tony Blair, believed the Kantian prophesy and tried to accelerate the route of history. The wars in Yugoslavia, Afghanistan, Iraq and Syria would bring democracy and human rights to these 'dark' parts of the world. They would be the last wars before the emergence of the age of peace and plenty. Most cosmopolitan plans in the past started with good intentions and unfailingly morphed into versions of imperialism.[1]

Hegel discovered the necessity of historical change in actuality. History moves through the clash between subject and object. The need for radical change emerges first in social being and later moves to social consciousness. Human action gives the final push to the old. In France, for example, the contradiction between Enlightenment principles and feudal monarchy had undermined the social and political regime well before the revolution. The *ancien régime* had become obsolete and harmful; the revolution completed the job. For Hegel, modernity aligns the progress of the spirit with historical movement. In the move from classical Athens to modern civil society to the moral state (*sittlichkeit*), humanity ascends towards self-consciousness. History ends when philosophy realizes that history is nothing more than the gradual unravelling of spirit and that rational reflection coincides with the empirical world. Adam Smith and the Scottish Enlightenment had argued that the engine of historical movement is the economy. Marx adopted from Hegel the idea of the historical march and from Smith the emphasis on the economy and 'turned Hegelian idealism on its head'. When the relations of production advance, historical epochs change.

After the catastrophes of the twentieth century, however, it is hard to believe in the necessarily progressive motion of history. The forward march of reason and history was halted; then we realized that it was always a mirage. What remains from the philosophy of history? What is the role of agency in the historical movement? These questions have become even more pressing with Syriza's aspiration to help end the advertised 'end of history'. Can history 'teach' anything?

Let me begin with personal history. I went to London in July 1974 for graduate studies. The idea of staying permanently in England had not entered my mind. It happened without planning or desire on my part. I received my PhD from the London School of Economics in 1981 and sent back to Greece my household goods, fifty tea-chests full of books. As I was preparing to return to Greece, the Head of a Law Department offered me a year's contract replacing a colleague on sabbatical. The rest, as they say, is history. The tea-chests are still in a damp storage room, the books feeding the wisdom of mice and worms as I did not acquire an apartment big enough to house them.

The unpredictable, the unexpected, the accidental lurk in every corner of individual and collective life. Our coming into the world, the most important fact of life, is absolutely contingent. If our parents had not met, we wouldn't have come to the world. Still, this accidental arrival into this family of doctors or farmers, this or that neighbourhood, Hampstead or Peckam, this or that country, Greece or Haiti, determines life's trajectory. Despite the social mobility rhetoric, most people stay, physically and metaphorically, in the place they were born. A recent study by the International Economic Forum found that rich Greeks spend five times more than the poor on the education of their children. As expected, you would say. However, it doesn't seem obvious to those who cannot understand the class privilege of private schools. The most accidental fact of our lives is at the same time the most decisive.

Important life decisions – whom to fall in love with, whether to have children or not, what profession to follow – are often taken by fate or others. You enter a bar, and you see a stranger in the corner. The way she smokes her cigarette, how she drinks her whisky, the song she picks to play on the jukebox, a silent smile allure you. Love at first sight strikes on the forehead – a *coup de foudre*. Later, we tend to forget that we were called and consider our act the outcome of free choice. Later again we re-interpret as necessary or fateful the contingent events that led to the encounter. Freedom and determination, will and submission go hand in hand. Freedom is the insight into necessity; autonomy the understanding of heteronomy, to paraphrase Marx. This is how personal and collective histories work.

13.1   The reversed time arrow

When we abandon faith in historical necessity, history appears open, unforeseen, contingent. The historical trajectory is not written in advance as a linear and inexorable progress. It is composed retrospectively after the provisional end of a sequence of events. When they occur they often appear unrelated. Only later could they be recognized as links in a chain. This recognition is retrospective not because reality is too complex and incomprehensible. The reason is that we cannot predict in advance how our own intervention into reality might change the historical route. Events that appeared to their participants embedded in unrelated causal sequences are retrospectively reconstructed as indispensable links in a chain of necessity. This retroactive causality reverses the time arrow, directing it backwards. Once an historical epoch has run its course, historiography integrates the steps that led to it. History becomes the tribunal of the world, the unravelling and judging of humanity's action. We narrate in the present the history that brought us where we are. We don't just make our history in conditions not of our choosing, as Marx said. We write today – we give narrative form to – what happened earlier and led us to our present state. In this sense, the historical event creates its own pre-history. Future change creates the contemporary historical trajectory. We are parts of the future, which is still to come. More importantly we create or change the past that led to our present.

Let me give an example from law. Jurisprudence argues that norms precede temporally the facts they come to regulate; facts on the other hand have (or ought to have) ontological solidity. Facts happened. It is the job of courts and rules of evidence to discover and confirm them in order to subsume them under the relevant rule. But the temporal priority of law and the ontological rigour of facts are often challenged.

Take the distinction between void and voidable legal acts. A void contract is null from the beginning and cannot be enforced. A voidable contract on the other hand suffers from a smaller defect and can be avoided through a court decision. A marriage is void if one spouse is already married; voidable if it has not been consummated through incapacity or wilful refusal of one spouse. A contract to kill someone or to sell cocaine is void; a contract is voidable if it has been obtained by fraud. Voidable marriages and contracts can be annulled through the action of the injured party. Once the nullity has been declared, it is as if the contract had never happened. Its effects are retrospectively eliminated even though reality may have changed: the assassination has taken place, the coke has been sniffed. The contract as performative speech act changes the world; the declaration of nullity is a world-unmaking legal fiction. Like a time machine, it goes back and deletes what legally happened.

T. S. Eliot expressed the same idea brilliantly. 'No poet, no artist of any art has his complete meaning alone... You must set him among the dead... what happens when a new work of art is created is something that happens simultaneously to all the works of art that preceded it. The existing monuments form an ideal order among themselves which is modified by the introduction of the new work of art among them.'[2] To judge the new arrival, we must place the work in the pantheon of previous and dead poets. But, as the poetry edifice is finished and its archive complete before the new arrival, the new poet changes the whole canon. We cannot therefore read the old poets without referring to the work of the recent arrival. As Slavoj Zizek put it, 'each truly new artistic phenomenon not only represents a break with the entire past but retroactively changes the past itself.'[3] In Jorge Luis Borges' wonderful story 'Pierre Menard, Author of the *Quixote*', a twentieth century fictional French author decides to rewrite the ninth and thirty-eighth chapters of the first part of *Don Quixote* and a fragment from chapter twenty-two.[4] After learning seventeenth-century Spanish and the history of the period, Menard re-writes a text that is word-for-word identical with the original. It is, however, 'infinitely richer' and subtler because the later text has to be read through the lens of everything that happened in history, politics and philosophy since 1602. In this sense, every writer creates his own predecessors. As Borges puts it, we have 'to go through the Odyssey as if it were posterior to the *Aeneid*'. Something similar happens in philosophy and politics. The latecomers alter our understanding of the classics. Nietzsche changed Christ, Stalin Marx, Heaney Eliot. The past determines and constrains us; but we can change the past. History moves forward only for those who look backward. An event acquires historical significance when it severs the umbilical cord with its environment and alters the situation it emerged from. In doing so, it changes retrospectively the meaning of the past. Historical necessity emerges from today's contingency.

Let us test Syriza's rise. Many initially unrelated facts led to the left government. From the perspective of the present they were the necessary links of historical change although no one saw them like that at the time. Let me mention indicatively a few. 'Greek statistics' allowed the country to enter the Eurozone and, later, receive limitless credit; the murder of Alexandros Grigoropoulos in 2008; the election of the George Papandreou's government in 2009 with increased majority which led to hubristic arrogance; the first two bailout agreements and the associated austerity measures; the *indignados* occupations in Spain; the closure of ERT, the public broadcasting corporation; the creation in the late 2000s of the Syriza party out of many small groups; the election of Alexis Tsipras as Syriza leader; his statement on live TV in 2012, that 'the Left is ready to take power', something that came to him at the spur of the moment and so on. An important link was the occupation of Syntagma Square in 2011. It was the most fortuitous of events. On 25 March 2011, two hundred people demonstrated outside the Spanish embassy at the foot of the Acropolis in solidarity with the *indignados*. As they were breaking up, someone suggested that they move to nearby Syntagma to express their solidarity in a more public setting. Once in the square, the few protesters decided to spend the night. The following day the square filled. Syriza members participated, while other parties denounced the protest. The rise of Syriza was placed firmly on the agenda in a series of events unplanned by the party, which can now be seen as necessary pieces in the puzzle of historic change. The causal sequence and the coherence of facts and actions

that led to a major personal or historical change can be recognized only in retrospect, when the event is completed and
the travellers of history rest at the inn of 'temporary peace'.
Unlike Kant's cosmopolitan inn of 'perpetual peace', peace is
always temporary and precarious.

What role do agents have in this revisionist philosophy of
history? Ordinary people underestimate their own contribution. They have been taught to consider political participation as secondary and insignificant. Leaders and money make
the world. But if this were the case, history would be the
lineal progression of heroes and celebrities. It is not. History
happens because the 'little' people enter its archive with acts
of courage and sacrifice, generosity and solidarity.

Let us attempt a thought experiment inspired by 'catastrophe theory'.[5] Let us suppose that the worst has happened.
The left government was overthrown, the most reactionary
forces came back into power and Greece was turned into a
'special economic zone' and the first formal colony of Western
Europe, with citizens' rights and freedoms permanently suspended. The Left was destroyed for at least the following
generation, as Bill Frezza had advised. We find ourselves at
the end of the journey and, looking back, we try to spot the
crucial points, the rings of the chain that led to the disaster,
in an attempt to prevent the worst from happening.

It is ordinary people who can prevent this future catastrophe by taking action in the present. Ministers should stop
making policies without consulting with the party and MPs,
people should rejoin and moblize social movements, direct
democracy should be introduced at all levels of local and
central government. From the perspective of the future all
these initiatives will have become the grand stations that
frustrated the catastrophe. Preventing the worst can only
happen by working for the best. The struggle for social transformation is happening (or not) here and now. But as we
are weighed down by the hardships of everyday life and
the attacks of domestic and foreign elites we cannot see it
yet as an element in a significant historical trajectory. We
will fully know whether the radical transformation began or
whether the Left became another version of the 'third way'
only at the end of the process. The inability to predict the
future evaluation of the present makes us all accomplices in

success or failure. Those who denounce ideological retreats and political compromises, often with the immodesty that stems from the frustration of personal ambition, become Hegel's 'beautiful souls'. They do not commit themselves to work, they don't 'dirty' their hands to help change the route. They keep their conscience pure, happy to denounce their opponents in increasingly stringent language. They become 'formless vapour' that dissolves in the air, as the inimitable Hegel put it. For the rest, the pre-judgment of history is risky. We have to fight without guarantees and insurance policies. History's openness and unpredictability makes participation in the struggle a moral obligation and a personal responsibility. Radical change is nothing more or less than the persistence in our present determination to stop the inevitability of disaster in preparation for a future always to come.

14

The Cycles of History:
1949, 1969, 1989

Never in my wildest dreams did I expect that one pleasant January night I would meet at the yard outside the University of Athens Senate House old friends from the 1973 occupation of the nearby Law School and the many years in London, new friends from the resistance against austerity and the 2011 occupation of Syntagma Square, and strangers from France, Germany and Brazil chanting, talking, singing. Never in my wildest dreams could I have foreseen that people from all over the world would meet in Athens to celebrate the impossible that had become possible. In front of the Greek Academy building I saw an elderly couple. The man was sobbing. 'Why are you crying?' I ask. 'We didn't expect we would live a moment like this, son', the woman responds. The man adds, 'Lord, now lettest thou thy servant depart.' It was a magical moment. We called it 'historical'. But on that night personal emotions dominated; tears, hugs, kisses with strangers, dancing to Catalan and Scottish rhythms. 'Bella Ciao', 'Avanti Popolo', 'Paidia Sikotheite'. Not a single person among those Bakhtinian ca(rna)valiers, those Bacchic radicals, had joined the Left hoping to become a member of Parliament or minister.

History does not move in a linear fashion, as historicism has it. The present is not the culmination of an inexorable march of progress. As argued in the previous chapter, we can recognize the direction of history only after the completion of a sequence of events. Often history follows a cyclical movement, like that of the seasons or, even better, of successive waves on a lake that start where a pebble lands and move outwards one after the other. European and Greek history have gone through cycles of rise and decline.[1] Only now we can detect the Syriza victory as an important station in three such cycles. They started in 1949, 1969 and 1989. For all three, 2015 was a year of culmination and consummation.

14.1   1949

1949 was the year the Greek Civil War ended and the Cold War began. The long and politically anomalous period that followed culminated in the 1967–74 Colonels' dictatorship. In those hard times, the people who resisted the Nazi occupation were executed and persecuted, imprisoned and exiled in islands and concentration camps. Greece is the only country in which the majority of Nazi collaborators were not punished. Instead they moved seamlessly to the post-war political and economic establishment. The strong right–left divide dominated politics after the Communist defeat. The Right dominated and used the state to buttress its power. The Left retreated to trade-union activism, cultural politics and theoretical reflection. The right-wing hegemony was challenged by the rise of Pasok, the first Andreas Papandreou government and the legalization of the Communist Party. Pasok gradually became part of the establishment, however, overtaking New Democracy in its ability to mobilize the state for political advantage. To this day, most people approach Pasok cadres and former deputies in order to get a public sector job or jump the queue and get fast hospital admission. The party has left government for good but the state is still in its clutches. Pasok's assimilation into the power structure meant that the left–right political schism survived for seventy years as the disciplining and stabilizing structure of politics and society.

The resistance against the austerity measures imposed by the creditors and delivered by Pasok and New Democracy, the erstwhile 'lethal' enemies, was the first real challenge

to the old system of power. The 2011 Syntagma occupation attracted people from different social classes, ideological
and political backgrounds. Left and Right, nationalists and
cosmopolitans, the religious and the atheists converged in
the squares. Many had never participated in protest before.
When people from traditionally opposing ideologies found
themselves occupying the same square, marching the same
protest route or participating in the same rally, they had
an epiphany. They realized that unemployed rightists and
leftists suffer the same; that religious patriots and atheist
internationalists feel equally humiliated by the treatment of
European and domestic elites. They recognized that class
interests and the common good are stronger than family
loyalties. The wall separating Left from Right for seventy
years started cracking. After that politics could not be
the same. The economic crisis led to the collapse of the
ancien régime.

When the multitude of the squares were asked to become a
people and vote, they chose Syriza.[2] The protest party of four
per cent in 2009 rose to 36 per cent in 2015. Syriza's nine per
cent victory margin was largely the result of a direct transfer
of votes from Right to Left. The outgoing New Democracy
government sensed the sea change. Its election campaign
tried to resurrect the ghosts of the past. Greece under Syriza
would become like North Korea, stated the Premier Antonis
Samaras. We will protect 'by all means necessary' what our
fathers won with armed struggle, added a senior right-wing
minister. This raising of the dead did not work. As the old
ideological divide collapsed, the Left moved through its electoral glass ceiling. The significance of the occupations to the
end of the old system is evident in the vitriolic attacks by
established media and politicians. No opportunity is missed
to claim that the Chryssi Avgi fascists acquired their first
taste of national publicity in Syntagma or that Left and Right
were united in attacking Parliament and democratic institutions. Both accusations are part of the recent penchant for
post-truths or 'fake history'. The fascists were chased off the
square and were not allowed to have even a minimal presence. The multitude attacked the policies passed by the New
Democracy-Pasok government and not democracy. On the
contrary, the direct democratic procedures initiated during

the occupation gave the kiss of life to moribund democratic institutions.

More generally every class-based or populist division of a population will include both right and left-wing people on the popular pole. This is not a problem; it is an answer to the old attempt of capitalism to divide people belonging to the same class by using nationalist, religious or xenophobic ideologies. When peoples' personal imaginary is uncoupled from the myth offered by the collective imaginary of political ideology, political history takes a new path. In this sense, the January 2015 election marked the end of the post-civil war period and the homecoming of the Left. The Syriza coalition with the right-wing Independent Greeks confirmed this view. Most Greek leftists did not object to this unnatural coupling. They were worried that victorious Tsipras, short of a couple of MPs to form a government, would enter an agreement with the various centre-left splinter groups that had backed the previous government and are ideologically committed to neo-liberalism and austerity. When people were considering the possibility of a joint negotiating team including Varoufakis and Tsakalotos on the Syriza side and Venizelos and Theodorakis on the other, I was reminded of Sir Geoffrey Howe's resignation from the Thatcher government. His Commons statement was devastating for the Eurosceptic Premier. When I went to negotiate with the Europeans, he quipped, I felt like an opening batsman who, on getting to the crease, realizes that the captain had cracked my bat. The Pasok members of a coalition with Syriza would have stolen the negotiating bat altogether. The extreme anti-Syriza and Europe-at-all-costs attitude of Pasok and the other centrist parties precluded any thoughts of a centre-left coalition.

The Syriza-AnEll coalition partners agree on the negotiating line with the lenders. The right-wingers have entrusted strategy and economic policy to Syriza and have vehemently defended it against the opposition. However, the two parties fundamentally differ on a number of important issues. Identity politics and the rights agenda forms a key part of Syriza ideology. Throughout the many transformations of the party, democratic socialists have defended immigrants, refugees, gays and lesbians, prisoners, the Roma, drug addicts and all kinds of minorities. Every politically persecuted or arrested person would automatically turn to the Syriza 'political rights' section and its lawyers for advice, advocacy and legal representation. This commitment was confirmed through a number of legislative initiatives despite opposition from their AnEll partners. The government introduced the gay and lesbian civil union law, the law offering citizenship to second-generation immigrants, that abolishing high security inhumane prisons and the law establishing the first official mosque in Athens. The AnEll include a nationalistic, religiously fanatic and rabidly homophobic element. AnEll deputies have used highly discriminatory and homophobic language. Kammenos, their leader, has threatened to bring the government down if asked by the Archbishop who is vehemently rejecting government efforts to loosen the Church's hold on the state.

Syriza is a coalition of groups with a working-class and identity politics background. It has to pursue politics on both the economic and the rights front. The class agenda suffered as a result of the July defeat. The identity agenda on the other hand has been a success. This has brought to an end the long period of post-Civil War political anomaly and has started a second *metapolitefsi*. But the increasingly fractious relationship with the AnEll indicates that the left–right marriage of convenience may be running out of time. When the negotiations over the loan and the austerity measures accompanying it come to an end the coalition will come under intense scrutiny. Syriza cannot unfold its radical programme in a coalition with the culturally conservative right-wing even though it needed it in order to change the political and ideological parameters of the country. Economic development and the defence of the rights and culture of minorities will probably find willing collaborators on the centre-left. By the beginning of 2017, Pasok has started mitigating its anti-Syriza rhetoric and has voted for the first time with the government on a number of issues. The trauma of dissolution and the loss of power, the cement of an ideologically vacuous party, will not allow a real convergence despite the fact that European social-democracy has welcomed Tsipras to its meetings. Irrespective of petty political calculations, however, the historic demise of the right-left divide will survive the pending governmental divorce. As the political stage becomes dominated by the populist split between 'people' and 'elites', the ghosts of the anti-communist period of political anomaly have been exorcized among the people even though the elites have not followed yet.

14.2   1969

May 1968 symbolizes the cultural and moral rebellion of young people in Europe and America. 1969 was the year of the counter-revolution, the establishment's response to youthful zest and cultural insurrection. President de Gaulle defeated students and workers; Richard Nixon succeeded Lyndon Johnson and his 'great society'; we learned about the Soviet gulags; the anti-colonial revolutions started turning into one party states ran by corrupt elites. Idealism lost, the fight for social justice morphed into philanthropic campaigns and petitions supporting victims of torture and persecution. The Left entered a long winter of political defeat and theoretical failure.

The 'baby boomer' generation that led the 1968 rebellion became highly successful. They didn't change the world, as they had hoped in their youth, but they conquered the heights of power in the public and private sectors, in political parties and the media. Human rights, the toleration of difference and the rhetorical condemnation of discrimination became part of the vernacular but did not change the balance of power. Human rights replaced the struggle for socialism. In the early days, they had a moral almost religious ring. Everyone is against torture and imprisonment for political views or without trial. These questions have a right or wrong, black or white, answer. Political campaigning on the other hand is complicated, harder, calls for negotiation and compromise. The logical extension of turning every political campaign into a question of rights was represented in the phrase 'humanitarian' war: a war in which hundreds of thousands are killed in order to save 'humanity'.[3] The centrality of the individual and her rights gives capitalism a human face but does not challenge growing injustice. Human rights started as a cry of dissidents and rebels. They have now turned, in part, into the moral gloss of the successful capitalist and the ethical supplement of a multinational's CEO.[4] Idealism was defeated through its incorporation.

The Greek May '68 came late and was not completed. The 1967–74 Colonels' dictatorship hated equally the Left and counter-culture. Its slogan was 'fatherland, religion, family'; communications with Western Europe were restricted; it was equally problematic to read Marx or to listen to the Rolling Stones. The dictators left the Council of Europe preempting pending ejection after a devastating report by the European Commission of Human Rights detailing the blatant violation of every human right. Their defence was that they were condemned by a 'coterie of Communists and Queers'. Resistance combined therefore the politics of the Left and democracy with a faint echo of the May '68 events. Its high point was the Athens Polytechnic uprising in November 1973.

Greece joined the cultural revolution belatedly after the return of democracy in the *metapolitefsi*, the post-dictatorship period. A significant part of the dictatorship generation ruled the country for forty years. They accepted the '68 values but twisted them towards individualism and consumerism. The transformation of campaigns for social justice into the promotion of individual rights explains a common phenomenon of *metapolitefsi*. Many Polytechnic insurgents became successful politicians, academics or businessmen and turned into the most vitriolic enemies of the Left. The apostate is besotted with his past and youthful beliefs. At the same time, he hates this nostalgic craving he cannot leave behind. This existential impasse makes him vengeful, aggressive, brutal in his enmity. The prime target of attack is not his former comrades but his own young self. He must be punished and cleansed for his youthful errors and sins. As we know from psychoanalysis, the superego is the hardest sadist.

In Kafka's story *Before the Law*, the 'man from the country' spends his life without fulfilling his desire to enter law's house. The bulk of the Syriza cadres were resisters, protesters, defenders of the persecuted. They stuck to the Polytechnic uprising agenda of class struggle and human rights. In 2015, the poachers turned gamekeepers and entered the courtyard of the house of power. They are that part of the 1968 and 1973 generation which, while defeated time and again, did not change life commitments. They didn't expect any reward besides a calm conscience, the soothing feelings of friendship and the consolations of comradely company. The move from street to government mansion and Parliament is not easy. The greatest difficulty is not political. Undoubtedly power seduces – but not those who did not change their convictions for fifty years. Yet, as Kafka knew from the Jewish tradition, the house of law is empty, the book of law blank. Spending a life at the threshold keeps the desire to enter growing and the man alive. But what happens when the portals finally admit the man to a vacuous grandiosity? Perhaps, this is something we may come to learn at great personal cost.

The hardest test is therefore existential. How can the outsiders move inside, from the streets to the salons, where everything looks morally ambiguous, aesthetically questionable, the surface gloss of a power that is safely hidden elsewhere, beyond the line of vision and touch of the neophyte? How can a radical and noble conscience accept its new position as a – justified or not – target of the criticism that it has abandoned its values? There is no easy or obvious answer; Syriza leftists may never have a quiet night's sleep again. The hope is that they are returning and rekindling the May '68 and November '73 values. The Syriza victory was mainly the result of economic promises. Its long-term responsibility is the obligation to initiate a moral revolution and a cultural regeneration.

14.3   1989

The 2015 elections were caught in a third more recent historical cycle. It started in 1989 with the fall of the Berlin Wall. Francis Fukuyama and President Bush proclaimed the 'end of history' and presented liberal capitalism as the last stage in humanity's progress. This is the economic system in which, according to Oxfam, half the world's wealth belongs to one per cent of super-rich. It is the most shocking evidence of the intellectual bankruptcy and moral degeneracy of a type of ideology that has dominated Western capitals far too long and has destroyed the lives of millions. The Syriza victory rejects this catastrophic orthodoxy and, in a small way, puts history back on the road. The government's immediate adoption of a tranche of measures aimed at helping the most vulnerable shows that there is another way, that the TINA mantra could come to an end.

Nikolas Sarkozy promised in the 2007 presidential campaign to bring 'May to an end'. In Greece, right-wing Premier Antonis Samaras and his ministers copied this arrogant silliness in their election campaign. Realizing the importance of the Polytechnic uprising for popular imagination, they promised to end the *metapolitefsi* with its memories of resistance and struggles for social justice. Separating political from economic liberalism, they planned to sacrifice political liberties on the altar of market fundamentalism. Syriza put paid to these megalomaniacal hopes. Dreams consigned to memory and song returned.

2015 was the year of living out dangerous dreams. The elections did not bring the cycle of '68 to a close. On the contrary, they marked the end of the post-Civil War cycle, the second beginning of the May '68 values and Polytechnic legacy and the beginning of the end of the 'end of history'. In 2015 and 2016, we reached the threshold of *jouissance*, an intense pleasure beyond limit inextricably bound with angst, awe and fears. Pleasure drowned in anxiety is the dominant emotion, circling incessantly around a victory that could – and did – turn into defeat. We cannot predict history with its victories and catastrophes but we sense them when they appear on the horizon.

Part VI

From Grexit to Brexit

15

Putting the Demos on Stage

15.1   The mythology and the philosophy of 'nay'-saying

Humanity was born in acts of disobedience. Almost every creation myth has the humans defy gods and the law. In the book of *Genesis* from the Jewish tradition, Adam and Eve disobey God, are expelled from Paradise and inaugurate life in our vale of tears. In the Greek, Prometheus steals fire from the Olympian gods and sets the foundations for human civilization. Outraged Zeus bound Prometheus on the Mount Caucasus and had an eagle eat his liver daily, since the organ, ignorant of alcohol, revived nightly. St Paul discovers the psychological foundations desires of humanity on law breaking. 'What shall we say then? Is the law sin? God forbid. Nay, I had not known sin, but by the law: for I had not known lust, except the law had said, Thou shalt not covet' (Romans 7: 7). Freud's myth of origin, finally, has a band of brothers kill their primordial father, who kept all women to himself. The Oedipal murder and the guilt that descended on the parricides led to the creation of ethics and the superego, a self-disciplining device more fearsome and effective than the father's threats. We have invented gods and mythical legislators to give us the law so that we can break it. Disobedience, defiance, saying 'No' to higher power is what it means to be human.

Philosophy too discovers freedom in negation, in 'nay'-saying. The affirmation, saying Yes, consents to someone or something that precedes the subject temporally or hierarchically. When I obey a command or accept an offer, my participation is limited to accepting incorporation into a narrative constructed by another. The subject who affirms remains heteronomous, hostage to the other's wish. Autonomy, the essence of freedom, is to give the law to yourself. A pivotal moment of emancipation is to negate the other's imposition. There is more. For Hegel, the freedom of negation helps remove the secondary elements in a situation or the unnecessary and contingent additions to a notion. Negation starts the ascent from the specific to the abstract and from the particular to the universal. Refusal is an integral part of autonomy; abstraction and generalization are preparatory steps for free thought. History moves dialectically through denial; disobedience confirms the law it breaks.

15.2   Putting the demos on stage

Early Greek resistance culminated in the occupation of Syntagma and the other squares in June 2011; it came full circle on 5 July 2015. The *aganaktismenoi* brought to politics a new form of direct democracy. The first resolution of the occupation read: 'We will not leave the squares if the government, the troika, the banks, the memoranda and those that exploit us do not leave first.' A popular 'we' was born in 2011 and became the protagonist in 2015. This 'we' rejected the austerity memoranda acting as a counter-constituent power. In 2015, it became a positive force. The referendum created a strong compact between Syriza, Premier Tsipras and the people. The negative moment of resistance started turning into the positivity of political subjectivity. How did we get to the July referendum?

On 26 June, Alexis Tsipras returned from Brussels with a European 'take it or leave it' ultimatum. At midnight, in a dramatic televised message, he called a referendum on the European proposals asking people to reject them. Soon after, the government announced that banks will be closed on Monday and capital controls will allow people to withdraw just €60 a day. It was a necessary but desperate measure, as the ECB threats and a bank run would bankrupt high street banks. The referendum campaign lasted from Monday 29 June to Friday 3 July. In that long week, the whole domestic and European establishment told the Greeks to accept the European ultimatum. Jean-Claude Juncker, Martin Schultz, George Osborne and various other European heavy-hitters warned of the dire consequences of a No vote. The Greek media were awash with predictions of doom and gloom, if people rejected the offer. Polling organizations, negligently and perhaps fraudulently, were predicting a comfortable Yes victory. It was the beginning of a long period of political miscalculation and polling disaster. David Cameron, Hillary Clinton and Matteo Renzi did not learn from the Greek establishment's Yes debacle.

On the Tuesday morning, I received in London a worried phone-call from Syriza headquarters in Athens. I was asked to draft and circulate among international academics and intellectuals a petition supporting Oxi. The text concluded: 'We believe that [the European] ultimatum to the Greek people and democracy should be rejected. The Greek referendum gives the European Union a chance to restate its commitment to the values of the Enlightenment – equality, justice, solidarity – and to the principles of democracy on which its legitimacy rests. The place where democracy was born gives Europe the opportunity to re-commit to its ideals in the 21st century.' It was published on the *Guardian* website the same afternoon and in its pages the following day.[1] By Wednesday morning, when I flew to Athens, close to one thousand prominent academics had signed the petition. Moving messages of support and solidarity accompanied the signatures. A well-known Italian Law professor wrote that 'it would be important to have available Greek flags to hang on the balconies of the people through Europe in solidarity as we did with the Rainbow flags during the Iraq assault'. When the LSE Hellenic Observatory issued an institutional statement supporting the Yes vote, senior professors associated with the school, including Saskia Sussen, Richard Sennet and Conor Gearty, signed a letter condemning it and complained to Craig Calhoun, the LSE Director. While the European establishment was going all out in an attempt to cow the Greeks into submission, academics the world over saw the referendum as an opportunity for democracy. Irrespective of political ideologies – the signatories included Rowan Williams, the former Archbishop of Canterbury, and many liberal intellectuals – they stood with the government and the people.

Things started changing in Greece too. The Syriza machinery was initially taken by surprise and mobilized slowly. By Wednesday, when I arrived in Athens, it became clear that ordinary people had taken matters into their own hands. The turning point was the massive Oxi rally in Syntagma on Friday. The Square was filled with angry and hopeful citizens. They sang old and new resistance songs, strangers kissed and hugged, the elderly cried and the young laughed. On 5 July, the multitude became again a people and was united with the occupiers of 2011. The 61.3 per cent victory was won by ordinary people, many of whom adopted the No vote in a determined but silent manner. This is perhaps the reason for the failure of opinion polls to predict the Oxi vote dynamic until the very end. The people, weary of hostile media and employers, became 'Shy No Voters', not answering or disclosing their intentions to pollsters. When I campaigned for the Oxi, people would not engage openly, only to wink a minute later and do the V for victory sign after taking precautions not to be seen. It was understandable. Companies had threatened to sack people if they voted No or to close factories and offices and leave the country altogether if the No won. Real and immediate punishment was threatened, the scare tactics were not about future adverse consequences as with Brexit. But people resisted. It was a case of citizens against power, one of those rare occasions when a people hoodwinked first and then bloodied their 'superiors'. They made the Oxi their business and led to one of the biggest polling upsets and popular victories in Europe.

15.3   Oxi and hegemony

Let me start with a story. A man visits the Australian consulate in Athens and asks for a work visa. 'Why do you want to leave Greece?' asks the official. 'I am worried that Greece will leave the euro zone' answers the man. 'Don't worry', responds the consul 'I was talking to my German colleague yesterday who assured me that Greece will stay in the Euro.' 'This is the second reason why I want to emigrate.' The story expresses the tragic dilemma the government and the people faced in that hard summer of 2015. The choice was between a continuation of catastrophic austerity and Grexit, a prospect that would destroy the living standards of a people who had already seen their income halved. It was not a choice between good and bad but between the worse and the worst. Whatever the people chose, they and Syriza would be punished.

The initial shock at the unexpected scale of the Oxi led to an avalanche of interpretations. The people chose the populist anti-European side atavistically, opined the shocked Europhiles. Syriza's left faction adopted the other side of the same coin, arguing that the people had positively voted for Grexit. The government concluded that the vote was a decisive approval for Tsipras' negotiating position. All interpretations have a grain of truth. The beauty for some, the ugliness for others of a Yes or No, black or white, vote is its inscrutability. The meaning of the vote is exhausted in its outcome. There is no reasoning or justification behind it, allowing any number of interpretations and rationalizations. The voting population is a silent entity. It acts but does not speak. On the rare occasions that the people are asked to vote on some ill-defined question, they do so for multiple and unfathomable reasons. After the vote, politicians and commentators announce that the 'mute' population has 'spoken'. The problem is that the people speak 'in tongues' like some evangelical mystics. My name is legion, said the possessed Gadarene to Jesus. My reasons are myriad, repeat the people. The only safe conclusion is that the politician who calls the vote wins if the people follow him. Tsipras built a strong, almost personal, bond with the voters. Cameron and Renzi did not and had to go. Tsipras' outrageous gambit made him the decider of his and Syriza's destiny.

Everyone agreed, however, that the vote was largely determined by class. The map of Greece turned into the red of No except for a few posh suburbs in Athens and Thessaloniki. It is an obvious but inadequate interpretation. The referendum did not mirror a pre-existing social architecture. The Oxi vote acted as a hegemonic division of the social body, continuing the earlier resistance. Differences, tensions and conflicts between classes, professions and ideologies characterize the social field. There is division between public servants, private employees and professionals, between the employed and unemployed, high and low earners, Greeks and immigrants. A hegemonic intervention shapes the social field when it manages temporarily to attenuate tensions and conflict on the popular side and emphasize common interests. This happens when the political subject elects a line of division of the social field which can unite 'us' against 'them'. Popular politics emerges when 'we' are divided and confront 'them'. The 'people' do not pre-exist the hegemonic intervention; it is created through political division. Classes, sectors and groups on this side accept that the differences with those on the other are more important than their local and sectional tensions. An ensemble of demands, struggles and campaigns become linked in a chain of equivalences and congregate in a common place and time. This is exactly what the *aganaktismenoi* did in the 2011 occupations. The multitude adopted the triptych 'no to the memoranda', popular and national independence (again autonomy as negation) and direct democracy, paving the way to the end of the *ancien régime*.

What began in 2011 was concluded in 2015. On Sunday 5 July, after the amazing results started coming in, many of us converged spontaneously to Syntagma, the place where it had all began. Syriza cadres asked people to move to the party's referendum centre in a nearby square. It showed their inability to understand popular dynamics and symbolic links. I was so taken by the miraculous nature of the occasion that, without thinking much, I proposed marriage to Joanna, my delighted companion and muse. It was a small personal moment, which chimed with the great river of popular joy. Everyone soon returned to Syntagma to sing, dance and celebrate. It was further confirmation of the popular, non-partisan nature of the occasion. At these moments, the *demos* comes to the forefront. Referenda are the institutional expression of direct democracy in a parliamentary system. But the No vote was more. Citizens adopted it secretly and privately, individually and collectively, beyond party and ideology. They took their lives in their hands. That night, the old triptych 'No to austerity', independence and direct democracy returned. From Syntagma back to Syntagma and towards the democracy to come.

16

Grexit and Brexit,
Oxi and Leave

I arrived in London in July 1974. A few weeks later, while strolling in Brockwell Park I was approached by an elderly English gentleman. He had a tweed jacket, a Salvador Dali moustache and a serious looking bulldog. 'Where are you from?', he inquired. 'Greece'. 'Is Greece in Asia?' 'No', I replied, 'like England, in Europe'. 'England is not in Europe' he retorted angrily. 'There are five continents. If England is not in Europe where does she belong?', I murmured worried by the dog's aggressive turn. 'England stands on her own', barked the gentleman proudly.

The Englishman with the bulldog represents one part of the Brexit decision. 'Fog in the Channel, the continent is cut off', weathermen intoned until the 1960s. This was the period of 'spendid isolation', when Churchill reportedly told de Gaulle that every time we have to choose between Europe and the high seas, we will opt for the high seas. A people who believes that 'there's some corner of a foreign field, that is forever England' had to accept two difficult ideas. First, Britain has become a second-rate power after the end of empire, depending economically, politically and militarily on the United States, a former colony. Secondly, it had to join a club dominated by Germany, a power that Britain had defeated in two world wars.

The British psyche is still marred by a certain postcolonial malaise. The self-deprecation, light-touch humour and faint tristesse of the British are not unrelated to the rapid and violent departure from Asia and Africa. Add a sense of cultural superiority towards the materially dominant Americans as well as pride in the military prowess of a relatively small island nation and you get the sweet and sour scent of British melancholy. I encountered it in Northern working men's pubs and clubs, where men sat around telling stories of British military courage and trade-union struggle. The people had fought valiantly in wars and military campaigns only to see their eternal rulers leading them to purposeless sacrifice and decline. The workers had created the industrial revolution only to see capital flee its Northern home. I came across the same reserved sadness in early punk despite its surface raucousness. It expressed a growing alienation from mainstream society. The old was coming to an end but the new was still not to be seen. When the scary figure of Mrs Thatcher started something presented as the 'new' it was not based on the traditions of solidarity forged in wars, the NHS or free education. On the contrary, it promoted possessive individualism and consumerism. Old hegemony had died and the new was not interested in reviving the idea of community. 'Tell Syd', the advertising campaign for the pioneering privatization of British Gas, 'get a fast buck' and popular capitalism were the injunctions of the new age. The old aristocracy, the new 'loadsofmoney' culture and the political system had failed the British tradition of community. Brexit grew on the soil of this failure. It was the wrong answer to a wrong question.

The British are still mourning their postcolonial decline. The Greeks have not been through a colonial past but have now become a twenty-first century neo-colony. The attacks by European politicians and media, the continuous slurs and defamations, the questioning of their honesty, probity and work ethic have affected them deeply. They touched the rawest of nerves. Greece is a small country of few natural resources except its beautiful and ragged landscape and its classical monuments. A sense of pride and honour beyond market success is central to the Greek psyche. The glory that was Greece, the continuity of language and the ancient sites, for which modern Greeks are the custodians, form main-springs of national identity. It was this sense of pride and dignity, central to what it means to be Greek, that was deeply hurt by the European humiliations. It was as if the European elites, no longer the beneficiaries of classical education, attacked the softest spots of the Greeks to make them rise in response. They succeeded. The Oxi, whatever the intentions of voters, was about pride and dignity. A hurt people was given a rare chance to say 'enough is enough' to its domestic and European tormentors. Brexit was partly about a lost empire. Oxi was largely about being lost in a new empire.

16.1   Post-democracy, Grexit and Brexit

There are many similarities as well as some important differences between the 2015 Greek No and the 2016 Brexit referenda. The most obvious affinity was the concerted bombardment of the population by the assembled establishment in an attempt to cajole or scare Greeks and Brits into voting Yes and Remain. In Greece, every major newspaper and broadcaster, all opposition parties, the usual TV dons as well as big and small capital and trade-union barons threatened people with famine, earthquake and floods, if they voted Oxi. In Britain, all parliamentary parties, the CBI and the TUC, the Church and the banks, Obama and Schäuble, NATO and IMF, told the citizens that if they left the EU they would be destroyed. *Bild* and *Financial Times Deutschland* published articles in Greek just before the June 2012 elections telling people not to vote for Syriza. *Spiegel* considered the experiment successful and did the same in English before the Brexit referendum with the front cover pleading 'Please Don't Go.' First in Greece then in Britain, the political 'caste', as *Podemos* calls it, tried persuasion, intimidation and scare tactics. None worked.

As the date of the referenda approached, the elites panicked and brought forward even more experts, ex-prime ministers, industrialists and foreign dignitaries. It proved counter-productive. The people-who-always-obey-their-superiors defied them and voted against instructions. The complacent and arrogant claim that the British decided against the 'obvious' facts of the pro-Europe argument, ushering in the 'post-truth' society, misses the mark. If anything, the popular reaction was directed as much at the endless parade of experts and patricians telling them what to do as to the content of their admonitions. The *hoi polloi* did not admit their intentions to the pollsters as the power and vindictiveness of their 'superiors' are well known and considerable. They became the 'shy Oxi and Brexit voters' causing the pollsters another dismal failure. This silent revolt is not new. Every time European citizens are allowed to vote on some aspect of the European construction, they take the rare opportunity to say what they think about their rulers. It happened in core states such as France, Ireland and Poland and twice in the Netherlands. It was baffling, therefore, that the commentators neglected this consistent trend and politicians used in Britain the same campaign tactics that had demonstrably failed in less Eurosceptic countries.

There was a second similarity between Greece and Britain. Both Brexit and Remain campaigns shared with the 'We Remain in Europe' [*Menoume Europi*] Greek campaign several disreputable methods: terrorization of people, stigmatization of opponents, *ad hominem* attacks. The right-wingers of Brexit claimed that eighty million Turks would 'enter' the EU and flood Britain with Islamic terrorists; the health system would collapse; unemployment would rise as the foreigners would steal our jobs; England would keep losing in football and cricket. The Remainers followed similar tactics and mobilized the politics of fear when the opinion polls tightened. If we leave the EU the GDP will shrink, the sterling will devalue, pensions will be cut, unemployment will skyrocket, the City of London will lose its dominant position, it will rain throughout the year. The Europhiles had the better economic argument but the most unappealing lineup to put it across. The 'it's the economy, stupid' cliché did not work because people do not vote solely out of their pockets. The same disreputable tactics had been tried and failed miserably in Greece.

Lies against lies, extreme insults against outright slurs, allegations of deceit and treachery marred the British debate. Often, however, abuse for partisan gain backfires. Discrediting and slandering opponents delegitimizes the whole political

order. The claim 'that all politicians are the same', the cry
of anti-democratic forces all over Europe, encourages people
to think that politicians do not deserve respect; it leads to
heckling and jeering, disruption of public rallies and party
meetings. It promotes an infectious contempt for politics and
politicians. The murder of Jo Cox, whatever the motives of
her killer, was carried out on that poisoned soil.

16.2   Was Brexit predictable?

Six months before the British referendum, I was predicting
in Parliament and the media that Brexit would win. I stated
clearly that I do not support it but had every indication that
Britain was moving that way. After the referendum, people
said that I was able to predict the outcome because of my long
experience of British life. David Cameron and the Remain
promoters had lived in Britain longer and presumably understand the British psyche better than a Greek-born expatriate. The difference was not extensive empirical evidence but
theoretical tools. Two arguments led me to expect Brexit.
Both the Brexiters' attacks on immigrants and the Remainers'
scaremongering were consequences of the decline of the idea
of Europe. As Mahatma Ghandi said when asked his opinion
about the European civilization, 'it would have been a good
idea'. All great modern ideas, the nation, constitutionalism,
natural and later human rights, socialism were conceived and
launched by intellectuals. Later, they were adopted by people
and inspired their struggles. This has not happened with the
European Union. The elites have been 'Europeanized' but
the people have not followed. Industrialists, bankers, trade-
union barons and think-tank technocrats consider Brussels as their second home. But for Maria from Perama and
Mary from Peckham, Brussels is the centre of a distant and
scary power.

The second argument is about our post-democratic condition. Its missionaries are the commentators of the *Economist*,
the *Financial Times* and the *Wall Street Journal*. Their idea of
political progress is the convergence of centre-left and centre-
right into the extreme neoliberal centre. Complex social
problems, they argue, require optimal scientific solutions that

cannot be put into public deliberation or, even worse, the vote. The people cannot understand, they make mistakes; it is preferable to keep them far from decision-making centres. As a result, they promote the omniscience and support the omnipotence of technocrats. Our societies need broad alliances of technocratic and grand coalition governments. It is the main credo of the post-democratic condition. As parties and ideologies converge, people conclude that 'they are all the same'; elections make no difference. This derogatory treatment of ordinary people lies in part behind Oxi and Brexit. Michel Foucault wrote in a late text that critique is to cultivate 'the art of not being governed in this way.'[1] This contemporary 'art of resistance' was expressed in the massive popular mobilizations of the Arab Spring, the *indignados*, the *aganaktismenoi*, Occupy and the historic referenda. Reaction and defiance are not addressed at a single target – the Euro, the Europe Union, austerity. They target local and foreign rulers and the way we are governed as a whole. On such occasions, a population rises from class, sectional and professional fragmentation and becomes a political subject. Late capitalism promotes horizontal communications but not political collaboration, networking but not ideological convergence. When those rare 'constituent moments' come about, the people take their fate into their own hands. After the rebellious event, things go back to routine governance. But citizens and politics have risen to a higher level.

When the unemployed, the poor and the excluded, those without health or welfare coverage, the workers on zero-hour contracts vote Oxi or Brexit, they reject the way of life imposed on them. They do not necessarily have a clear view of the issues or an alternative. They rediscover, however, their dignity after years of humiliation. In both referenda, people rejected the way power operates and not just the 'remote' and 'scary' Europe. They voted against the rulers' advice for a million reasons: she had lost her job; his benefits were cut; the local council does not collect the rubbish regularly; the local MP avoids meeting them; England lost in the Euros; French cops treated them roughly on their holidays; and many others. For the *hoi polloi*, when the establishment supports massively a particular view, something is wrong. Given the chance to say so, they take it.

This 'insurrectionary' part of democracy, as Etienne Balibar calls it, emerges at critical moments in our history and keeps politics alive.[2] Regardless of outcome, such rebellions become the fertilizer that allows democracy to survive against vested interests, dynastic demands and corruption. The leaders may follow or not the popular will; but the political scene has irreversibly changed. Established parties and politicians fear such popular irruptions. This is why they do not stop attacking and demonizing the 2011 occupations and the Oxi vote in Greece. This is why every attempt will be made in Britain to reverse the referendum verdict.

Let me conclude with three remarks about my experience of the Greek debate on Brexit.

1. The Greek reporting on Brexit was littered with mistakes, silliness and ignorance. We were told that Nigel Farage is a member of the House of Lords, that the British electoral system is proportional representation, that Britain will be ejected from the Eurozone. In Greece, the less someone knows about an issue, the more he talks about it. It is said that all publicity is good publicity. Its Greek variation: all commentary, even the ignorant, banal or irrelevant, creates commentators. I should not have been surprised. The British discussion of the Greek crisis was more professional but equally replete of misunderstandings, prejudice, borderline racism.

2. Pontificating without theoretical knowledge and historical awareness as well as the slavish following of opinion polls without class and political analysis are doomed to fail. Numbers cannot replace thought, quantitative cannot become qualitative analysis, political desire is not a substitute for disinterested and unbiased understanding.

3. The citizens have learnt how to trick the connoisseurs, the experts and the pollsters. In the 2015 elections in Greece and Britain and in the Greek and British referenda, opinion polling, including the 'safe' exit polls, failed

spectacularly. If we discount fraud or gross incompetence, we can conclude that the citizens hid from the pollsters their intention to vote Oxi or Leave. These 'shy' voters found a way to reassure the elites, making them believe that the people were going to vote the way their betters told them to vote. We knew that opinion polls are often used to manipulate the public. In 2015, we learnt the public can also use them as weapons of resistance.

17

Brexit and Euroscepticism

17.1 The Right

Boris Johnson and Nigel Farage reacted to British decline with a nationalism of nostalgia and failure. Their slogans about 'taking back control', restoring sovereignty or 'repatriating' the constitution are idle promises in an age of globalization. In British constitutional doctrine, sovereignty belongs to Parliament not to the people. Any 'repatriated' powers would end up with the same political caste that the Leavers condemned. The limited success of nostalgic nationalism turned a part of the Brexit campaign towards xenophobia. This was the greatest difference between Greece and Britain. In Greece, the ideological divide was clear: all shades of the Left supported Oxi, with the right-wing and the centre-left voting Yes.

David Cameron argued that his opt-outs had achieved a kind a Europe *à la carte*, distancing Britain further from the European core. For Nigel Farage and Boris Johnson, the European concessions did not go far enough. Only out of Europe does Britain have a future, they argued. Fighting against an unimpressive David Cameron, they upped the ante, using anti-immigrant arguments bordering on racism. Immigrants 'swamping' the country became a key part of the unsavoury mix. The numbers game was reintroduced with some contemporary additions. Exploiting the refugee flows into Greece and Italy and the terror attacks in France and Belgium, the Brexiters condemned Islam and predicted atrocious acts of terrorism if the country stayed in Europe.

The public clash between the lesser and the greater 'little Englanders' and xenophobes dominated the European media headlines. We were told ad nauseam that Brexit was the result of British racism. I repeatedly stated on radio and TV that it is not necessary to have lived in Britain to know that the people are among the most multicultural and tolerant in Europe. More than one hundred and forty languages are spoken in London; almost 50 per cent of its population was born outside Britain. Every country has a few diehard racists. But the English working class, its trade unions and professional bodies are internationalists and have repeatedly expressed their solidarity with struggles around the world. The problem lies elsewhere.

Cameron's government continued Thatcher's assault on the welfare state for purely ideological reasons, since the UK is not in the Eurozone nor in an IMF-run structural adjustment programme. The tens of thousands of Poles, Bulgarians and Romanians let into the country as a reserve workforce settled into cities and towns with high unemployment, few places in schools, fewer beds in hospitals and mutilated social services. This is fertile ground for xenophobia. Working people have legitimate worries about work, the prospects of their children, a decent life. They are justifiably concerned about the massive settlement of immigrants in devastated regions. These legitimate concerns can turn into racism only as a result of conscious ideological intervention and wilful misinformation about the effects of immigration. This is what right-wing Brexiters did in Britain using EU immigrants; this is what the right-wing attempts in Greece using Asian and African refugees. A great paradox characterizes anti-immigrant rhetoric. Right-wing politicians and their austerity policies have destroyed jobs and the welfare state. They then mobilize xenophobia and the foreign 'invaders' argument in a fake attempt to 'defend' the indigenous 'victims' from the effects of their own actions.

The anti-immigration argument is false both in Britain and Greece. European immigrants into Britain are net contributors to UK finances. They are better educated and healthier than the British and draw much less in benefits than the average citizen. The Office for Budget Responsibility has advocated long-term net immigration of 140,000 per annum in order to make the health service and social security viable.[1] The same argument applies to Greece. The fertility rate needed for the reproduction of a population is 2.1 per woman of child-bearing age. The Greek rate is only 1.3. In 2015, the number of deaths was for the first time higher than births. The EU predicts that on current trends, the Greek population of eleven million in 2011 will decline to nine million by 2050. The population is ageing and is not being replaced. Greece must import the people, whose contributions will pay for the pensions and social welfare of the ageing population. The refugees who come to Greece are a god-send answer to its acute demographic problem. The many thousands trapped in the country can become the pool that helps contain rapid and inescapable decline. Immigration is not a problem. It is the solution to a problem.

The Leavers won in the great Tory civil war. As the party of power, the Conservatives soon covered their differences, got rid of some unsavoury characters and crowned the 'moderate' Theresa May, calling her at the same time Iron Lady Mark 2. As I have learnt from my short politician's life, when the cement of a political party is power rather than ideology, the most intense disagreements are rapidly patched up in the quest for the only thing that matters.

17.2 The Left

The Labour party was the great loser of Brexit. Jeremy Corbyn and Labour were given a great opportunity to present themselves as the unifiers of the nation against a ruling party riven by internecine conflict. They could do that by adopting the Syriza position: 'We are not for or against Europe; we are for another Europe.' This line was compatible with both sides of the Brexit debate. On the Remain side, which was chosen by Labour, the party should have adopted a stance of aggressive reformism. The Europhiles argued that Corbyn's late and lukewarm intervention misfired and led to Brexit. The main problem, however, was the lack of a clearly articulated left alternative whether Britain stayed in or left Europe. Using the anti-democratic attacks on Greece and other countries, Labour could have campaigned for a reversal of austerity and a deep reform of EU institutions towards greater democratic accountability. Had Remain won, Labour would have been able to articulate and represent left Euroscepticism, becoming the standard bearer of the legitimate grievances of working people throughout Europe. If Brexit won, as it did, it would have been in pole position to represent those who, for various reasons, do not trust the European Union. In the current difficult situation after Jeremy Corbyn's second emphatic victory, Labour needs to mount a constant and robust anti-racist struggle, which does not downplay the size of the problem for British workers, nor does it abandon the marginalized and alienated people to those whose policies led them to despair. Despite Corbyn's left turn, the party was not adequate to the task of representing the unrepresented. Labour's ideological and policy failure will follow the party for many years to come. It was a case of snatching defeat out of the jaws of victory. The great Tory civil war may end with the destruction of Labour as a politically relevant organization. It is the great tragicomedy of our times.

One final point. Silence is always better than conceited verbosity or vain ignorance. Various European politicians rushed to demand an immediate British exit, as if they own the EU. Light-weight politicians like Jean-Claude Juncker, the President of the Commission and former Prime Minister of Luxemburg, and Donald Tusk, the Polish President of the Council, should show greater respect and restraint. Britain is one of the great European civilizations; alongside the Soviets and the Americans, she saved Europe from the Nazis. Luxemburg, the size of Croydon, is the banking centre of a large tax-evasion scheme. Poland is acting towards women and refugees in the most un-European way. Luxemburg and Poland's former prime ministers have little moral or political standing to teach the British a lesson or gainsay their democratic decision. They could do it to the Greeks because of the dire economic straits and size of the country. Bullies find their nemesis when they overstretch their reach. Trump's victory may be just that nemesis for the complacent Europeans.

Part VII
The End of Europe?

18

Finis Europae?

How different Europe looks today from fifteen years ago. In 2002, Jürgen Habermas and Ulrich Beck hailed the dawn of the new 'European' century to replace the 'American' twentieth century.[1] Many were the successes of the Union, they claimed. Old nationalisms and xenophobia had been left behind; former enemies collaborate in peaceful competition creating the most successful economic region in the world. The European Union's principles of democracy, solidarity and social justice are a beacon of hope. Europe is the model for the future of humanity.

The reality is so different today. The European Union has become a dysfunctional organization that has abandoned its founding principles. Every crisis brings to the surface presuppositions and premises that had become hidden during the period of normality. The exception teaches how the rule works, the emergency allows us to comprehend normality. This is how the late Ulrich Beck opened his last book *German Europe*: 'Today the Bundestag will decide the future of Greece.'[2] Beck was aghast to hear this opening line on the midday news in February 2012. It did not happen in 2012 or in the following years. But it is true that the fate of Greece is being decided in capitals far from Athens. Mrs Merkel, taking her cue from Wolfgang Schäuble, her hawk Finance Minister, has stated on occasion that she would prefer Greece to be removed from the European top tables. Intermittently, Merkel has kind words for the Greeks, particularly after the refugee crisis. Mostly, however, she does not reveal her wishes. The Greek elites, placed in the position of a desperate and jilted suitor, tried to divine the lady's wishes. In good psychoanalytical fashion, they had raised Mrs Merkel into their ego ideal. Between 2009 and 2015, under the Pasok and right-wing governments, Greek politicians competed to make themselves desirable or at least acceptable to the lady. For Sigmund Freud, the question 'What does the woman want?' is unanswerable. Jacques Lacan, developing the theme, argues that desire works as a continuous and failing attempt to imagine the other's wishes and fashion ourselves according to her desire. While the gambit fails because we cannot fathom what the other wants, the misfiring efforts keep desire and subjectivity going.

Something similar happened in the relationship with the lenders. The Greeks kept adopting the prescribed medicine of fiscal discipline and internal devaluation hoping to please Mrs Merkel. The Europeans did not reciprocate the slavish obedience to their orders. They acted like the Protestant Pastor in Micahel Haneke's 2009 moral tale 'The White Ribbon'. The more the Greeks obeyed, the more barbaric the punishment became. The unprotested acceptance of every slap and kick led to increased cruelty. It is a typical case of sadistic punishment meted out to a pliant masochist. This obscene behaviour came to a symbolic end with the Syriza government. As Giles Deleuze explains, in sadism the master is sovereign of the subject's fate. Masochism on the other hand works on the basis of a contract of submission between master and slave, which the slave can terminate.[3] The election of Syriza and the referendum were attempts to stop the sadistic punishment and its masochistic acceptance by the submissive elites which found parts of it pleasurable. As right-wing politicians repeatedly stated during their reign (and conveniently forgot later), 'if the Memorandum did not exist, we would have to invent it'. Syriza made clear that any further infliction of pain is unacceptable; but it failed to stop it. For the first time, however, the victim insists that the quantum of punishment and the degree of pain toleration are no longer the prerogative of the master.

What did we learn from the European blackmail that led to the third Greek austerity memorandum? On 16 July, immediately after the agreement, Jürgen Habermas said in an interview: 'I fear that the German government, including its social democratic faction, have gambled away in one night all the political capital that a better Germany had accumulated in half a century.'[4] It was a stark judgment that applies equally to all European leaders who ganged against Tsipras and the Greeks in order to defend their dogmatic ideology. The coup against Greece revealed a number of highly problematic developments. First and foremost, it highlighted the EU's increasingly authoritarian character and its disrespect for democracy. The Greek referendum, which rejected the earlier European plan, was dismissed by the ruling European elites. This authoritarian attitude delivered a devastating blow to the idea of Europe and to the democratic credentials of the Union. As Habermas put it, 'the de facto relegation of a member state to the status of a protectorate openly contradicts the democratic principles of the EU.'[5] The oft-lamented EU 'democratic deficit' was shown to be a benign euphemism. When it comes to hard decisions, Europe is not just deficient; it lacks democratic legitimacy at the supra-national level and is quite lackadaisical about democratic decisions at the domestic. Secondly, the determination of the ruling group to visit the Greeks with punishment instead of solidarity and assistance indicates their inability to learn from the European history of conflict and their careless attitude towards the threat of nationalism and fascism. Finally, the *coup d'état* against Greek democracy marked the end of the marriage of convenience between capitalism and democracy of the post-war social contract. In the 1960s and 1970s, the social state and the European Union had been one of the most successful instances of the truce between capital and workers. As the next part details, this uneasy compromise came unstuck in the 2000s.

German-Jewish philosopher Edmund Husserl argued in his famous 1935 Vienna lecture 'Philosophy and the Crisis of European Man' that the 'idea of Europe' represents truth and the universal, what transcends local and parochial attachments and commitments.[6] The project of Europe is to construct a genuinely universal humanity. In this sense, Europe is not just a landmass but an ideal, a 'spiritual geography'. Humanity will be reached when the idea of Europe becomes global. Europe is the *telos* of humanity; Europeans, the functionaries of spirit. While the universal vocation of truth, philosophy and science does not belong to any particular nation, Husserl claimed, their Greek birth and European heritage make them unique in their universality. No similar idea or vocation worthy of the name philosophy has emerged in India or China. 'Therein lies something unique, which all other human groups feel with regard to us: constantly to Europeanize themselves, whereas we, if we understand ourselves properly, will never, for example, Indianize ourselves.'[7] If Europe designates the unity of spiritual life and creative activity, the Eskimos or Indians of the country fairs or the constantly wandering gypsies do not belong to it. It is a strange conclusion for a Jewish philosopher who had just been expelled from his university. It shows how the dark side of Europe always followed its spiritual ascent.

18.1   The rise and decline of Europe

In the second decade of the twenty-first century the European nations are sick, Europe is in a critical condition. There is no European leadership or vision, the Union's institutional architecture is cracking. We, Europeans, feel old, tired, running out of time and ideas, relying on our ancient laurels, many of them ill-gotten. Yet, the present predicament comes from a long way back. The current European crisis is the culmination of three concentric and overlapping historical cycles, which, in a dialectical fashion, both created and are now leading Europe to its decline. The pioneering work of Etienne Balibar on the European Union and its teleologies is crucial.[8] The first and longest cycle started in the fifteenth century and is still with us rapidly coming to a close; the second was the short twentieth century. Finally, the third and shortest cycle, that of the 'end of history', started in 1989. European history has developed through these three overlapping temporalities; one slow and long, the others shorter and faster. Their combined and uneven effects unravel in the present. For Balibar, historical teleology is 'imagined circular processes, where a certain historical configuration can be said to have "returned" to the conditions of its constitutions, in order to reiterate the origin or, more frequently, to exhibit its displacement and reversal'.[9] In this retroactive narrativization of history, each cycle has a structuring principle and develops a unique type of (normative) universality. Europe invented and owns the universal, 'framing a system of categories for the representation of the world in the same gesture in which it identified itself with a dominant position. In doing so it generalized certain cultural codes, equating them with civilization, transforming other systems of perception, expression, and belief into "subaltern" discourses, which faced an alternative of repression of translation.'[10]

The first cycle started with the Renaissance and the European discovery and conquest of the New World. The dialectics of the Enlightenment inaugurated the great values and scientific achievements of European modernity as well as imperialism, colonialism and the atrocities against indigenous people. Using terms developed by Jacques Derrida and Dipesh Chakrabarty, it is the cycle of European 'capitalization' and 'provincialization'.[11] This historical movement started in the European centre and was then exported and expanded all over the world. Over five centuries, Europe became the capital, both the metropolis and the centre of capitalism. As Husserl put it, Europe is the *telos* of humanity. In its midst, the Mediterranean, the *medium terra*, formed the bright centre from where ships sailed carrying commodities and ideas. The Europeans developed and then exported all over the world capitalism as the economic system and the (nation) state as its political organization. They became the foundation of great empires. When the colonial masters started departing, the two forms had already been embedded in the newly independent postcolonial world. Dialectics and the cunning of history worked their magic however. The colonials adopted the two principles and turned them against the masters. Europe was 'a founding "myth" for emancipatory thought and movement' in the colonies.[12] The freedom struggles from the American War of Independence to the anti-colonial revolutions of the 1950s and 1960s used the national-patriotic ideology and, after independence, the state form to remove the domination of the metropolis.

This first and longest cycle is felt in our day as an evolving process of European decline. Violent economic development, the destruction of traditional communities, the artificial nature of the new states and imported consumerism condemned parts of the developing world into obscene inequality and a near permanent state of exception, giving rise to huge population movements. The recent arrivals of large numbers of refugees alerted the Europeans to a problem that is endemic to Africa, Asia and America. It was seen as a 'problem' only after the Europeans felt its impact. These population flows towards the North and the West are symptoms of a wider change in the balance of forces. Economic, political and even military power has been shifting gradually from the North and the West to the South and the East. The huge inequalities and the imbalance in living standards and expectations are gradually being reduced internationally but increased domestically. The Greeks lost on average up to 50 per cent of their pre-crisis income. This violent pauperization in a short five-year period was an experiment testing how much economic punishment can a people tolerate. Europe-wide austerity policies are effecting a similar type of correction albeit more gradually and with less resistance.

The northbound population flows are part of the same historical movement. According to the UN, seventy million refugees and two hundred million economic migrants are on the move globally looking for a safe haven and a dignified life. This moving humanity, the ethnic minorities in postcolonial countries and the unstoppable influx of refugees and immigrants are symptoms of the shift. The East and the South have become an integral part of the North and West. Long-term decline cannot be stopped by fences, walls or warships pushing back the boats of immigrants. 'Fortress Europe' and the Visegrad leaders' racism can only temporarily slow down the flow by threatening migrants with cruelty and death. The historical trajectory set up by the Western conquests and reversed by the great anti-colonial struggles will continue regardless. People fleeing poverty and disaster are as unstoppable as water as the contemporary King Canutes will soon discover. We live the endgame of five centuries of European domination. The British and French post-imperial *tristesse*, evident in Brexit and the rise of nationalism in France, Germany and Italy testifies that the decline is irreversible. Europe is turning from

Husserl's 'spiritual geography' into a landmass, a promontory attached to Asia and depending heavily on its hitherto colonies. No philosopher or historian could claim today that Europe represents the universal destiny of the world.

During this first long cycle, still with us, the Europeans discovered the inferior, exotic, uncivilized other, Husserl's Chinese, Indians and Eskimos who must 'Europeanize' themselves. The belief that the Other is culturally or racially inferior led to atrocities, genocides, the Holocaust. It became clear that enslaving and dehumanizing the different leads to unimaginable evil. The invention of the idea of universal humanity and of the institution of human rights was in part a normative response to evil. The elevation of humanity to the position of the universal both expanded and contracted the normative horizon. It expanded it because the universality of humanity replaced that of citizenship, which remains the privileged bearer of moral dignity and legal entitlement. Historically, however, every age has developed its own definition of what it means to be human. Humanity has always existed against a background of 'conditions of inhumanity', which exclude those of the wrong colour, gender, religion, sexuality or economic standing. The idea of humanity introduced normative universalism; it was also used to separate empirical flesh-and-blood humanity into higher and lesser parts.[13]

The historical cycle opened with the Mediterranean boats of discovery is now closing with the sinking of the flimsy dinghies of refugees. In a strange twist, European nations are returning to the hedgehog-like version of national identity that the idea of Europe and the European Union had helped undermine. In the refugee crisis, the Greeks and the Italians are almost alone in defending international law and the values of solidarity and morality. As always, a particular speaks for the universal; if it succeeds politically, it may turn the particular into the hegemonic version of the universal. The Mediterraneans, who created the idea of Europe, are fighting to save the honour of the name.

18.2   The short twentieth century

The second cycle is the short twentieth century between 1918 and 1989, the century of the European civil war. First, the war between Germany and the European powers and, secondly, the clash between capitalism and communism. The two conflicts overlapped but also followed their own internal logic. Wars finished with the defeat of Germany and its pacification with the rest of Europe. The ideological conflict ended with the defeat of communism. Today it would be inconceivable to call what were in essence European conflicts 'world wars'. The twentieth was the last European century. Only the Americans could call today their baseball championship the 'world series'.

The social state and the European Union were direct consequences of the two conflicts. They promised to leave behind the ethnic and ideological wars that raged over the last century. In this sense, they mark the culmination of five centuries of European history. The social state dialectically 'sublates' the ideological war precariously synthesizing the two sides. The European Union symbolizes the determination to leave behind ethnic strife and turn military conflict into regulated economic competition. The lore of European ideology claims that the EU is moving towards a federal post-national state, the cosmopolitan conclusion of old ethnic divisions. The process of convergence would be facilitated by the sharing of economic prosperity. The Common Agricultural Policy and the various structural and convergence funds aim at reducing regional inequalities through moderate capital transfers from the wealthy North to the poor South. By the 2010s, these policies were gradually abandoned alongside their Keynesian theoretical foundations. The rapid expansion from six to twenty-eight members added to the club post-Communist states, which were economically, culturally and politically distant if not incompatible with the European core. The aspiration of integration is a constant mantra in Brussels communiqués but is no longer a real possibility. As Alan Milward and Perry Anderson have persuasively argued, the Union is the last major attempt to save the nation-state.[14] When the inability of the Union to integrate populations economically became evident, ethnic tensions returned. The European periphery saw Germany's assertion of economic dominance as a claim to national hegemony. The existential crisis engulfing the EU is a symptom of the decline of European domination and of its claims to historical and normative

universalism. The departure of Britain is a further sign of
the disintegration of the latest and probably last project of
European exceptionalism. Followed by the pan-European
rise of extreme right-wing nationalism and protectionism, it
symbolizes the end of the 'United States of Europe' project,
a somewhat quixotic idea from the start.

A similar trajectory marked the rise of the social state. It
was a post-war creation and an exceptional achievement. No
similar regime guaranteeing collective social, economic and
workers rights exists outside Western Europe and a few other
advanced capitalist societies. The American travails over
Obamacare emphasize the unique achievement of Western
European social democracy. Its post-WWII life started with
the Labour victory in the 1945 British elections, the Beveridge
report and the foundation of the National Health Service. It
was a major victory for the working class, the trade unions
and the Left. The social state added to the long-established
civil and political rights a raft of social and economic entitlements. It was also a concession by capital to the dynamic
working-class movement, presenting a superior alternative to
Soviet communism.

The social state became the European growth and redis-
tributive engine. It is capitalism with a human face, a marriage
of convenience between capitalism and socialism. It combines
the operation of the market with its putative correction by
principles of social justice. Capitalism distributes according
to market decisions expressed in prices and property entitlements. According to classical economics, the market is an
efficient and fair mechanism of wealth distribution. Those
who fail in the marketplace are condemned to destitution and
the consolations of philanthropy. Social justice on the other
hand distributes the national wealth according to cultural
norms, the ethos of a society and epoch and collective ideas
of fairness and reciprocity. People are entitled to a minimum
standard of dignified life irrespective of productivity, competitiveness or success in the marketplace. Wealth distribution
is carried by decisions of formal and informal institutions,
which correct the harshness of the market. As Wolfgang
Streeck put it, the marriage of convenience worked because
politics intervened in the economy and mitigated market decisions in favour of working people.[15] Democratic politics is

the means for legitimizing the moderation of market decisions and the imposition of restrictions on property rights; elections have been the political expression of social justice.

The two principles of wealth and income distribution are antithetical and fought each other for two centuries. In the nineteenth century, the conflict took the form of laissez-faire capitalism versus democracy. Liberal democracy is an historical latecomer. The great liberals, John Locke, Jeremy Bentham, the Mills, Alexis Tocqueville and Benjamin Constant opposed the extension of the franchise to working men and women because they were considered a mortal danger to private property. Similarly, the post-war combination of capitalism and social justice has been an uneasy alliance, leading both to attack the social state for betraying the unadulterated basic values of each side. It should be added that past and contemporary transfers of value from the colonies assisted the compromise. The social state and the class truce in the West were built in part on the brutal exploitation of workers in the South and the East. Today when people ask what happened to the European working class, the precise answer is that it has moved to China.

But the all-conquering dialectic worked its magic again. In the West, the qualified acceptance of the social state was a direct result of the ideological Cold War. When the Communist states adopted Western liberalization and the market mechanism, they accelerated their demise. In turn, this freed the West from its lukewarm commitment to the social state. What started as the great compromise of our times has finished with the end of both social systems. Soviet communism is dead and the social state has not been feeling very well either.

What specific form did normative universality take in the twentieth century? Citizenship at the level of the individual, mass democracy at that of institutions. The democratic citizen is not the abstract human of humanism and human rights but a concrete subject with history and body, needs and desires. Social and economic entitlements supplement legal rights recognizing the importance of class and the uniqueness of individuals. Mature democracy and the social state are the outcome of the entrance of the excluded into politics. The Athenian *demos* became *kratos* when those who had no qualifications for the of exercise power because they were not rich or wise, elderly or prudent, demanded to become partners in decision-making. The *demos* was both the people, the whole of society, and the excluded who had no credentials or entitlement to rule. Democracy emerged when a particular class demanded and succeeded to be raised to the universal. It was completed when citizenship turned from limited legal protection into claims to active political participation and fulsome social recognition. These major achievements are under threat at the closure of the second historical cycle. Social and economic rights are on the way out while, as Habermas and Streeck agree, the advance of democracy has been halted. Technocrats are replacing politicians, private universities and health plans public and free education and health. The repeated attacks on 'populism' are often attacks on the people, on those who demand participation in decision-making and consideration of their interests. They mark the end of the social state.

18.3   The 'end of history' cycle

The second cycle closed after the end of the Cold War with the unravelling of the marriage of convenience between capitalism and social justice. The 'end of history' cycle started in 1989. Fukuyama's claim was both arrogant and pathetic. It returned to the disgraced idea of a universal European history and turned the decline of the West into a terminal station for the history of the whole world. In this sense, the third cycle is not a distinct historical epoch but a virtual creation of Western desire, an attempt to re-establish Western hegemony at a time of retreat. Democracy has been marginalized and markets have been freed from correction by social justice. This retreat of democracy was the cause and effect of the Greek crisis. The impotence, indeed irrelevance, of elections was confirmed by the treatment of the Syriza government. If the people vote the wrong way the rulers will elect another people, said Berthold Brecht. The current European rulers have updated Brecht: they will try to elect another government. Economic performance, productivity, competitiveness and the repayment of debt have been prioritized over the needs of people. As the social state withdraws, people must be turned into entrepreneurs of themselves and their families. We have to provide for our education, health, old age and social care. The rights and entitlements of the post-war social contract are undermined, state institutions and services are privatized, governments have become collection agencies of international capital against their own citizens.

Citizenship has drifted alongside the social state. People have withdrawn from democratic politics, which they justifiably consider unable to change much. The much-trumpeted European citizenship has been abandoned, surviving only in the glossy brochures of Brussels. We observe the same process of retreat in the other great achievement of the Union, the pacification of ethnic disputes. It has come under great stress from the economic crisis and is unravelling as a result of the refugee crisis. When the refugee flows increased in 2015 and 2016, a number of states prioritized national interests and the needs of their election cycle over legal obligations or moral considerations. Europe is returning to old nationalisms; spheres of influence and groups of nations of an ideological and ethnic nature have started competing for dominance. At the height of the economic crisis, large parts of the European press wrote about the Greeks in racist and orientalist terms. Samuel Huntington's 'clash of civilizations' popularized the idea of a political and cultural conflict between the rational, civilized and Protestant West and the irrational, lazy and corrupt Christian Orthodox and Islamic East. The Orientals are unwilling to join the Northern march of reason, we are told. In this vein, European leaders and commentators spoke disparagingly about Greek sloth and corruption, lack of efficiency and trustworthiness. Legitimate economic or political criticism slid into cultural racism. The attacks on Greeks, the alpha PGS among the Southerners, paved the way for a reconceptualization of economic problems and political difficulties as racial defects. The ethnic European wound, which had re-opened the Yugoslav wars, started bleeding again.

In another strange twist of dialectics, the victory of the West in the Cold War undermined its greatest success, the post-war social contract. Had the Cold War lasted longer, had the victory of capitalism been delayed, perhaps Europe could have moved towards political union, the ultimate defence against the Soviets. This did not happen. The successive enlargements of the EU coupled with its federal architecture preclude the movement to the 'ever closer union'. Mr Cameron won a British opt-out from this aspiration for political integration. It did not stop Brexit. The centrifugal and nationalist forces have spread everywhere. Europe is moving to an ever more distant disunion. The enduring memories of national, cultural and military conflict have resurfaced.

The combined effects of the three historical cycles are still with us. The longest first cycle created the idea of the human, of the full humanity and of its inferior versions. The short twentieth century concretized the moral recognition and the legal entitlements of humanity and conferred them to the citizens of democratic states. What remains of the universal in the dense temporality of the virtual end of history? Humanity and citizenship have been replaced by commodities and money. Neoliberalism, the bastard progeny of classical liberalism and social democracy, is presented as the last stage in human development. No conflict of historical proportions has survived, the last engine for historical movement has come to an end. As Chapter 12 explains, the Euro and money more generally have been elevated into the 'sacred and holy' of our time.

Dialectics and the cunning of history intervened again to upset the dominant model. The aggressive greedy neoliberal capitalism unleashed by the defeat of the ideological civil war inscribed dialectically in the European Union the seeds of its own destruction. The emancipation of market from social justice, the impoverishment of populations and the undermining of democracy are leading the end of history to its end. The Greek answer to austerity, recession and the refugee crisis has been the left alternative. Unfortunately, it was followed in 2016 by the extreme Right's reaction to the neoliberal disasters. Brexit, the rise of xenophobic nationalism in France, Holland, Italy, Germany and Donald Trump's victory challenge the free movement of capital and people, cardinal principles of globalized neoliberalism. They confirm that the 'new world order' will be the shortest in history. Four dates mark its provenance and probable demise: 1989, the triumphant commencement of the new global economic

and political dispensation; 2008, the banking and then economic crisis, direct effects of the economics and politics of the
new order; 2011, the Arab Spring, Puerta del Sol, Syntagma,
Occupy Wall Street, the world Occupy movement: the Left
and popular insurrection against neoliberalism; 2016, Brexit
and Trump: the right-wing reaction to neoliberalism. The
wheels of history have started turning again. The destination
is not yet known. But the popular rejection of the establishment's 'business as usual' approach indicates that the struggle
for the soul and the future of Europe will be fought between
the radical Left and the nationalist Right. Every fascist victory
will be the result of the failure of democracy and the Left.

In March 1938 after *Anschluss*, Sigmund Freud wrote in
his notebook 'Finis Austriae'. If Europe does not change soon
it will move towards its end.

19

The Left and the Future of Europe

Euroscepticism is spreading throughout Europe like wild-fire, as a recent report by the Pew Research Center details.[1] Right-wing rhetoric prevailed on both sides of the British referendum; it did not encounter strong countervailing arguments from the Left. The repeated and historic failures of the European establishment in the recent crises have created an unprecedented existential crisis. The Europe of second-rate political leaders and centralized and distant bureaucracies is on the retreat. The panic-stricken elites, trapped in the ideological straitjacket of fiscal discipline and internal devaluation, have neither the theoretical imagination nor the interest or will to move in a radically different direction. The Europhiles go back to the experience of past crises, which tended to lead by stealth to greater integration. Without great conviction they hope that the overcoming of the present travails will almost automatically lead in the same direction. It was evident in the complacent statements of European leaders after Brexit. The unprecedented rise of the nationalist right wing, however, indicates that this is not a 'normal' crisis. The British, the Italian and the Austrian voters rejected for good the 'ever closer union' mantra. The multiple crises had delegitimized the federal European plan. Brexit delivered the *coup de grâce*. Economic integration and political convergence have been scuppered at least for a generation. It is the final victory of the Thatcher plan, according to which Britain, a trading nation, would benefit from a continuously expanding single market. The cultural, economic and political gap that relentless expansion would create between old and new states guarantees that political union will never happen. Mrs Thatcher's plan to seek a grocer's advantage and derail the political union succeeded, however, a little too much, threatening the whole edifice as well as Britain's future.

The failures of the elites have created an unexpected opportunity for the Left. It has the responsibility to articulate and represent both popular scepticism and a new project for Europe. The Left must abandon (if it still believes) the project of political integration. The democratic guarantees for the protection of the interests and rights of working people, if state sovereignty is further weakened, are lacking. A move towards political integration would further enhance and constitutionalize neoliberalism; it would perpetuate the myth that late capitalism can become fairer, if obstacles to supranational governance were removed. Globalized capitalism intensifies socio-economic inequality in order to compensate for stagnating productivity and profitability. As Claus Offe puts it, 'Europe thought its "negative" model of integration consisting in the abolition of borders, "barriers to trade", and modes of distribution and social protection within members states that markets judge "inefficient". It is a machinery of market liberalization that disempowers states and their democratic constituencies.'[2] A federal EU would continue and consolidate its integration into the global financial and capitalist circuit. On the other hand, a return to full state sovereignty is both impossible in a globalized world and undesirable for the internationalist Left.

Stark juxtapositions have dominated the debate over the European future so far: for or against the Union, ever-closer union or return to the nation state, Euro or Drachma. These simplistic bipolarities distort our vision. The Left can neither accept the current EU nor return to old nationalisms. We need a different politics in a different Europe. The Greek Left in particular, with its institutional naiveté and youthful insolence, should take the initiative and suggest a number of institutional reforms and democratic initiatives that could inspire the European citizens. A European public space for debate and action must be created for developing and launching a new plan for Europe. This debate should leave behind the clichés of Eurocrats and European studies textbooks. It should develop an alternative vision for the Union with emphasis on reversing austerity, enhancing sustainable and just development, deepening democracy and recognizing cultural differences. The task is to rebuild Europe from the bottom up as a community of democratic nations and peoples opposed to the current one-size-fits-all top-down construct. The battle for the soul of Europe will take place on three fronts.

First, the Union must reverse its austerity policies, which have led to permanent recession and huge unemployment, particularly among the young. Wide political alliances are necessary in order to confront catastrophic austerity. Many centre-left and social-democratic parties have gradually moved against the dominant German policies. The European left and centre-left parties, which resist neoliberalism and German domination, should come together in a loose alliance and agree a new social compact which would guarantee a minimum living income for all and protect work, social rights and cultural identities. Second, a campaign to welcome and integrate refugees and immigrants should be launched throughout Europe. The next enlargement of the EU should be an enlargement of people, through the settlement and integration of refugees and immigrants. They should be welcomed, given education, work and life chances in order to contribute, as so many immigration waves in the past, to the renewal of an old and tired continent. This is perhaps the only area where the idea of 'European citizenship' might acquire some significance. If some governments are not prepared to consider even second and third-generation immigrants for nationalization, Europe could return to its founding values by considering the creation of a special status citizenship for refugees and immigrants.[3]

An important part of the new European project is the creation of a Mediterranean pole prepared to confront the anti-immigrant campaigns of the Visegrad, Baltic and Balkan governments. The economic and refugee crisis have affected the Mediterranean more than other parts of Europe. Its peoples share histories and traditions and are closely linked with the ideals of the radical Enlightenment. As Chair of the Hellenic Parliament Standing Committee of Defence and Foreign Relations, I have helped create a 'Med Group' of corresponding parliamentary committees. In September 2016, at an inter-parliamentary conference in Bratislava, the Mediterranean delegations objected strongly to the absence of any reference to the refugee crisis in the conclusions of the conference. Slovakia, Hungary, Poland and the Czech Republic have refused to take the refugees allocated to them by the EU. A Greek amendment calling the Union to implement a Council decision distributing refugees to all twenty-eight states according to size and GDP and, alternatively, to fine those states not receiving their allotted number was rejected. It was resubmitted by the Mediterranean states and was inserted in the text after the seven delegations stated that they would not accept the conclusions otherwise. The Germans backed the amendment. It was a small victory; parliamentary resolutions do not change much. It showed, however, that if people stand up to the bullying tactics of the xenophobes wider support may be attracted. The refugee crisis is the greatest challenge to the EU since its inception. Greece and Italy showed to the world how to react to such an existential and moral challenge. The Mediterranean shores, where the idea of Europe was invented, are again its main defenders.

Finally, the Union needs to reboot its constitutional structure. Europe has failed to create a *demos* or a working democracy. It was unable, despite half-hearted attempts, to generate a sense that Europeans belong to a common cultural, political and economic space. Every time the European citizens were asked to vote on federalist constitutional plans they determinedly rejected them. In the corridors of Brussels, the word 'referendum' has the effect of garlic on vampires. Secondly and closely related is the euphemistic 'democratic deficit', in reality the almost total absence of democracy. The signs of the democratic decline are striking. The European Parliament has limited legislative powers, while its control of the executive branch is cosmetic. Institutions outside the constitutional structure have proliferated and have acquired a dominant role. Summit meetings of leaders, the Council of Ministers and the Coreper committee of member state representatives have become the ultimate decision-makers, making national priorities the deciding criterion. The Eurogroup and the Euro-Working group of Eurozone Finance Ministers and technocrats have increased their powers by stealth. The Eurogroup has no proper constitutional or legal status but makes the key decisions about the countries in bailout programmes. Yanis Varoufakis revealed that the Eurogroup has no set rules of procedure, minutes are not taken and the decisions are reached through an arcane method of nudges and winks. As the former minister put it, the Eurogroup is a 'body that does not even exist in European law, that operated on the basis that the "the strong do as they please while the weak suffer what they must" … and whose only rule is that its deliberations are confidential – that is, not to be shared with Europe's citizenry.'⁴ Total lack of democratic accountability applies also to the troika, which imposes terms on debtor countries and oversees their compliance. These groups stand outside the law but set the legal obligations of countries in programmes.⁵ According to Carl Schmitt, sovereign is he who can impose the state of exception. The Eurogroup and the troika are both outside – setting the law – and inside some vague European constitution. They act like a super-sovereign that stands above the formal sovereignty of states.

The most important task for the Left is to re-politicize politics at the European and domestic levels after the long post-democratic interval. The World and European Social Forum trained a group of young militants into activism, solidarity and the defence of working people. Imaginative forms of resistance and solidarity from the *indignados* to *Bloccupy* and *Cant Pay Wont Pay* developed all over Europe. They have created a rich experience of transnational collaboration and itinerant activism. It must be raised to a higher plane. A radical restructuring of politics involves the substantial upgrading of democratically legitimate institutions. Parliaments, including the European, should become independent of the executive and exercise more energetically their role of controlling the state and holding the government to account. Direct citizen participation in decision-making should be introduced at the local, national and European level. Local and regional authorities should develop direct democracy institutions, such as local referenda, citizen assemblies and collective budgeting. Alternative networks of solidarity, innovative forms of grassroots associations and social economy indicate new avenues for progressive action that disrupt capitalist domination and shift the balance of power. These initiatives will improve citizens' everyday life and will raise their interest and participation in the European construction. Europe should become a union of people with full recognition of local histories and traditions; many powers and competencies should be devolved from Brussels to national capitals. Perhaps the idea of a confederation of European homelands to replace the failed federal plan should be part of this debate. Such ideas and initiatives can only come from those challenging the tired European establishment.

The Greek government launched in late 2016 a major public debate and consultation about a full-scale amendment of the Constitution. People are asked to participate in discussions in Town Halls and squares, universities and working places. The consultation will gather ideas and proposals which a committee of experts will then formulate into a set of rules to be decided by Parliament. This debate will determine the nature of the twenty-first century polity. It is a European novelty and the natural continuation of the popular dynamic that led to Syriza's victories. The opposition denounced the initiative arguing that constitutional rules restrict the amendment process to Parliament. Popular participation terrorizes the political establishment. The people must be kept away from decision-making; they must be confined to the position of obedient subjects and insatiable consumers. In early modernity, the rulers and the wealthy were scared of riots and mobs in the street. Today, they fear the eruption of people on the political stage. Whenever it happens it spells a serious challenge and often the end of a system of power.

We should imagine and plan a similar process at the European level. A wide public debate should lead to a peoples' congress, a pan-European constituent assembly. The Left must reconfigure and energize popular power outside the formal rules of the Union. Such a constituent initiative will bring movements, parties, and people together in a struggle to expand the borders of what is considered properly political. The insurrectionary moment of democracy achieved such an expansion in the resistances of the 2010s. The very survival of the EU has now been placed on the historical agenda and depends on the democratic awakening of its citizens.

Part VIII
Cities of Refuge

20

Europe Between Two Infant Deaths

2015 and 2016 were marked by the heart-breaking images of a moving humanity of refugees and migrants who left the battlefronts of Syria, Iraq, Afghanistan and Libya to come to Europe, their imaginary Arcadia. Greece is a transit point on the way to Northern Europe. Over one million refugees entered Europe, with some 850,000 landing on the Greek islands of Lesbos, Chios, Kos, Agathonissi, Farmakonissi and Lemnos. On the way from Libya to Italy and from Turkey to Greece, five thousand perished and some 150,000 were rescued. Photographs of drowned dead bodies lying on the beaches of Greece, Italy and Turkey have been published regularly. The image of dead three-year-old Aylan Kurdi on a Turkish beach on 4 September 2015 went around the world and became the icon of the refugee crisis. Britain's chief rabbi, Ephraim Mirvis interviewed on radio stated, 'for far too long, we have related to these suffering individuals as if they are people who are living on Mars. Thanks to that image, that desperately sad and tragic image, it's moved our hearts...It's an image of that boy that has brought us to our senses and we must respond adequately.'[1]

Yet the first known refugee casualty of 2016 was an unnamed two-year-old boy who drowned on New Year's day when the crowded dinghy he was travelling in broke on rocks off Greece's Agathonissi Island. Later in January, a six-month-old baby was found close to the island of Samos. He had drowned on 29 October 2015 alongside eighteen others. He was dragged for two months by the currents and was found eigthy-five miles from the place where the boat sank. He was finally identified through a DNA sample given by his father who had survived the tragedy. 'Nothing can prepare you for the horrific reality of what is going on. Today we came face to face with one of the youngest victims of this ongoing refugee crisis. It is a tragic reminder of the thousands of people who have died trying to reach safety in miserable conditions', said Christopher Catrambone a migrant support NGO officer.[2] Between the first and the second dead infant, thousands braved the sea and hundreds drowned.

The image of the little dead body floating on the waves and then lying on the beach was powerful. Yet Aylan's image did not have the same effect on European politicians as on the Rabbi. Germany temporarily opened its borders, receiving around a million refugees. But when the political climate started turning the borders were closed again. In September 2015, an EU Council meeting reluctantly agreed a relocation plan for 160,000 refugees from Italy and Greece. They were to be distributed to the twenty-eight EU states, according to size and population. At the time of writing, only four thousand refugees have been relocated to the rest of Europe. Immediately after the agreement, a number of states refused to take refugees. Hungary built a fence on the border with Serbia and declared that it cannot accept the moral blackmail of Germany. Hungary held a referendum in October 2016 in which 98 per cent of Hungarians rejected the European migrant quota plan, which would have sent a few hundred refugees to their country. But as the turnout was less that the required 50 per cent of registered voters, the decision was not legally binding. György Schöpflin, a Hungarian ruling party MEP, has suggested that pigs' heads and human faces made from root vegetables should be placed along Hungary's razor wire border fence to deter migrants. The Slovak Premier Robert Fico opened his 2016 election campaign by inaugurating a new fence on its borders. Poland declared that it would only accept Christian refugees. The Polish leader Jarosław Kaczyński claimed that Muslim immigrants bring into Europe microbes, parasites and eradicated diseases. 'They could try to impose sharia law and turn our churches into lavatories', he added.[3] When Austria closed its borders in March 2016, Croatia and the Former Yugoslav Republic of Macedonia followed suit. They were successor states after the collapse of the Austro-Hungarian Empire in 1918. A new anti-immigrant empire is being constructed in Central Europe. Denmark, on the other hand, one of the wealthiest nations of Europe, passed a law authorizing the confiscation of the pitiful valuables of refugees to cover the cost of offering basic services to them.

The Greek people took everyone by surprise with their response to the influx of suffering humanity. Battered by six years of austerity, record unemployment and falling income, the islanders came out in numbers to help. They rescued the shipwrecked, welcomed those landing on their shores and looked after their immediate needs. For the Greeks, the refugees are not invaders. When others build walls and fences, Greece constructed reception centres and schools to provide a basic decent living for refugees. Their solidarity was recognized by global public opinion. The Pope, the General Secretary of the UN and many politicians, artists and intellectuals came to Lesbos to pay homage to the simple people who saved the honour of Europe.

Early in 2016, the flows from Turkey to Greece increased. On some days more than three thousand would land on the Greek islands. In March, after Austria stopped refugee entry, the West Balkan route was sealed with soldiers patrolling the border between Greece and FYROM. Greece was effectively cut off from the rest of Europe, turning into a 'prison' for refugees. Some 70,000 refugees were 'trapped' in Greece in the summer of 2016. Forty-six per cent of the refugees are children, many unaccompanied. Those already in the country and any future arrivals will not be able to leave.

After the closure of borders, the EU entered an agreement with Turkey, which promised to stop the flow of refugees into Greece. Turkey would accept the return of economic migrants and failed asylum applicants from Greece and would send an equal number of Syrian refugees to European countries for resettlement. In return, Turkey would be given over €3bn in aid for the care of Syrian refugees in its territory and, more importantly, a visa waiver for Turkish citizens travelling to

Schengen area. The deal initially worked with the flows to Greece substantially reduced. But Greece is on tenterhooks. The hostile European response to Erdogan's purges after the failed *coup d'état* in Turkey may scupper the agreement. In such a case, Greece will become a new Lebanon, with hundreds of thousands of refugees permanently stuck in the country.

The European Union has unilaterally declared itself closed to outsiders, against international and European law. It has become a physical 'Fortress Europe'. It has externalized immigration management by delegating the control and security of its borders to Turkey, a country which, according to human rights organizations, is not safe. The survival of the idea of Europe depends on the Union's response to the greatest humanitarian crisis since its inception. If Fortress Europe continues, with its violation of international law and basic principles of humanity, the EU does not deserve to survive.

20.1   The refugee as bare life

Hannah Arendt understood the fate of refugees. In the *Origins of Totalitarianism* she wrote:

> If a human being loses his political status, he should, according to the implications of the inborn and inalienable rights of man, come under exactly the situation for which the declarations of such general rights provided. Actually the opposite is the case. It seems that a man who is nothing but a man has lost the very qualities which make it possible for other people to treat him as a fellow-man.[4]

Arendt was referring to the wandering ethnic minorities in the inter-war period after the dissolution of the Ottoman and Austro-Hungarian empires. The modern political principle that every nation should have its own state and each state a dominant ethnicity has led to the proliferation of minorities no longer welcome in the places they had lived for centuries. Population exchanges helped some to move to their ethnic state where they usually encountered hostile reception by the local population. When there was no homeland to receive them, large groups of people wanderend around the Balkans looking for a place to settle. Arendt, a German-Jew and herself a refugee, describes the treatment of those wandering people in the darkest colours. No state would accept them, no law would protect them, the ethnically 'pure' people rejected them.

Refugees escaping dictatorships, wars, ancient and recent conflicts face a similar hostility in many countries today. Despite the legal instruments introduced after the Second World War, most governments and the European Union do not treat the contemporary wandering populations much better. Even the slaves in ancient Athens had more rights than those without a homeland, Arendt added in her descriptive and prophetic text. Their masters had the obligation to provide food, shelter and basic care, not to work them to exhaustion. Nothing from that list was given to the minorities of the inter-war period and very little to migrants nowadays.

In Hegel's famous master and slave dialectic, the master obtains his position by taking the struggle for recognition to extremes, risking his own life. At that point, the servant fearing for his life concedes and accepts his subjugation. Refugees reverse the dialectic.[5] Fleeing dictators, wars, traffickers and gunboats, they find comfort in the freedom of risk-taking. They are the 'degree zero' of humanity, quasi slaves who risk their lives in order to survive. Before the closure of the West Balkan route, they embarked in flimsy crafts sailing to Lesbos or Chios. They then headed North on foot in the rain and cold, following the trajectory of their predecessors in the 1920s and 1930s. A snake-like line of people walked, without stop, towards their imaginary land. The walking line brought to mind images of genocides, atrocities, ethnic cleansing.

Throughout the refugee crisis many photographs emerged capturing its tragic nature. In one such picture from 2015, two Italian soldiers carry the simple coffin of a drowned refugee. 'Body No. 132' is written on it. In another from the same incident, twenty-four numbered coffins are surrounded by men in black. They are European officials, like those who discontinued the *Mare Nostrum* Mediterranean naval search and rescue operation for financial reasons in 2014.

An ancient Mediterranean practice calls on women – mothers, sisters, wives – to mourn their dead and care for their body. Antigone, the grieving women of Mani, Sicily and Sardinia carry out the libations necessary to have the loved-one embark in Charon's boat on the way to the other side. But there will be no wake for 'Body No. 132', no mourning eulogies; his mother will not sing farewell songs. The island of Lesbos has run out of burial space. Several bodies lie in the mortuary with a number and the place they were found as only markers of a spent life. Graves stand unmarked, as the name and nationality of the buried are unknown. In my capacity as Chair of the Foreign Relations Committee, I have received letters and visits from ambassadors and family members of people who have disappereard on the passage to Greece. They are begging for help to trace and identify their bodies and give them a proper burial. Some 550 bodies have not been identified at the time of writing.

Refugees are the unmourned victims of the latest humanitarian catastrophe. As Antigone knew, the dead must be honoured at all costs. Those who are not form the most extreme case of life outside the protection of law. Some people are not entitled to the rites of mourning, says Judith Butler.[6] Their life is worthless, meaningless, as Athena Athanassiou puts it.[7] Bare life, *homines sacri*, life outside humanity. Such are the people who board the flimsy dinghies on the way to the West, the way others boarded the trains to Germany. Hostages without future in the countries of departure, hostages without past in their unknown destination. Wandering and drowning, eternal sailors in the waters of Lethe, companions of the mermaid.

20.2   Cities of Refuge

And yet this callousness is modern. Asylum and protection for the persecuted is an ancient tradition. Throughout history, temples and cities have been places of protection. The tradition started with the six 'cities of refuge' listed in the Priestly and Deuteronomy codes of the Old Testament. The Jewish cities were places of refuge for those persecuted for crimes, usually homicide. Priests would question the supplicant and, if the criminal act was not intentional, the city would offer protection from the relatives of the victim who wanted to exercise the age-old *lex talionis*. A similar institution existed in Ancient Greece. Someone who had committed a crime or was persecuted could ask for *a-sylum* – protection from *syle* or harm. The plea was made to a temple or city. The supplicant had to perform certain rituals, which placed him under the protection of the gods, in particular the *Ikesios* or hospitable *Zeus*. Examples of supplication are found in Homer; *The Supplicants*, Aeschylus' masterpiece, describes the ritual and political operation of the institution. The fifty daughters of King Danaos fleeing the proposed incestuous marriage with the sons of King Aegyptos seek asylum from King Pelasgos in the city of Argos. The prudent king hesitates, initially fearing that the barbarians might attack the city to abduct the maidens. But if he does not offer protection, he will offend *Ikesios Zeus* and will bring a curse on the city. The King takes the issue to the assembly of the demos, which votes to grant asylum. Argos welcomes the Danaids, protects them from evil and, as a result, Zeus blesses the city.

Cities continued offering asylum. Before the consolidation of state sovereignty, Italian, Hanseatic and Ottoman cities – the places of early European urbanization – gave refuge and protection to the persecuted. Thessaloniki was a typical example. It gave refuge and protection to thousands of Jews fleeing religious persecution in Portugal and Spain. After the creation of the modern state, asylum became a privilege granted by the sovereign as a sign of mercy or out of political interest. Protection was no longer solely a moral obligation. It was legalized and soon became a tool in ideological rivalries. The 1951 Geneva Convention on Political Asylum was a typical creation of the Cold War. Asylum was granted only to refugees from Europe who had fled their home country before 1951 and was extended to all refugees only in 1967. These restrictions allowed Western Europe to offer protection to people persecuted by the newly established Communist regimes. This is why the Convention stipulates that those protected must have fled their country of nationality because of a 'well-founded fear of persecution' on the basis of their race, religion or political views. The Convention creates an individualized process of processing asylum applications, excluding those who flee for non-Convention reasons – such as discrimination on grounds of sexual orientation or extreme poverty – or economic migrants who leave their home country to improve their lives. International law turned political asylum into a legal institution. Its scope and extension was seriously restricted, however. The Geneva asylum system is limited to the exclusively listed grounds of persecution, creating a presumption of rightlessness for non Geneva-grounds migrants. The division of people coming to Europe into those who may seek political asylum and receive limited protection and economic migrants who have none is highly artificial. Its historical reasons no longer apply; the individualized Geneva process cannot deal with the contemporary population flows. People fleeing war may receive protection, those fleeing poverty not. Yet extreme inequality and poverty almost always lead to war; war further impoverishes people in a vicious spiral of destruction. The international community needs to re-examine the legal and social treatment of migrants and to combine the legal regimes of asylum and immigration.

Jacques Derrida, Pierre Bourdieu, Toni Morrison, Salman Rushdie, among many great intellectuals, revived the tradition by founding in Strasburg in 1994 a contemporary network of 'cities of refuge'. Their aim was to protect oppressed intellectuals and artists. At the time of the initiative, artists and writers feared possible persecution by an incoming Islamic regime in Algeria. Great cities like Barcelona, Hamburg and Liverpool joined the initiative, creating a group of cities offering protection and hospitality to persecuted intellectuals. The organization still survives but has become relatively inactive and its focus is limited to the protection of people of letters. The city of refuge idea has historical and material resonance. Urban protection avoids the tension with local societies associated with state sovereignty. It recognizes that the settlement and integration of foreigners takes place within the city web, where anonymity and privacy allow traumatized refugees to acquire gradually the necessary confidence in order to restart life in a foreign country which will become their second home.

Europe should be offering protection to the persecuted of our age irrespective of educational or social background. A new network of cities of refuge is urgently called for. They would undertake to host a number of refugees and offer them shelter, food and care for basic needs helping them settle in their new home. The cities of refuge initiative should be expanded throughout the continent. The civic authorities of European cities should ask their citizens to follow the steps of the Argeian demos. It is not just an issue of humanitarianism, philanthropy or solidarity. The asylum is the foundation of every kind of religious, normative or utilitarian morality. The face of the other who suffers lies behind the identity of each and every one of us.[8]

There are good policy reasons for such initiatives. Europe needs new blood and new ideas. The refugees knocking on Europe's door are educated, dynamic – this is always the case with people who go through all kinds of hardship to get to their imagined utopia. Repulsion, xenophobia and racism show not only meanness and lack of morality but also ignorance of basic facts about population needs. The European pension and social protection regimes are no longer viable. It was argued above that the demographic data are worrying.[9] First, the fertility rate is very low, 1.5 births per European female in child-bearing age – and only 1.3 for Greeks and Germans – when a 2.1 rate is needed for the reproduction of the population. Second, life expectancy has increased, putting pressure on pensions, social care and health provision. Finally, the ratio between working and out of work population has deteriorated. The EU predicts that Europe needs around sixty million new immigrants in the next forty years in order to reproduce its active population. Angela Merkel understood this problem and without grandiose statements accepted around one million refugees, the employees of the future. Her lead must be taken up by other leaders.

The contemporary supplicants must be welcomed. They flee bombs, death and oppression, to which Western policies have contributed. They are ready to work hard in order to build a new life. The great European cities must become shelters and places of settlement for these new Danaids. Hospitality does not mean solely temporary stay but policies of inclusion and integration. This is what the values of solidarity and the reality of demographic decay demand.

The Greek government has put into place a plan to integrate those refugees prepared to settle in the country. Those who want to leave but cannot are being spread around Greece in small numbers and are housed in reception centres and flats while the process of registration and examination of asylum applications lasts. Twenty thousand children have been allocated to reception classes in town and city schools teaching Greek, a second language, maths and art. Laws are prepared to offer the new settlers work permits and social security benefits. A new and prosperous Greece and Europe of solidarity could be built around the settlement of refugees. As Etienne Balibar put it, such a settlement would be a new type of moral enlargement of Europe that will change the definition and the purpose of the Union.[10] The signs, however, are not encouraging.

21

Human Rights for Martians

In November 2015, I attended a European Parliament conference to discuss migration flows in the Western Balkans. It was my first participation in the roundtables of Europe. The experience confirmed reservations I had formed in libraries and academic meetings. Most international meetings and conferences MPs attend have no obvious purpose besides networking. They are a type of parliamentary tourism which allows people with rather large egos to feel even more important. It became painfully clear at the meeting that many Northern politicians consider refugees as invaders. The European Union, and Greece as its border guard, should prevent entrance and repel these dangerous intruders. I explained at the meeting that the Greek position, inspired by solidarity and Enlightenment principles, is the exact opposite. We welcome the refugees, register them, start the asylum determination process and do everything possible to make their lives bearable while in the country. It is a huge task for a small and economically ravaged country.[1] A Northern deputy retorted that the Greek port police should prevent entry into Europe by 'pushing back' the flimsy refugee dinghies. I explained that 'pushing back' entails ramming these boats with the risk of sinking them, something the Greeks would not do. My interlocutor changed tack. The patrol boats should allow refugees into the country but turn back

'illegal' migrants. I explained again that the Greek government is not prepared to tolerate more deaths in the Aegean.
Moreover, the separation of asylum-seekers from economic
migrants in rough waters is impossible even if some inhuman
administration were to adopt the plan.

Jami and Barzo, two failed asylum seekers living in the
London shadows, give a succinct answer to the European
politician. In a video accompanying coverage of a report
by the refugee charity Parfras, which details the life of an
underground humanity without shelter, food or the right to
work and survives on less than one dollar a day, Jami who
sleeps in parks, quietly contrasts himself with his friends
who have 'papers' and implicitly to the rest of us. 'We both
have two hands, two eyes, two legs. They are human like
me.' Barzo concludes his heart-rending description of destitution and homelessness by quietly addressing people like us
who, from our comfortable homes, keep proclaiming 'human
rights, human rights. But where are the human rights for the
asylum seekers?'[2] In haunting and halting sentences, these
natural philosophers state an indisputable truth: we may all
be human but humanity has always excluded, despised and
degraded some of its parts. Humanity is not one: it has always
been split between full and lesser humans. Immigration law
distinguishes between refugees and migrants, placing the
former in a precarious position of rhetorical protection while
abandoning the 'illegals', as if there are 'illegal' human beings.

21.1   Split humanity

How can we understand this paradox that not all humans
have humanity in a human rights world? The inflation of
rights-talk has obscured the terms. To understand what Jami
and Barzo tell us – and Aylan proves – we need to start
again. The term 'human rights' combines law and morality.
Legal rights have been the building block of Western law. As
human, rights refer to a type of morality and to the treatment
individuals expect from public and private powers. Human
rights are a hybrid category, which introduces a number of
paradoxes at the heart of the polity by bringing together law
and morality.

Let me start with legal rights. Contractual and property rights were introduced in early modernity. They emerged fully with capitalism and contributed to its success. Modernity led to what Alasdair MacIntyre has called a 'moral catastrophe'.[3] It destroyed premodern communities of virtue and duty. In capitalism, restraints on private egotism must be external because no universal moral code exists. Criminal law, tort and legal rights achieve precisely that. The law empowers individuals to enforce their rights, limiting their exercise so that all have, in theory, an equal amount. When disputes arise, it is the business of lawyers and judges to resolve them and, of the police and prison guards to restrain the rampant egotism of capitalist man.

Legal philosophy has propagated the commonly held view that laws and rights are fact-like. They have 'objective' meaning, which can be discovered by rule experts and applied by administrators. This way legal rights turn social and political conflict into a 'technical' problem about the meaning and application of rules. It is an illusion. Legal rules and rights do not come with their meaning on their sleeve. Human rights provisions in particular are general and abstract. They must be interpreted in order to be applied. Most rights disputes involve at least two contradictory but plausible legal meanings. Interpretation does not mean, therefore, discovering the 'real' meaning of the rule hidden in its text. Rather, the business of interpretation is about constructing a meaning that can attract a majority of the judges. In this process, the moral, ideological and aesthetic beliefs of the judges become all important. Take the 'right to life', which opens most Bills of Rights and Human Rights Conventions. The statement does not answer questions about abortion, the death penalty, euthanasia or whether this right protects the prerequisites for survival such as food, shelter, health care or a safe passage to a place of asylum. To decide such controversial questions, the 'right to life' and every other right must be placed within a wider theoretical framework about the importance of freedom, autonomy and morality in a democratic polity. Such discussion would then allow the construction (and not the discovery) of a meaning that could decide whether abortion, for example, should be allowed. This is the reason why, during the 2016 American presidential election, so much discussion referred to the power of the President to appoint Supreme Court justices and thus affect future decisions with abortion rights at the top. The Americans fully understand that key legal decisions are not just legal and that the Constitution is what 'the judges say it is'.

A human rights claim is the beginning rather than the end of a dispute about the protection it may offer or its standing vis-à-vis conflicting rights. Deciding conflicts between liberty and security, for instance, so important after the recent terrorist attacks, involves assumptions about the way a democratic society works. Non-legal considerations necessarily enter the legal argument. Removing these decisions from politicians and giving them to lawyers, with their usually homogeneous outlook, does not change this basic fact. The law supposedly uses argumentation and precedent to make the exercise of power neutral. The proud claim of Western law is that it expelled 'subjectivist' morality from its empire in order to give a neutral and acceptable answer to social conflict. But the repressed 'subjectivism' always returns. Rights adjudication is ambiguous, open, a contested site. Law's job is to provide order not to support morality. And if anything, there are multiple moralities.

'Human rights', recognized or not by the law, are primarily moral claims. A Chinese dissident who asserts the right to free political activity or a refugee who claims the right to safe passage to a place of protection are both right and wrong. The dissident's or immigrant's 'right' does not refer to an existing legal entitlement but to a claim about what morality (or ideology, or international law or some other higher source) demands. In this sense, morality is in potential conflict with law. Legislated rights confound the real and the ideal. Take Article 1 of the Universal Declaration of Human Rights: 'All human beings are born free and equal of right.' But, as Jeremy Bentham noted first, newly born infants depend for survival on their carers, while the statement that people are born equal flies in the face of huge disparities in the world. Biological and social nature distribute their wares unequally; it is an unavoidable result of the accidents of birth and history. Heredity, the standing and economic (dis)advantage of family and community largely determine our lives. Equality on the other hand is unnatural and must be fought for. Similarly, the

refugee's claim to the right to life does not create an inde-
feasible expectation of survival. Ramming a dinghy may be
interpreted as a violation of refugee rights or as a necessary
protection of national security. Human rights statements are
prescriptions: people are not free and equal; they ought to
become so. People do not have a right to life; they ought to
be given the necessary means for survival. Equality is a call
to action not a description of a state of affairs.

21.2   The human rights paradox

Human rights are a subcategory of legal rights protecting
important values and goods. We are told that they are given
to people on account of their humanity rather than membership of narrower categories such as nation, community or
class. They promote, therefore, the morality of a universal
humanity. Yet, the history of natural and later human rights
does not support this assertion. The French *Declaration of
the Rights of Man and Citizen*, the manifesto of modernity,
opens with a statement about the free and equal rights of
men. It proceeds to bestow these rights to French citizens
only. From that point on, statehood, sovereignty and territory
follow the fate of nations and their pathologies: nationalism, xenophobia, ethnic cleansing. The gap between universal
'man' and national citizen is inhabited by immigrants, refugees, the stateless. They do not have rights because they are
not citizens and because they don't have rights they are lesser
humans. The 'man' of the 'rights of man' has no concrete
characteristics, except for free will, reason and soul.[4] These
universal elements secularized the Christian sacredness of life
and endowed humanity with dignity and respect. This 'man'
is an abstraction without body, colour, gender or history,
as Hegel, Burke and Marx agreed. Yet the empirical man
who actually enjoys legal rights is literally a well-off, white,
Christian, urban, propertied man. He condenses the abstract
dignity of humanity and the privileges of the powerful.

Full 'humanity' is constructed against a background of
exclusions and inhumanity based on nationality, class, gender,
race, religion or sexual orientation. If rights were universal,
refugees, the *sans papiers* immigrants or the Guatanamo Bay

prisoners should enjoy humanity's entitlements. They have very few, almost none. They are bare unprotected life. Every historical age has used its philosophical or empirical definition of what it means to be human to separate between rulers, ruled and excluded. Those who don't speak our language, share our religion, belong to the wrong class, gender, colour or sexuality, have always been left outside locally defined 'humanity'. These categories of exclusion are still active. They have been joined by the 'bottom billion', the economically redundant humans, the rejects of neoliberal capitalism. Human rights do not belong to humans, they construct a hierarchized or graded 'humanity'.

The human rights movement can be seen as the on-going but failing struggle to close the gap between the abstract man of the Declarations and the empirical human being. Has it succeeded? Yes and no. The concept of a common 'humanity' introduced the vocation of universal dignity. Jami, Barzo and Aylan teach us, however, that there is nothing sacred about any definition of humanity and nothing eternal about its scope. The paradoxical relationship between law and morality has been resolved through the elimination of the moral command.[5] While refugees bleed and hurt like the rest of us, they are not fully human.

Those who defend Jami, Barzo and the refugees who arrive daily in the Greek islands are the latest expression of a human urge to resist domination, oppression and the intolerance of public opinion. They are part of a long and honourable tradition, which surfaces in the struggles of the despised, enslaved or exploited. On the other hand, those who use human rights rhetoric to defend the 'human' rights of powerful companies in the developing world contribute to the banalization and eventual atrophy of rights.[6] This atrophy paradoxically follows the triumph of rights. Human rights have mutated, expanded and turned into a vernacular touching every aspect of social life. Rights have become ubiquitous at the cost of their specificity and significance. They are seen as a key concept in morals, politics and subjectivity. Claiming rights is the main form of morality.[7] Responsibility, virtue and duty on the other hand have been confined to backwardness and fanaticism. In politics, rights have become a tool of policy and site of intervention. Group claims and ideological positions, sectional interests and global campaigns are routinely expressed in the language of individual rights. But when rights trump state policies and collective priorities, allegedly to support the liberty of the individual, society starts breaking up into a collection of atoms indifferent to the common good. Politics is depoliticized; both liberty and security suffer.

In postmodern societies, rights are the main instruments of identity politics. Every lifestyle choice, every consumer preference and demand can be expressed in the language of rights. I desire something and I have a right to it have become synonymous. This linguistic inflation weakens the association of rights with significant human goods. A politician recently argued that we have a human right to properly functioning kitchen appliances; another to a regular collection of trash. The right to choose our kids' school or mobile phone is as important as the right to be free of torture or to have food on the table. This inflation of rights-talk has nothing to do with the Enlightenment tradition of emancipation and self-development or with the radical tradition of dissent and social justice. When every desire can be turned into a legal right nothing retains the dignity of a higher law.

Finally, the issue of human rights has become the last universal ideology. It unites the North and the South, globalizing imperialists and anti-globalization protesters, first-world liberals and third-world revolutionaries. Human rights are used as a symbol or synonym for liberalism, capitalism or individualism by some and for development, equality or peace by others. In the South, rights are seen primarily as collective, social and economic; in the North as individual, civil and political. The South prioritizes social justice, the North liberty. Does the victory and ubiquity of rights indicate that they transcend conflicts of interests and the clash of ideas? It is a comforting idea daily denied in news bulletins. If there is something perpetual about our world, it is the increasing wealth gap between the metropolitan lands and the rest, the yawning chasm in income and chances between the rich and the poor, the strictly policed walls which divide the comfortable middle classes from the 'underclass' of immigrants, refugees and other assorted undesirables. If anything, our world looks increasingly more hostile and dangerous and the administration of justified or imagined fears has become a major and common tool of governments.

Human rights introduce morality into law and offer limited legal enforcement to moral claims. But as morality is not one and the law is not a simple exercise in reasoning, moral conflict enters the legal archive and legal strictures regiment and control moral responsibility. Jami, Barzo and Aylan remind us of the purpose of human rights. Their sad soliloquies attest to the fact that when seen as alien Martians they are turned into sub-humans without humanity or rights.

At the end of this journey through the rise of a radical left government in the midst of a European and world crisis, we have to conclude that the fates of Syriza, Greece, refugees and Europe are in some strange way linked. It is only if the alternatives offered by the Left succeed internally and are adopted internationally that the unbearable suffering of refugees and of humanity with them will be soothed. The prospects of success are in the balance. The rise of the racist right-wing throughout Europe indicates that the Syriza moment has not caught yet. The anti-establishment anger is there, the indignation about the decline of the social state and globalization's loss of jobs and inequality has become stronger, the rejection of remote powers and unaccountable technocrats is widespread. It is not the Left, however, but the xenophobic and racist right-wing that reaps the benefits of popular disapproval. Let me repeat: every victory of fascism emerges on the ruins of a radical left defeat. Syriza may be forced by domestic and European powers back to its pre-2012 marginalization. In such case, Greece will rejoin its earlier vicious spiral, the refugees will be treated again as aliens from Mars and humanity will exclude a large part of humans. The liberal, social-democratic and radical Europeans have a responsibility to stop such a catastrophe. The Greeks will continue fighting against long odds. The only struggle that always fails is the one that has not been joined.

Notes

1 From Utopia to Dystopia and Resistance, a Short Run

1 Costas Douzinas, 'The poverty of (rights) jurisprudence' in Connor Gearty and Costas Douzinas eds. *The Cambridge Companion to Human Rights Law* (Cambridge University Press, 2012), pp. 56–78.
2 Christian Marazzi, *The Violence of Financial Capitalism* (Los Angeles, Semiotext(e), 2007, p. 40.
3 Naomi Klein, *The Shock Doctrine* (Penguin, 2008).
4 Joanna Bourke, *What it Means to be Human* (Virago, 2012), p. 98.
5 'The State murders HIV Women' at http://www.provo.gr/loverdos_dolofonos/
6 Costas Douzinas, *Philosophy and Resistance in the Crisis* (Polity, 2013).

2 Hunger Strikers and Hunger Artists

1 Franz Kafka, 'A Hunger Artist' in *Stories 1904–1924* (J. A. Underwood trans.) (Cardinal, 1981), pp. 242–52.
2 Jean-Jacques Rousseau, *The First and Second Discourse* (R. and J. Masters trans.) (New York, St Martin's Press, 1964), p. 5.
3 MacSwinney quoted in Maud Ellman, *The Hunger Artists: Starving, Writing and Imprisonment* (Harvard University Press, 1993) at p. 60.

4 Jean-Luc Nancy, 'Church, State, Resistance' in Hent de Vries and Lawrence Sullivan, *Political Theologies* (Fordham University Press, 2008), pp. 102–12.

5 René Girard, *The Scapegoat* (Yvonne Freccero trans.) (Johns Hopkins University Press, 1988).

6 Ellman, *The Hunger Artists*, pp. 83–9.

7 Kafka, 'A Hunger Artist', pp. 251–2.

3 Radical Philosophy Encounters Syriza

1 Douzinas, *Philosophy and Resistance in the Crisis*, ch. 9.

2 Quoted in Jessica Whyte, 'Michel Foucault on revolution, neo-liberalism and rights' in Ben Golder ed., *Re-reading Foucault: On Law, Power and Rights* (Abington, Glasshouse, 2013), p. 208. Whyte and Golder have rescued Foucault's radical theory of law and rights from persistent attempts to present the late Foucault as a liberal supporter of rights.

3 Maria Kakogianni and Jacques Rancière, 'A precarious dialogue', in M. Kakogianni ed., *The Greek Symptom* (Nissos, 2014, in Greek), p. 181; *Radical Philosophy*, September–October 2013), p. 18.

4 Michael Hardt and Toni Negri, *Declaration* (e-book, 2012), p. 78.

5 Howard Caygill, *On Resistance: A Philosophy of Defiance* (Bloomsbury, 2013), p. 208. Caygill's book offers a history and classification of types of resistance but does not discuss or analyse recent events.

6 Slavoz Zizek, *The Year of Dreaming Dangerously* (Verso, 2012), p. 127. Zizek moved to a more positive assessment of the prospects of a left victory after the Turkish uprising in 2013 and the rise of the Greek Syriza party. See 'Trouble in Paradise', vol. 35, no. 14, *London Review of Books* (18 July 2013), pp. 11–12.

7 Gilbert Leung, 'Rights, politics and paradise', *Critical Legal Thinking*, 14 March 2012, at http://criticallegalthinking.com/2012/03/14/rights-politics-and-paradise-notes-on-zizek/

8 Alain Badiou, 'Our contemporary impotence', 181 *Radical Philosophy*, September-October 2013, p. 43.

9 Alain Badiou interview with Maria Kakogianni, 'On the occasion of the publication of *The Greek Symptom*', 27/4, 2014, Avgi (in Greek) at http://www.avgi.gr/article/2414442/alain-mpantiou-me-tin-eukairia-tis-kukloforias-tou-tomou-«to-elliniko-sumptoma» (my translation).

10 See chapter 8.

4 A Philosophy of Resistance

1 Françoise Proust, *De la Résistance* (Paris, Cerf, 1997). Penelope Deutscher has translated into English Proust's Introduction and 'The line of resistance' both in vol.15, no. 4 *Hypatia* (2000), pp. 18–37.
2 Proust, 'Introduction', *De la Résistance*, pp. 1–2.
3 Gilles Deleuze, *Foucault* (University of Minnesota Press, 1988), p. 89.
4 Costas Douzinas, *The End of Human Rights* (Oxford, Hart, 2000), chs. 8 and 9.
5 Costas Douzinas, '*Adikia*: Communism and rights' in Costas Douzinas and Slavoj Zizek eds., *The Idea of Communism* (London, Verso, 2010).
6 Michel Foucault, 'Is it useless to revolt?' in Janet Afay and Kevin Anderson eds., *Foucault and the Iranian Revolution* (Chicago University Press, 2005), p. 266.
7 Daniel Bensaid, 'Je résiste donc je suis' in *Résistances: Essai de taupologie generale* (Fayard, 2001), pp. 29–46.
8 Douzinas, *Philosophy and Resistance*, ch. 6.
9 Costas Douzinas, 'The "right to the event". The legality and morality of revolution and resistance', vol. 2, no. 1, *Metodo: International Studies in Phenomenology and Philosophy* at http://www.metodo-rivista.eu/index.php/metodo/article/view/65
10 Douzinas, 'Philosophy and the right to resistance' in Costas Douzinas and Conor Gearty, *The Meanings of Human Rights* (Cambridge University Press, 2013).
11 Foucault, 'Is it useless to revolt?' n. 30, p. 263.
12 Foucault, 'Is it useless to revolt?', p. 266.
13 Badiou, *Metapolitics* (Verso, 2012), p. 24.

5 A Very European Coup

1 http://www.theguardian.com/commentisfree/2011/nov/06/greek-spring-europe-contagion-resistance
2 http://www.theguardian.com/commentisfree/2012/may/01/greece-vote-european-spring
3 http://www.theguardian.com/commentisfree/2014/jun/03/syriza-future-greece-europe-radical-left
4 This is the difference between tax revenues and state expense minus the servicing of public debt.

5   Independent Evaluation Office of the IMF, *The IMF and the Crises in Greece, Ireland and Portugal*, 8 July 2016 at http://www.ieo-imf.org/ieo/files/completedevaluations/EAC__REPORT%20v5.PDF, para. 70.

6   Ambrose Evans-Pritchard, 'IMF admits disastrous love affair with the Euro and apologises for the immolation of Greece', *Telegraph*, 26 July 2016 at http://www.telegraph.co.uk/business/2016/07/28/imf-admits-disastrous-love-affair-with-euro-apologises-for-the-i/

7   http://reports.weforum.org/global-competitiveness-report-2015-2016/economies/#indexId=GCI&economy=GRC

8   Douzinas, *Philosophy and Resistance*, ch. 9.

9   http://www.theguardian.com/commentisfree/2011/jun/15/greece-europe-outraged-protests

10 Kevin Ovender, *Syriza* (London, Pluto, 2015) offers a fair history of the party and an accurate description of the 2015 events up to the September elections.

11 Chris Mullin, *A Very British Coup* (Serpent's Tail, 2010).

12 http://www.forbes.com/sites/billfrezza/2011/07/19/give-greece-what-it-deserves-communism/

13 http://www.kathimerini.gr/894943/article/proswpa/synentey3eis/ant-samaras-monh-lysh-h-prosfygh-stis-kalpes (in Greek).

14 Carl von Clausewitz, *On War* (Wordsworth Editions, 1998).

15 Ian Traynor, 'Three days to save the Euro', *Guardian*, 22 October 2015, pp. 29–31 is the most complete account of the days when Greece and the Euro went to the edge.

16 Costas Lapavitsas and Sebastian Budgen, 'Awakening the European Left' and 'Greece Phase Two', *Jacobin* at https://www.jacobinmag.com/author/sebastian-budgen-and-costas-lapavitsas/

6   Contradiction is the Name of the Governing Left

1   Traynor, 'Three days to save the Euro', p. 31.

2   Michalis Spourdalakis, 'Rekindling hope: SYRIZA's challenges and prospects', *The Bullet*, E-Bulletin 1213, 27 January 2016 at http://www.socialistproject.ca/bullet/1213.php

3   Costas Douzinas and Adam Gearey, *Critical Jurisprudence* (Hart, 2005); Evgeni Pashukanis, *Law and Marxism: A General Theory* (Pluto, 1987).

4   John Holloway and Sol Picciotto, *State and Capital: A Marxist Debate* (Edward Arnold, 1978); Bob Jessop, 'Marx and Engels on the state', in S. Hibbin ed., *Politics, Ideology, and the State* (London: Lawrence and Wishart), pp. 40–68, 1978.

5 Nikos Poulantzas, *State, Power, Socialism* (New Left Books, 1983), pp.128–9.

6 Bob Jessop, 'The Strategic Selectivity of the State: Reflections on a Theme of Poulantzas', *Journal of Hellenic Diaspora*, 25/1–2, 1–37, 1999.

7 Gunther Teubner, *Constitutional Fragments: Constitutionalism and Globalisation* (Oxford University Press, 2012); Sandro Mezzadra, 'Seizing Europe. Crisis Management, constitutional transformations, constituent moments' in Oscar Agustin and Christian Ydesen eds., *Post-Crisis Perspectives, The Common and its Powers* (Peter Lang Verlag, 2013).

8 https://www.opendemocracy.net/can-europe-make-it/athena-athanasiou/performative-dialectics-of-defeat-europe-and-european-left-afte

9 http://www.newstatesman.com/world-affairs/2015/07/slavoj-i-ek-greece-courage-hopelessness

10 James Galbraith, *Welcome to the Poisoned Chalice: The Destruction of Greece and the Future of Europe* (Yale University Press, 2016), pp. 13–14.

11 https://www.opendemocracy.net/can-europe-make-it/stathis-gourgouris/syriza-problem-radical-democracy-and-left-governmentality-in-g

12 Spourdalakis, 'Rekindling hope'.

13 Etienne Balibar, *Equaliberty* (James Ingram trans.) (Duke University Press, 2014).

8 Learning from Ideology

1 Sigmund Freud, 'Mourning and melancholia' in *The Standard Edition of the Complete Works of Sigmund Freud* (Hogarth, 1957), vol. 14, p. 249.

2 Walter Benjamin, 'Left-wing melancholy' in Anton Kaes, Martin Jay and Edward Dimendberg eds., *The Weimar Republic Sourcebook* (University of California Press, 1994), p. 305. See Wendy Brown, 'Resisting Left melancholy', *Boundary 2* 26.3 (1999), pp. 19–27 for a brilliant use of the Benjamin essay.

3 Walter Benjamin, *The Arcades Project* (Harvard University Press, 1999), pp. 462–3.

4 Slavoj Zizek, *In Defence of Lost Causes* (London, Verso, 2008), p. 7.

5 Costas Douzinas, *The End of Human Rights* (Oxford, Hart, 2000).

6 Samuel Moyn, *The Last Utopia* (Harvard University Press, 2010).

9 The Curious Incident of the Missing TV Licences

1 Members of the Conference are the Speaker and Deputy Speakers of Parliament, former Speakers, the Presidents of the six Standing Committees and one representative from each parliamentary party. The main work of the Conference is to set Parliament's agenda and carry out various housekeeping tasks. There are ten Syriza MPs in the Conference out of a total membership of twenty-four.

10 The Ethos of the Left

1 Douzinas, *Philosophy and Resistance*, pp. 64–6.
2 Hans Georg Gadamer, *Truth and Method* (Seabury Press, 1975).

11 Greeks or Europeans?

1 Soti Triantafyllou, 'Representative democracy and Jacobinism', *Athens Voice* 1-4-2015 at http://www.athensvoice.gr/politiki/antiprosopeytiki-dimokratia-kai-iakovinismos
2 Alexandra Bakalaki, 'Chemtrails, crisis, and loss in an interconnected world', *Visual Anthropology Review*, vol. 32, 1 (2016), pp. 12–23.
3 Costas Douzinas, *Human Rights and Empire: The Political Philosophy of Cosmopolitanism* (Routledge, 2007).

12 The Euro, the Sacred and the Holy

1 Jean Luc Nancy, *The Sense of the World* (University of Minnesota Press, 1998).
2 Ernst Kantorowicz, *The King's Two Bodies: A Study in Mediaeval Political Theology* (Princeton University Press, 1998).
3 Maurizio Lazzarato, *The Making of the Indebted Man* (Semiotext(e), 2012).
4 Galbraith, *Welcome to the Poisoned Chalice*, p. 149.

13 The Left and the Philosophy of History

1 Costas Douzinas, *Human Rights and Empire*.
2 T. S. Eliot, 'Tradition and individual talent' in *The Sacred Wood: Essays on Poetry and Criticism* (Methuen, 1920), pp. 43–4.
3 Slavoj Zizek, *Absolute Recoil* (Verso, 2014), pp. 187–8.
4 Jorge Luis Borges, 'Pierre Menard, author of the *Quixote*' in *Fictions* (Andrew Hurley trans.) (Penguin, 1998), pp. 33–43.

5　Jean-Pierre Dupuy, *A Short Treatise on the Metaphysics of Tsunamis* (Malcolm Debevoise trans.) (Michigan State University Press, 2015).

14　The Cycles of History: 1949, 1969, 1989

1　Chapter 20 below.
2　For the difference between multitude and people, see Douzinas, *Philosophy and Resistance*, ch. 10.
3　Douzinas, *Human Rights and Empire*.
4　Anna Grear, *Redirecting Human Rights: Facing the Challenge of Corporate Legal Humanity* (Palgrave Macmillan, 2010); Upendra Baxi, *The Future of Human Rights* (Oxford University Press, 2008).

15　Putting the Demos on Stage

1　Costas Douzinas et al., 'Greeks, don't give in to the EU's austerity ultimatum', *Guardian*, 29 June 2015 at https://www.theguardian.com/world/2015/jun/29/greeks-dont-give-in-to-eu-ultimatum

16　Grexit and Brexit, *Oxi* and Leave

1　Michel Foucault, 'What is enlightenment?' in Paul Rabinow ed., *Ethics* (New York: New Press, 1997), p. 315.
2　Etienne Balibar, *Masses, Classes, Ideas* (James Swenson trans.) (Routledge, 1994); Douzinas, *Philosophy and Resistance*, ch. 6.

17　Brexit and Euroscepticism

1　John Lanchester, 'Brexit blues', 28 July 2016, *London Review of Books*, p. 4.

18　*Finis Europae?*

1　Jürgen Habermas, *The Divided West* (Cambridge: Polity, 2006), p. 43; Ulrich Beck, *Cosmopolitan Vision* (Polity, 2006).
2　Ulrich Beck, *German Europe* (Polity, 2014), p. 1.
3　Giles Deleuze, *Masochism: Coldness and Cruelty* (Zone Books, 1991).
4　Philip Oltermann, 'Jürgen Habermas's verdict on the EU/Greece debt deal', 16 July 2015, *Guardian* at https://www.theguardian.com/commentisfree/2015/jul/16/jurgen-habermas-eu-greece-debt-deal

5   Oltermann, 'Jürgen Habermas's verdict'.
6   Edmund Husserl, 'Philosophy and the crisis of European man'. At   http://www.users.cloud9.net/~bradmcc/husserl_philcris. html
7   Ibid., p. 15.
8   Etienne Balibar, 'The rise and fall of the European Union: temporalities and teleologies', *Constellations* vol. 21, no. 2(2014), pp. 202–12.
9   Ibid., p. 203.
10   Etienne Balibar, 'Ideas of Europe: civilization and constitution', IRIS, [S.l.], pp. 3–17, May 2009 (ISSN 2036-6329).
11   Jacques Derrida, *The Other Heading: Reflections on Today's Europe* (Indiana University Press, 1991); Dipesh Chakrabarty, *Provincializing Europe: Postcolonial Thought and Historical Difference* (Princeton University Press, 2007).
12   Chakrabarty, *Provincializing Europe*, p. xiv
13   Costas Douzinas, *Human Rights and Empire*, chs. 3 and 8.
14   Perry Anderson, *The New Old World* (Verso, 2009), Part I; Alan Milward, *The European Rescue of the Nation-State* (Routledge, 1999).
15   Wolfgang Streeck, *Buying Time: The Delayed Crisis of Democratic Capitalism* (Patrick Camiller trans.) (Verso, 2014).

19   The Left and the Future of Europe

1   http://www.efsyn.gr/arthro/brexit-or-not-brexit-2-eyropi-kai-ellada
2   Clauss Offe, *Europe Entrapped* (Polity, 2015), p. 118.
3   Etienne Balibar, 'Europe et Réfugiés: L'élargissement' in *Europe, Crise et Fin?* (Le Bord de l' Eau, 2016), pp. 177–82.
4   Yanis Varoufakis, *And the Weak Suffer what They Must* (Bodley Head, 2016), p. 221.
5   Giorgio Agamben, *State of Exception* (Kevin Attell trans.) (Chicago University Press, 2005); William Rasch, *Sovereignty and its Discontents* (Birkbeck Law Press, 2006).

20   Europe Between Two Infant Deaths

1   http://www.theguardian.com/commentisfree/2015/sep/06/photograph-refugee-crisis-aylan-kurdi
2   http://www.theguardian.com/world/2016/jan/03/toddler-becomes-europes-first-refugee-casualty-of-2016
3   'The alliance of the unwilling in Visegrad and the Balkans', 28 February 2016, *Avgi* newspaper, p. 46 (in Greek).

4 Hannah Arendt, *The Origins of Totalitarianism* (Harvest, 1979), p. 300.
5 G. W. F. Hegel, *Phenomenology of Spirit* (A. V. Miller trans.) (Oxford University Press, 1976).
6 Judith Butler, *Precarious Life: The Power of Mourning and Violence* (Verso, 2006).
7 Αθηνά Αθανασίου, *Η Κρίση ως "Κατάσταση Έκτακτης Ανάγκης"'* (Σαββάλας, 2014) ['The Crisis as "State of Exception"'].
8 Costas Douzinas and Ronnie Warrington, ' "A well-founded fear" of the other: The momentary principle of justice' in *Justice Miscarried* (Harvester, 1994), pp. 211–41.
9 Chapter 17.
10 Etienne Balibar, *Europe, Crise et Fin?* (Le Bord de l'Eau, 2016), Chapter 6.

21 Human Rights for Martians

1 This was the case before the closure of the Northern borders of Greece in March 2016. After the closure, the situation has changed radically and the government's efforts have been transferred to the effort to settle people likely to stay in the country for long periods.
2 http://www.theguardian.com/uk/2009/mar/16/asylum-seekers-immigration-poverty
3 Alasdair McIntyre, *After Virtue* (Duckworth, 1981).
4 Costas Douzinas, *The End of Human Rights* (Hart, 2000), chs. 8 and 9.
5 Costas Douzinas, 'The paradoxes of human rights', *Constellations*, vol. 19/2 (2013)
6 Danny Nicol, *The Constitutional Protection of Capitalism* (Hart, 2010); Anna Grear, *Redirecting Human Rights: Facing the Challenge of Corporate Legal Humanity* (Palgrave Mac-Millan, 2010).
7 Costas Douzinas, 'Philosophy and the right to resistance' in Douzinas and Gearty, *The Meaning of Rights* (Cambridge University Press, 2014), pp. 85–104.